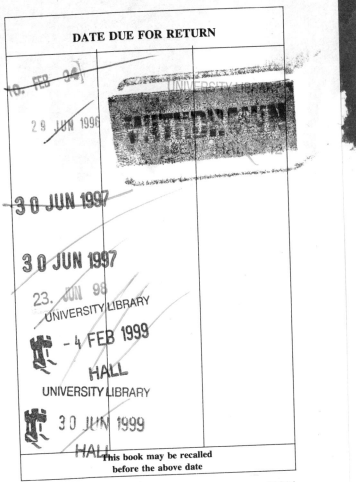

Elites in France

Elites in France:
Origins, Reproduction and Power

Edited by

Jolyon Howorth
University of Aston

Philip G. Cerny
University of York

Frances Pinter (Publishers), London
for the Association for the Study of
Modern and Contemporary France

First published in Great Britain in 1981 by
Frances Pinter (Publishers) Limited
5 Dryden Street, London WC2E 9NW

ISBN 0 903804 90 5

Typeset by Anne Joshua Associates, Oxford
Printed and bound in Great Britain by
Redwood Burn Ltd., Trowbridge, Wiltshire.

CONTENTS

Introduction

En l'église Saint Clotilde, a eu lieu, hier, 23 février, le mariage de Paul Coulon, ancien élève de l'Ecole polytechnique, sous-chef de bureau à la Caisse des dépôts et consignations avec Mlle Andrée Delatour, fille du conseiller d'Etat, directeur général de la Caisse des dépôts, commandeur de la Légion d'honneur et de Mme née Ferrus. Les témoins du marié étaient le colonel Lenoir, chef du personnel du génie au ministère de la Guerre, le commandant Augier, commissaire du gouvernement près le conseil de révision de la Seine. Pour la mariée, Paul Delombre, député, ancien ministre du Commerce et le commandant Ferrus, ancien membre de la section technique de l'artillerie. Parmi la nombreuse assistance on notait, MMmes Rouvier, Goyaux née Félix Faure, René Berge, Leroy-Beaulieu, MM. Casimir-Périer, Abel Combarieu, Ballot-Beaupré, Forichon, de Selves, Moreau, Lesieur, Derode, Pallain, J. Siegfried, Cheysson, de Foville, Pr. Raphaël Blanchard, de Liron d'Airolles, Chomereau-Lamotte, de Trégomain, Payelle, Louis Martin, Guernaut, Coquelin, et d'autres personnalités de l'administration, de la politique et de la finance (. . .).

This is an extract from the *carnet mondain* of the *Figaro*, for 24 February 1905 (and it is reproduced in *Les Hauts fonctionnaires en France au XIX siècle*, presented by Christophe Charle, in the Collection Archives [Paris, 1980]). In this we can see how the bridegroom has connections amongst the higher officials of the Ministry of War, since he has chosen them as his witnesses. His father-in-law, who is the son of a *percepteur*, is the President of the Association des Anciens Élèves de l'École Libre des Sciences Politiques and is in charge of the section of the Ministry of Finance where he works. His mother-in-law is the daughter of a *receveur des finances* and, as the bride's witnesses reveal, has connections with the army. Those present include, among the women, the wife of a former Minister of Finance (Rouvier), the daughter of a former President of the Republic (Félix Faure), the wife of Paul Leroy-Beaulieu (of the Collège de France and of l'École Libre des Sciences Politiques); amongst the men there is a former President of the Republic, a former Secretary-General of the office of the President of the Republic, the first President of the

Cour de Cassation, a member of the Cour de Cassation and a Senator, the Prefect of the Seine, several *directeurs* or former *directeurs* of the Ministry of Finance, the Governor of the Bank of France and two Deputy Governors, members of the Chamber of Commerce, a Professor at the Faculté de Médecine de Paris, two Professors at Sciences Politiques who will shortly become members of the Académie des Sciences Morales et Politiques.

The ceremony of marriage has long been recognised as an occasion which elicits the truth. It is clear that we have an example here of a governing class, of a centre of direction, the capitalisation of a world of relatives and contacts. In other words, of an *élite*.

This is not only an elite. It is a self-conscious elite. Not many years earlier, a writer well known in his time, Courcelle-Seneuil, had attacked '*le mandarinat*' of the administrative services, as a caste and as a separate, privileged group which wielded an undue influence in France, and an influence which he regarded as unfortunate.

Ceux qui entrent par cette porte son élevés dès leur enfance pour une fonction déterminée; ils n'ont jamais expérimenté ni rêvé une autre condition que celle de fonctionnaire public. Ils ont sucé avec le lait l'esprit de corps et sont convaincus dès la jeunesse de leur supériorité de lumière et de moralité sur tous les non-fonctionnaires. Ils constituent, dans leur opinion, une classe dominante et gouvernante. Ils n'ont d'ailleurs ni ne peuvent avoir la moindre connaissance de la vie ordinaire dans les fonctions libres de l'agriculture, de l'industrie et du commerce. Ces fonctions, ils les dédaignent autant qu'ils les ignorent et ne se doutent pas que ceux qui les exercent, c'est-à-dire les agriculteurs, les industriels et les commèrçants, constituent la nation, dont les fonctionnaires publics doivent être les instituteurs. La préparation aux fonctions publiques par les écoles et les concours (...) a donc un effet moral déplorable et qui ne peut être corrigé, parce qu'il est inhérent au système. Fournit-il au moins des garanties de capacité? Non, puisqu'elle consiste presqu'exclusivement en exercices de mémoire et ne développe pas le jugement. Autre défaut, aussi peu susceptible de correction que le premier, parce que l'expérience de la vie seule peut former le jugement.

(quoted in Guy Thuiller, *Bureaucratie et bureaucrates en France au XIXe siècle* [Geneva, 1980]).

How is an elite formed? Why does one elite persist and endure, whilst others fade away? Historians and many other social scientists have long puzzled over these problems. In the study of French history it has often seemed that it was particularly crucial to discover who, effectively, was important in France — where power really lay. It seemed that in France, perhaps more than in other countries, the historian was confronted with a society made up of different groups which were in rivalry, one with another, creating what General de Gaulle has called France's '*démons intérieurs*'. French history too, as has long been recognised, offered the spectacle of being interspersed by revolutions, upheavals, dramatic changes, whilst at the same time demonstrating many of the characteristics of stability and continuity.

For a long time historians concentrated on social classes. It seemed that power in France lay, in the Eighteenth Century, with the aristocracy, and that in spite of the Revolution, this power persisted. Other historians looked to the bourgeoisie, and saw the French Revolution and the subsequent developments of French history in terms of the emergence of an *haute-bourgeoisie*, successfully and continuously asserting its power irrespective of the excitements and flurries of politics and diplomacy which so often caught the eye of the historian. As terms like 'aristocracy' and 'bourgeoisie' revealed their confusions and inadequacies, historians sought for other words, and it became customary to speak of '*notables*' or '*notabilités*'. As one of the first historians to make a detailed scholarly use of this concept put it, 'la société française au milieu du XIXe siècle ne repose pas sur la prépondérance incontestée d'une seule valeur.' Hierarchy depended upon birth, upon wealth (whether inherited or personal), upon relationships and upon the various means which existed whereby a preponderance could be established, including '*les capacités intellectuelles*' (André-Jean Tudesq, *Les grands notables en France 1840-1849*, 2 vols. [Paris, 1964]). Amongst these notables was clearly the official, the administrator, the bureaucrat — and certain historians have focused their attention on whether or not there was continuity in the organisation of these administrative services. (See, for example, Edward A. Whitcomb, *Napoleon's Diplomatic Service* [Durham, North Carolina, 1979] and Clive H. Church, *Revolution and Red Tape: The French Ministerial Bureaucracy 1770-1850* [Oxford, 1981]).

It seemed appropriate, therefore, that the Association for the Study of Modern and Contemporary France, which had been founded at a meeting held at the University of Aston, should take the subject of elites as the theme of its first annual conference. This volume, which has been edited by Dr. Philip Cerny and Dr. Jolyon Howorth, contains the papers which were presented to this conference, which was again held at the University of Aston from 18-20 September 1980.

I would like to take this opportunity of thanking the University of Aston for their help and generosity in organising this conference, especially

Professor Dennis Ager, Dr. Jolyon Howorth, and Dr. Michael Palmer, from the Department of Modern Languages. I would also like to thank the Franco-British Council, especially its Secretary, Mr. James Hadley, for a generous grant towards conference expenses.

Douglas Johnson
Professor of French History,
University College London.

President of the Association for the Study
of Modern and Contemporary France.

PART I ORIGINS

1 The French nobility in the nineteenth century — particularly in the Dordogne

RALPH GIBSON
University of Lancaster

The chief difficulty with any discussion of the French nobility — in any period — is that it is impossible to know, in any precise way, what one is talking about. 'Nobility' was usually a fairly loose concept, and if it was clear that some people were definitely *nobles*, and others definitely *roturiers* (commoners), there was nevertheless a pretty large grey area in the middle. Furthermore, the nobility was always going through a continuous process of *'déstructuration et restructuration'*, described by Pierre Goubert for the Beauvaisis in the seventeenth and early eighteenth century,[1] but going on in all other places and times as well. In more modern jargon, the nobility was in a continuous process of *devenir*.

This was even more true of the nineteenth century, after such judicial definitions as had operated under the Ancien Régime had been largely wiped out. Article 71 of the charter of 1814 did, it is true, state:

> la noblesse ancienne reprend ses titres. La nouvelle conserve les siens. Le roi fait des nobles à volonté mais il ne leur accorde que des rangs et des honneurs sans aucune exemption des charges et des devoirs de la société.

More specifically, the Restoration established a *commission du Sceau*, with some legal powers to prevent *usurpation de titres*. But this was — not unexpectedly — abolished by the July Monarchy in 1832, and the 1858 decree forbidding such usurpations does not seem to have been very effective.[2] In any case, the problem was less one of people appropriating titles, than of making free with the *particule*. Names beginning in D could be split, and if the existing name was recalcitrant to such *anoblissement orthographique*, then it was a simple matter to add another. At least until the Third Republic, it was easy enough to get the courts legally to emend one's *état civil*.[3] Thus, for example, when the *périgourdin* general Dupuch, of good but distinctly bourgeois family, married the daughter of the Marquis de Foucauld (whose ancestor had represented the second estate of the Périgord in 1789), he profited from the occasion by adding to his own patronym that of one of his wife's uncles, thus emerging as the general Dupuch de Felez.[4] Some of these mutations have become famous, even on this side of the Channel:[5]

Delatre	: de Lattre de Tassigny
Millon	: (Millon) de Montherlant
Franchet Desperey	: Franchet d'Esperey ('desperate Frankey')
Beau	: Beau de Loménie (even he!)
Giscard	: Giscard d'Estaing

It thus became increasingly difficult, in the course of the nineteenth century, to distinguish between families *d'ancienne chevalerie* and those whose glories were of a more recent origin. To many writers this has not mattered very much, because they are concerned with the nobility *in the nineteenth century*; they accept that in the absence of a judicial definition, such a nobility could only be defined subjectively, and that the presence of the *particule* (indicating that its user thought of himself as noble) is thus sufficient evidence of 'nobility'. Louis Girard and his collaborators can accordingly write, in their study of the *conseillers généraux* of 1870, that

> . . . la noblesse nous intéresse comme phénomène d'opinion. De ce point de vue, le noble se définit par la prétention nobiliaire, plus que par la tradition familiale; il est plus important de se vouloir noble que de l'être réellement.[6]

Other writers, despairing of sorting out the lineages of hundreds of families (many of whom had an interest in obscuring their ancestry), have simply given up, and plumped for the *particule* as evidence of nobility, on the grounds that the application of any other criterion would prove hopelessly laborious.[7]

While I sympathise with this easy way out, I have found in looking at the nobility of the Dordogne that it is both possible and necessary not to adopt it. *Possible*, because of the existence of a local research tool which, while not utterly reliable, does make it feasible to sort out the recent genealogies of the notable families of the department in the nineteenth century.[8] *Necessary*, because I am here interested, not in a new conglomerate nobility steadily creating itself in the course of the nineteenth century, but in the survival of the nobility of the Ancien Régime. I have therefore taken the term 'noble' to refer exclusively to the descendants of families that voted with the order of the nobility for the Estates General in 1789.[9] It isn't always possible to know with certainty whether one is looking at the same family, and it is sometimes unclear whether the family concerned did in fact vote with the nobility. But in principle at least, the definition is a precise one.

This kind of precision is necessary, at least if one is going to talk about the survival of the Ancien Régime nobility. The following table is an example of why:[10]

Table 1.1 The conseillers généraux of the Dordogne, 1820–1900

	1820	1840	1860	1880	1900
% noble (as defined above)	29.2	20.0	12.8	8.5	4.3
% with particule	25.0	36.7	29.8	27.7	15.2

Looking only at the names with a *particule*, one would get the impression that the July Monarchy – and even the nascent Third Republic – appealed to the nobility more than did the Restoration. But under the Bourbons many old families did not feel the need to use the *de* in their name; conversely, after 1830, many newer families acquired one which they had not had before. The result is that the second line of the table is grossly deceptive – at least if one is interested in the continuing power of families that had been noble under the Ancien Régime.[11]

The major question that I want to try to answer in this paper is, therefore: to what extent, and in what forms, did the economic, social and political power of the families of the nobility of 1789 survive in the period between the Revolution and the First World War? Such original work as I have done on this question comes almost entirely from the department of the Dordogne (where I have been working on the role of the Church). Instead of merely presenting the tedious results of yet more monographic research, however, I would like to try and collate material from other areas, and to set my own as far as possible in a national context.

Before trying to measure the extent to which noble power survived, it will first be necessary to establish that the nobility remained a distinct entity after the Revolution. It has become pretty fashionable – in the wake of the magisterial studies of André-Jean Tudesq – to argue that already in the first half of the nineteenth century 'nobles' (however defined) and '*grands bourgeois*' were well on the way to being amalgamated into a large amorphous mass of '*grands notables*'. Tudesq is careful to make allowances, but his conclusion is clear:

Après 1830, le conflit aristocratie-bourgeoisie ne se pose plus sur le plan national, mais seulement dans quelques départements de l'Ouest, du Midi et du Centre de la France. Les familles nobles . . . continuaient à détenir une part importante de la propriété foncière et des hautes fonctions publiques, tandis qu'une forte proportion de la bourgeoisie censitaire ne jouissait que d'une direction illusoire de la vie politique du pays. Mais alors qu'au XVIIIe siècle la noblesse absorbait peu à peu la plus riche bourgeoisie, au XIXe siècle la noblesse n'est plus que l'un des éléments (le plus nettement différencié, certes) du monde des notables. Les grands notables — riches bourgeois et aristocrates — détiennent la direction économique du pays par leur richesse, la direction politique et sociale par leur influence. Dans le débat qui opposa progressivement au cours du siècle grande et petite bourgeoisie, ensuite prolétariat, la noblesse ne se distingue guère de la grande bourgeoisie; aristocrates et grands bourgeois, encore rivaux parfois, mais de plus en plus souvent alliés, composent précisément ce monde des grands notables.[12]

A lot of reflection, and a certain amount of evidence, have convinced me that this conclusion has been overdone. In the first place, it rests upon a loose definition of 'nobility', which in fact includes the imperial nobility, and (so far as I can make out) a number of other families whom we might nowadays be more likely to refer to as *dynasties bourgeoises*. It is thus not surprising that certain elements of this 'nobility' are to be found under the July Monarchy making common cause with the '*grande bourgeoisie*'.[13] In the second place, Tudesq himself is forced to make considerable concessions to the old picture of a coherent and isolated nobility.[14] In the third place, it is easy to find one's own counter-examples, of which I shall mention just a few.

Nobles were, much more than wealthy *roturiers*, given to residing in châteaux.[15] Noble families remained resolutely endogamous throughout the nineteenth century: Tudesq himself has found, for example, in a sample of 20 noble families between 1800 and 1860, that only 11 out of 146 marriages involved a non-noble partner.[16] Nobles favoured certain professions: in the Chamber of Deputies of 1837–9, 62.2 per cent of deputies from the old nobility were engaged in *la terre et l'épée*, whereas 60.6 per cent of bourgeois deputies were engaged in *le code et l'argent*.[17] Nobles preferred their *richesse foncière* to the *richesse mobilière* of the bourgeoisie; de Maistre spoke for them in 1819 when he declared himself

très peu partisan des fortunes en argent, grandes et petites: elles ont toujours quelque chose de précaire qui m'alarme, indépendamment d'un certain air mercantile qui me paraît avoir quelque chose de vilain.[18]

Table 1.2

	1829 (all 47 cantons)				1838/40 (43 cantons)			
	All electors		Electors paying > 1000 fr.		Electors paying 300–1000 fr.		Electors paying > 1000 fr.	
	Noble	*Roturier*	*Noble*	*Roturier*	*Noble*	*Roturier*	*Noble*	*Roturier*
Propriétaires	75	434	20	48	167	650	58	71
Cultivateurs					1	8	–	–
Agriculteurs	1	2						
Fermiers								
Titres honorifiques seulement								
Gens de loi	110	139	49	10	22	20	12	–
Militaires	16	158	6	23	8	197	4	25
Clergé	28	27	11	2	23	22	9	4
Autres professions libérales	1	5	–	4	1	4	–	–
Fonctionnaires	10	59	2	–	2	88	–	2
Industriels	–	37			–	37		5
Commerçants	–	81		6	–	122	–	9
Banquiers	–	12						
Maîtres de forge	–			4	1	10	–	5
TOTAL	241	954	88	97	225	1158	83	121

Such memories of *dérogeance* make it not surprising that of the 157 electors of the Manche in 1831 who exercised a 'profession économique', only *one* was a noble.[19] The electoral lists of the Dordogne for 1829 and 1839/40 tells a similarly predictable story (Table 1.2).[20]

Nobles also had different politics: those of legitimism (i.e. of support for the Bourbon monarchy). Recent studies of legitimism have, it is true, tended to deny this, and they have some evidence to back up their denials. Robert Locke, studying the legitimist deputies elected in 1871, finds that 45 per cent of them were *not* descended from the nobility of the Ancien Régime, and that their articulate leaders tended to be drawn from the professional bourgeoisie (e.g. Kolb-Bernard and Chesnelong).[21] His analysis is however rather spoiled by a generous definition of what constituted being a legitimist: his 'legitimists' might be better categorised as 'supporters of a moral order'. The percentage of nobles among the real *ultras* was much higher.[22] Tudesq has also found a large number of non-nobles and pseudo-nobles among legitimists.[23] Most authoritatively, Michel Denis has calculated that only 44 of his 110 legitimist families in the Mayenne after the Revolution were *privilégiés de l'Ancien Régime*,[24] and he evokes a legitimist milieu rather different from the picture I am trying to give here:

> Ancienne noblesse, noblesse récente et roture s'y coudoient; larges fortunes et situations plus discrètes s'y rencontrent. Ils ont en commun d'être tous des propriétaires, vivant plus ou moins de leurs rentes, mais il s'en faut de beaucoup que les anciens privilégiés l'emportent.[25]

This is a weighty testimony, but it is not uncontested. Patrick-Bernard Higounet, analysing the Chamber of Deputies before and after 1830, comes up with a very significant correlation between noble status and *ultra* convictions. The analysis of the 1827 chamber (see Table 1.3) will serve as an example.[26]

Table 1.3

%	Ancienne noblesse (titré)	Ancienne noblesse (sans titre)	Noblesse imperiale	Bourgeoisie avec particule	sans particule
gauche	15	6	17	14	48
droite governementale	38	18	5	14	25
ultras	42	21	2	15	21

Higounet concludes that 'l'on peut opposer de façon rigoureuse la droite gouvernementale et nobiliaire à la gauche essentiellement bourgeoise'.[27]

What appears to be true on a national level is certainly true of the Dordogne. After the 1830 revolution, 112 *maires* and *adjoints* resigned rather than swear allegiance to Louis-Philippe; 33 of them were nobles (*stricto sensu*), as against only three of the 112 replacements.[28] In 1836, when the *Gazette de France* opened a national subscription in favour of the legitimist advocate Berryer, the first list from the Dordogne contained 36 names, of which only two were *roturiers*.[29] In 1853 a 'tableau des fonctionnaires publics déclarés démissionnaires pour refus de serment' (mostly *maires* and members of *conseils municipaux*) included 44 legitimists, of whom 35 were noble (*stricto sensu*) and another two had a *particule*.[30] In 1871 the sub-prefects of three of the five arrondissements of the Dordogne made notes on the politics of the *maires* under their surveillance: of 22 legitimists, 19 were noble.[31] Clearly, the legitimist movement in the Dordogne was quite disproportionately aristocratic, at least in its *cadres*. Perhaps matters may have been different in the Mayenne, where popular support for the Comte de Chambord made legitimism a more attractive option to non-nobles. But in a non-royalist area, it was only the nobles who remained faithful to their king.

The nobility was therefore an objective reality, right through the nineteenth century. It had its own patterns of residence and marriage, its own professional activities, and (in many cases) its own politics. As a group, it doubtless diluted itself by welcoming new recruits whose credentials did not extend back to the Ancien Régime. It is not possible, however, to go so far as to say that it simply dissolved itself in the world of the *grands notables*. The nobility remained an identifiably separate and self-conscious element of French society. Social and political necessities may have forced it to make alliances — particularly in the defence of 'order'.[32] But alliances they remained, and not amalgamations.

How powerful, then, was this nobility in the aftermath of the Revolution? The Baroness Orczy image of that revolution as an aristocratic blood-bath has been well and truly laid to rest. Donald Greer calculated long ago that only 8¼ per cent of all victims of the Terror were of noble birth,[33] and an exhausive list of *périgourdins* condemned to death by revolutionary tribunals anywhere in France includes only 29 nobles (of whom 8 were priests) out of a total of 99.[34] Clearly, however, aristocrats did not do well out of the 1790s. Some noble families *were* badly hit by executions; many more opted or were virtually compelled to emigrate. The most reliable official lists of *émigrés* add up to 31,766.[35] Donald Greer, using the most extensive lists, provided departmental totals adding up to 124,994; he further estimated that 17 per cent of these were nobles.[36] For the Dordogne, a printed list of 1793 contains 616 names of *émigrés* (excluding priests), of whom 364 (59.1 per cent) came from families that had voted with the nobility in 1789.[37] Vidalenc gives the figure of 1396 as the total of the most reliable archival list of *émigrés* from the Dordogne,[38] and Greer makes it a round 2000.[39] André Gain, working from the lists of indemnities accorded in the *milliard des émigrés* of 1825, thought that there might have been as many as 200,000 *émigrés* from France as a whole.[40] Not all of these were nobles, but Gain estimated that the majority were, and gave detailed figures from five eastern departments, ranging from 26.9 per cent nobles in the Doubs to 72.5 per cent in the Côte d'Or.[41] The *milliard* lists for the Dordogne contain 405 names, of whom 69 per cent were nobles (*stricto sensu*), and they walked off with 87.6 per cent of the loot.[42] Wherever the real truth lies in this conflicting array of statistics, it is clear that emigration affected an important section of the nobility. Robert Forster (using Greer's figure of 16,431 *émigré* nobles) calculated that perhaps one noble family in four was affected — even more, if the calculation is based on the *milliard* statistics.[43] Furthermore, emigration was not exactly a picnic: it meant, in principle at least, loss of lands — a loss which the *milliard* of 1825, for various reasons, never succeeded in making good.[44] A poignant illustration is Pierre Massé's study of the de Marans family and their domaine of Varennes (Vienne); the land was lost, and the family effectively obliterated.[45] And even where the land was not lost, seigneurial dues certainly were: Forster has calculated that a typical noble of Toulouse, with an income of 8000 livres in 1789, found himself in 1830 with only 5200 francs (at constant prices) — including his part of the *milliard*.[46]

Many authors, however, have been able to show that by and large the French nobility did *not* lose its landed base during the Revolution. David Higgs thinks that 'the nobility retained or regained land after 1795 to an extent which has been substantially underestimated' — and is able to cite numerous (though minor) examples.[47] Maurice Agulhon, from his list of 235 families of the future department of the Var identified (by various criteria) as noble in 1789, has been able to find 157 who remained active in the department after the Revolution, plus another 42 who survived but broke their links with the department.[48] Claude Brelot, for the three departments of the Franche-Comté, concluded that 'la propriété foncière de la noblesse fut plus souvent amoindrie par les ventes révolutionnaires qu'elle ne fut complètement ruinée', and that after the Revolution the major landed fortunes were still in the hands of the nobility.[49] Paul Bois, in a sample of 28 communes from the south-west of the department of the Sarthe, has found that noble property scarcely declined at all: 13,270 hectares in 1777, 13,024 in 1830 — although the noble families were not necessarily the same, and the number of proprietors was fewer.[50] He even concludes that the *local* rôle of the nobility was more important after the Revolution than before:

> La noblesse a rapidement reconstitué, à peu de choses près, son ancienne fortune foncière. Elle est revenue vivre à la terre, même avant 1830, et elle a aspiré à y jouer un rôle politique et social auquel elle ne pensait pas avant la Révolution.[51]

For the neighbouring department of the Mayenne, Michel Denis estimates that perhaps 60 per cent of confiscated noble property had been recovered *before the milliard des émigrés*, and that the final loss of land by *émigré* families was probably only about 10 per cent.[52]

Denis also describes some of the mechanisms for avoiding (or compensating for) loss of land, which must have been fairly universal, since almost identical wheezes appear in the Dordogne. One simple method was for *émigrés* to leave a younger brother behind: of 175,000 livres worth of land belonging to the de Gastebois sold in the year III, one Louis de Gastebois purchased 18,300 livres (10.5 per cent).[53] That may not seem much in itself, but the other purchasers were probably straw men, because none of them appear among the 4 per cent of the richest proprietors of the commune at the time of the cadastral survey of 1829, nor in the *listes censitaires* of 1840 − whereas Louis de Gastebois (born 1778) possessed (in 1829) 148 hectares in that commune alone, and appeared on the electoral list as paying 1470 francs of direct taxes.[54] This system of understanding between siblings did, it is true, have it dangers. Three de Gimel brothers (including an abbé) emigrated; one was shot at Quiberon. The youngest brother stayed in France, and bought up much of the family property when it was confiscated and put on sale. When his two remaining elder brothers returned, however, he refused to share out, and they had to live under Napoleon by banditry − which did not prevent the abbé from fulfilling important clerical functions under the Restoration.[55] A surer method was to exploit the revolutionary legislation on divorce: great catholic ladies did not hesitate formally to divorce their absent husbands in order to conserve the property. Mme de Saint Astier, *née* de la Baume, divorced her husband the marquis in order to preserve the château des Bories for her son (whose own son died childless in 1891, and bequeathed the lovely château to a grandson of Louis-Philippe, who sold it to another).[56] Conversely, a dispossessed noble might reconstitute his fortunes after the Revolution by a judicious marriage. A daughter of the prestigious de Beaumont family married one Robert Paul Coignet, *capitaine du génie*, but above all director of the asphalt mines of Pyrimon-Seyssel

(Ain), and as such the wealthiest man in the 1839/40 electoral lists of the Dordogne (10,947 francs in direct taxation).[57] The comte de Rochechouart had pulled off an even more spectacular coup, for Elizabeth, comtesse de Rochechouart, was *née* Ouvrard; in the commune of Jumilhac alone, she possessed 1,158 hectares, one of the largest properties in the Dordogne, purchased by her husband with just over half the million she had brought him as her dowry.[58]

Others – perhaps the majority – survived the turbulent years by simply keeping a low profile. Typical of them was the comte Chapt de Rastignac, owner of the staggeringly beautiful Renaissance château of Puyguilhem. Visitors to the château today are told that its dilapidated state before restoration in the 1950s was largely due to depredations committed at the time of the Revolution. The partial ruin that confronted the inspector of the *Monuments historiques* was however much more the consequence of nineteenth century neglect, the attached property never having been sufficient to support a château of such magnificence.[59] What really happened in the 1790s was described by the local curé some sixty years later.[60] Contrary to the printed sources, which had the count staying in emigration until the disbanding of the army of the Princes, he returned to the Dordogne on his father's death in 1791, and established himself at Puyguilhem.

Il partagea son temps entre ses diverses terres, se montrant dans toutes, et ne négligeant pas de s'y rendre populaire. Il prit la direction de la forge de Firbeix, et se fit donner une commission du gouvernement pour y fondre des bombes et des boulets pour le service de l'état. Cette attitude, dans laquelle il sut se tenir sans rien perdre de sa dignité dans des démonstrations exagérées, lui fit passer les mauvais jours sans trop de périls. Il trouva du reste . . . une population sympathique et bien disposée, et il en garda un bon souvenir toute sa vie. Le château de Puyguilhem en fut quitte pour le sacrifice de quelques girouettes à fleurs de lys.

In a relatively calm department like the Dordogne,[61] there was in fact little danger, and not much provocation which would drive the nobility to leave. Of course many did leave – members of perhaps 300 noble families, to judge by the *milliard* statistics – and the Dordogne appears to have been harder hit than many other areas.[62] It is possible, however, that a significant number stayed, and managed to sit out the Revolution quietly at home.

Having either sat it out, or left brothers behind, or divorced, or married well, or repurchased from straw men (or from speculators), nobles in the Dordogne – as in much of the rest of France – were left in the early nineteenth century in possession of very sizeable chunks of real estate. Provided one is prepared to do a great deal of work, it is possible to calculate from the cadastral survey a fairly precise figure for the surface area of a department that was in noble hands in the first half of the nineteenth century.[63] Georges Dupeux has made such a calculation (without, unfortunately, defining the term 'noble') for the Loir-et-Cher: 22.7 per cent (by area) of that department was owned by the nobility — although noble property tended on the whole to be less valuable than other property.[64] For the Pas-de-Calais, Ronald Hubschner (who is equally reticent about what he means by 'noble') arrives at the figure of 16 per cent.[65] Gilbert Garrier, basing himself on regional samples from the cadastral survey of the department of the Rhône, estimates that the nobility ('*catégorie très artificielle*') owned between 0 and 21 per cent of the surface area (depending on the region).[66] Gabriel Désert (who defines 'noble' as having a *particule*), by a complex calculation based on the *listes électorales municipales*, has estimated that 17 per cent of the surface area of the Calvados was owned by nobles.[67]

The figure for the Dordogne, laboriously arrived at from the *cadastre* (and sticking to the strict definition of 'noble'), is almost exactly 10 per cent; it would probably be significantly higher, if one were to use a looser definition of nobility, such as appears to be operated by Dupeux.[68] Perhaps more interesting, and certainly easier to calculate, is the noble status of the most heavily taxed landowners in each commune (again according to the cadastral survey). In 41.7 per cent of communes, the richest proprietor was noble; in more than half (53.6 per cent), at least one of the two richest was noble. That is to say, not only did the nobility own a significant (though minority) fraction of the land, but they were not far from being a majority among the richest landowners of the Dordogne in the first half of the century.

Another way of looking at the strength of the nobles' economic base in the first half of the nineteenth century is to consider the electoral lists of the censitary monarchy. Tudesq has analysed the lists of seventy-seven departments (excluding Paris) for the July Monarchy, and comes up with the following figures:[69]

Table 1.4

Contribution (in francs)	Nobles	Total
> 10,000	40	50
8–10,000	43	52
5–8,000	183	285

Since direct taxes were mostly on land, the major landowners were clearly noble. Tudesq also gives a number of departmental breakdowns, for the percentage of nobles among those paying over 1,000 francs; they range from 11 per cent in the Haute-Garonne, to 45 per cent in the Ille-et-Vilaine.[70] But Tudesq's concept of 'nobility' covers a very wide range, not to say a multitude of sins. The following figures (even though none of the authors concerned defines his understanding of the term 'noble') may be more satisfactory:[71]

Table 1.5

Author	Department	Date	% of nobles among those paying > 1,000 francs
Désert	Calvados	1821	60
Garrier	Rhône	1829	34
Hilaire	Pas-de-Calais	1846	64
Hubschner	Pas-de-Calais	1846/7	79
Vidalenc	Eure	1847	29
Dupeux	Loir-et-Cher	1848	40

The situation in the Dordogne is given in rather more detail in the following table (remember that after 1831 the *cens* was lowered from 300 to 200 francs):[72]

Table 1.6

Paying:	200–300 fr.		300–500 fr.		500–1000 fr.		> 1000 fr.		Total	
	Noble	Rot.	Noble	Rot.	Noble	Rot.	Noble	Rot.	Noble	Rot.
1829 (47 cantons)	–	–	64	568	*85	288	92	98	241	954
1839/40 (43 cantons)	34	1014	56	695	86	342	83	121	259	2172

It seems safe to conclude, from the *listes censitaires*, that among the very rich landowners (i.e. those paying more than 5,000 francs in direct taxes) nobles were a clear majority, and that among the merely wealthy (over 1,000 francs) they were a very sizeable minority.

Like everything else in France, of course, it depended a lot on where you were. Unfortunately, interdepartmental comparisons on the basis of the *listes censitaires* are made tricky not only by varying definitions of nobility, but also by varying percentages of nobles opting to vote in the department where they owned the land concerned,[73] and by other technical factors — to say nothing of the fact that in a number of departments the lists have simply not survived. To get some idea of the geographical distribution of the noble presence, therefore, I have turned to a curious document deposited in the Bibliothèque Nationale.[74] In 1820 the genealogist Hozier borrowed from the Ministry of the Interior the electoral lists of all departments, and copied out by hand all the names that he considered relevant for his studies of the French nobility. It is clear from the list of names for the Dordogne that he included a number of pseudo-nobles whose families had been very much third estate in 1789, but at least his private definition was consistent from department to department, and nearly all departments are represented. I have simply added up the number of names in each case, and expressed it as a proportion per ten thousand of the departmental population in 1821.[75] The result is the accompanying map, which gives at least some idea of the differential distribution of the French nobility under the Restoration. Blue blood was evidently concentrated around Paris, in Normandy and the western interior (but not the Armorican peninsula), in the centre, in the old towns of the Midi, and in a rather inexplicable straggly line down the hinterland of the western seabord (including the Dordogne).[76] Conversely, nobles were relatively thin on the ground in mountainous areas, and in the East. This map exhibits certain similarities — but also marked differences — with the map of large-scale property in 1826 drawn by Georges Dupeux.[77] It is not entirely satisfactory (given the nature of the source), but it is the only distributional map of the nineteenth century nobility of which I know.

The two great classic sources on social structures of the first half of the nineteenth century (*cadastre* and *listes censitaires*) thus make it clear that the nobility came out of the Revolution in a position of strength, geographically variable but still imposing, at least in so far as its economic base in the land was concerned. Some nobles, it is true, were poor — as some had always been. In the Calvados, Jacques François de Bras de Fer, *capitaine en retraite, chevalier de Saint Louis*, had an annual revenue estimated in 1825 at only 2,000 francs (in emigration, he had worked as a watchmaker); Wambez de Fleurimont, *écuyer, chevalier de Saint Louis*, who had served in the *émigré* armies, had to survive under the restored Bourbons on 2,600 p.a. (which did not prevent him from having 'quelquefois chez lui deux ou trois filles publiques').[78] The Dordogne in particular was known for the pullulation of (relatively) impoverished *hobereaux*. 'Fatigué d'ensemencer des gentilshommes sur le beau royaume de France' (wrote the curé of Carlux in 1860), 'le bon Dieu vida le fond de son sac sur le Périgord'.[79] Less colourfully, but more convincingly, the

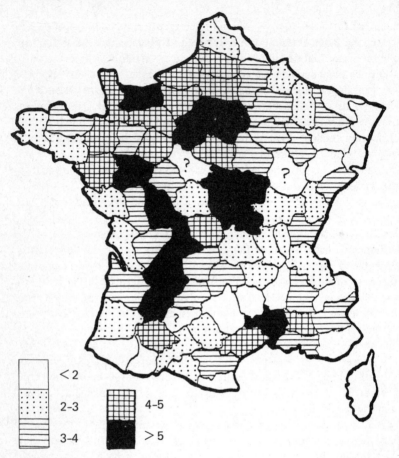

Fig. 1.1 Noble electors in 1820 per 10,000 of population

censitary lists for 1839/40 contain only 24 nobles taxed at more than 2,000 francs – of which only 7 between 3,000 and 5,000, and none at more than 5,000. Really massive landed fortunes – whether noble or bourgeois – did not exist in the Dordogne.

The attempt to *vivre noblement* on the strength of only a moderate fortune was especially hard on the women. In particular, it was hard for noble girls to make a suitable marriage. Acceptable men cost money: Joseph Cosson de la Sudrie, for instance, himself a younger son, turned down the daughter of the marquis de Sanzillon, who could bring only 45,000 francs and a hundred *pistoles* a year.[80] Even Eugène le Roy, the republican and anticlerical novelist of the Périgord, who is usually considered as a bitter critic of the nobility, had considerable sympathy for the plight of the (relatively) impoverished and frustrated *châtelaine*. In his youth he had loved just such a girl,[81] and her portrait turns up in many of his novels: la Galiote (*Jacquou le Croquant*), la demoiselle de Ponsie (*Le Moulin du Frau*), and particularly the eponymous heroine of *Mlle de la Ralphie*. He once told a friend, in a remark stimulated by their encounter with the never-married but sensationally beautiful Charlotte de Lostanges of the château du Sablou:

> Ici, nous avons des filles de hobereaux bien extraordinaires. Leurs revenus étant minces, elles ne trouvent pas de maris, dans leur monde s'entend, et, ma foi, elles pratiquent l'amour à la bonne franquette, s'éprennent de rustres qu'elles délaissent aussitôt. Leur orgueil s'oppose aux durables liaisons avec des gens qu'elles tiennent pour inférieurs. Au demeurant, bonnes filles, charitables mêmes, victimes seulement d'une société mal faite. Et il me revient un mot de l'une d'elles que je veux vous citer, parce qu'il est à lui seul une synthèse. Il ne restait à la demoiselle en question qu'un cheval pacifié par l'âge, tête basse et jambes incertaines. Or, il advint qu'elle rencontra un parvenu. Ce parvenu se montra grossier, et flattant la bête: le beau pur sang que vous avez là! – Savez-vous quelle fut la riposte? – Monsieur, le pur sang est dans la voiture.[82]

Le Roy almost certainly knew the history of the eldest daughter of another prestigious noble family of the *Sarladais*, a well-made woman whose sensuality is still perceptible from an old photograph, who in 1888, at the age of 33, gave birth to a child by the coachman. She died, unmarried, in 1921. The child is still living; he is the present marquis. The coachman was found dead, shortly afterwards, at the foot of the cliffs behind the lovely Renaissance château which had sheltered these particular victims of a badly constructed society.[83]

Neither the sad story of one particular noble girl, however, nor Le Roy's memories of youthful love affairs, nor the harsher statistics of the *listes censitaires*, should blind us to the fact that the vast majority of nobles (in the Dordogne as elsewhere) were not poor. Most of them had preserved their land through the *tourmente révolutionnaire*, and constituted an important element of the elite of a pre-industrial society.

How well did they manage to maintain this situation, up until the First World War? This question has received much less attention than that of the survival of the nobility during the Revolution, but some authors have had a stab at it. Philippe Vigier has the impression that in the Alpine region noble property was already suffering under the censitary monarchies, which he sees as the great period of speculation in real estate (by the celebrated *bandes noires* in particular); in the department of the Vaucluse, the number of nobles in the electoral lists paying more than 1,000 francs in direct taxes declined from 48 in 1832 to 39 in 1847.[84] For the Mayenne, Michel Denis finds similarly that the *grands seigneurs* of the Ancien Régime, having largely avoided the confiscation of their lands, nevertheless disappeared in the early nineteenth century; most had already been absentees before the Revolution, and now they sold off their provincial property to establish themselves definitively in Paris.[85] Studies of other regions, however, when considering the end of the century, suggest that noble property held up remarkably well. For the Calvados, Désert's sampling of the *mutations par décès* of 1895 concludes that 17.8 per cent of the land was still in noble hands — compared with 17 per cent at the beginning of the century.[86] It is true that he does also find that three-quarters of the nobles concerned (owning 58 per cent of the property) were absentees of one sort or another,[87] and concludes:

> Il semble qu'après un retour à la terre au lendemain des journées de juillet 1830, l'aristocratie foncière, dans une forte proportion, ait repris goût à la vie urbaine où elle vit en rentière du sol.[88]

Georges Dupeux' conclusions for the Loir-et-Cher are not dissimilar. His study of the cadastral revision of 1914 shows that nobles on the eve of the war still owned 104,577 hectares, as against 114,868 at the time of the initial cadastral survey (first half of the nineteenth century); the decline is only of about 10 per cent, over a period in which large properties (> 100 ha.) declined by about 15 per cent.[89] The most durable noble properties, however, were the very large ones (> 2,000 ha.), and

> l'impression d'ensemble est que la noblesse du Loir-et-Cher est en déclin à l'exception d'une minorité de très puissantes familles qui, seules, accroissent leur fortune foncière.[90]

Ronald Hubschner, from his sampling of the same cadastral revision in the Pas-de-Calais, finds that the nineteenth century saw only an 11 per cent decline in the land owned by the nobles (apparently defined by the *particule*); the decline came essentially from the sale of one or two privately owned forests. He concludes that 'au début du XXe siècle, la puissance de l'aristocratie foncière du Pas-de-Calais reste pratiquement intacte'.[91]

How was it in the Dordogne? Noble property was certainly under threat from a variety of sources. The first of these was the social pretentions of the nobles themselves. In reply to the 1886 agricultural enquiry, the *notaire* Gaillard pointed out that

> dans la Dordogne, la grande propriété est grevée d'hypothèques dans une notable proportion. Les emprunts ne sont pas consacrés à une amélioration de la propriété, mais à un tout autre emploi. Les grands propriétaires s'illusionnent souvent sur leur fortune, ils font des dépenses exagérées, et il vient un moment où ils sont obligés d'avoir recours aux emprunts.[92]

Being over-extended might not have mattered so much in the halcyon days of French agriculture under the Second Empire, but when the phylloxera and the agricultural crisis of the late nineteenth century arrived almost simultaneously, a number of noble proprietors had to sell up and leave — especially as commercial and industrial wealth was providing purchasers, who looked to the land as a symbol of status that movable wealth could not confer. Thus la Lardimalie, the old seigneurial property of the Foucald de Lardimalie, was bought in 1880 by M. Honoré Secrestat, who had made a fortune at Bordeaux in the liqueur trade. The 414 hectares domaine of the Dulau d'Allemans, together with the château de la Côte, was sold in 1869 to Charles Edouard Dethan, *négociant*. The château de Fleurac, with almost 300 hectares belonging to the de Beauroyre family (an old aristocratic family of the *Sarladais*) was bought by the principal creditor, M. Normand, an industrialist from Romorantin.[93]

The nobility of the Dordogne (as, for that matter, the rural bourgeoisie) was exposed not only to the combined dangers of poor management and agricultural crisis, but also the triple menace of mortality, contraception, and the attractions of city life. The abbé Bernaret, describing the diocese in 1863 for the benefit of the incoming bishop, warned him of what was happening:

> Il y a dans la plupart des paroisses quelques familles bourgeoises ou nobles. Elles étaient plus nombreuses il y a 25 ans; le nombre devient de plus en plus restreint, soit par extinction, soit par la misérable manie d'habiter les villes au grand détriment des campagnes.[94]

'Extinction' was a real danger. Emigration (together with the general disruption of the revolutionary years) and the Napoleonic wars had often delayed the matrimonial projects of the nobility until they were no longer fruitful.[95] We know, furthermore, that the *grands notables* in general were already showing in the first half of the nineteenth century a marked tendency to limit their posterity,[96] and the partible inheritance legislation of the Revolution and Empire could only have encouraged them in that direction.[97] In an age when calculations in matters of reproduction were necessarily haphazard, it was possible to be *too* careful. Thus certain noble families disappeared simply because they failed to have (male) children, and old mortality eventually caught up with them.[98] Of many examples from the Périgord, the best known will be that of the Baron de Damas, owner of the massive pile of the château d'Hautefort, himself one of ten children, but who died in 1888 without posterity, and the château was sold off to a distant *roturier*.[99]

Even those who managed simultaneously to content both their curé and their desires, such as 'la vénérable famille de Boysson, où il y a 12 ou 14 enfants, que Dieu les protège',[100] were likely to share in 'la misérable manie d'habiter les villes'. Villèle, the most successful politician of the 1820s, himself a southern landowner, had warned the Prince de Polignac as early as 1824:

> Personne ne veut vivre à la campagne sur ses biens; tous nos gentil-
> hommes se font bourgeois tant qu'ils peuvent, en passant à la ville
> six ou neuf mois, pour y jouir de la société, de l'aisance et des facilités
> de faire élever et de placer leurs enfants. Ils ne sont plus assez riches
> pour avoir tout cela à la campagne.[101]

He was probably thinking of Toulouse. Périgueux, under the Restoration, was a less attractive prospect; certainly the wife of comte Wlgrin de Taillefer found it

> la plus vilaine de toutes les villes et ne ressemblant à Paris que par la
> crotte qu'on y trouve aussi chaque fois que je m'y perds en équilibre
> sur les cailloux pointus (sic). Je me demande comment des personnes
> riches peuvent se décider à habiter un pareil trou, passe pour des
> malheureux comme nous, au reste le loyer et quelques autres petits
> articles exceptés tout y est aussi cher qu'à Paris en ce moment-cy.[102]

But Périgueux, like most French towns, was reconstructed in the nine-teenth century,[103] and when the bishop up-dated his address book in 1864, 18 of the 40 new noble addresses that he added were in the *chef-lieu*.[104] Not all nobles abandoned their rural roots, but there was a clear move in that direction.

Mortality, contraception and migration thus combined with poor management and agricultural crisis to undermine the landed base of the Dordogne nobility. The abbés Bernaret and Brugière, successively official historians of the diocese, in the lists of *bonnes familles* that they drew up towards the end of the Second Empire, complained bitterly.[105] At Château l'Evêque they noted the disappearance of four notable families;

'les villages dont elles portaient les noms sont habités par des riches pro-priétaires'. At Ajat they could list a dozen former families of distinction, but 'aujourd'hui le bourg d'Ajat n'est qu'un nid de pauvres'. At Sarrazac, five old families 'ont disparu et ont été remplacées par des petits bour-geois'. At Sainte Orse, finally: 'Plus de familles aujourd'hui à citer. Celle qui dépasse les autres est la famille Brachet, dont le père conduisait la charrue dans sa jeunesse.'

To try to quantify this decline in noble landownership and rural residence, I have turned first to the individual tax rolls, which are kept (in principle) for every tenth year from 1890 onwards.[106] For a rather limited sample of 51 communes, I have compared the wealthiest land-owner of 1890 with his predecessor of the time of the first cadastral survey (1810–45) – an exercise which produces the following table:

Table 1.7

Wealthiest landowner at the time of:		
First cadastral survey	1890	Number of communes
Noble	Roturier	16
Noble	Noble	11
Roturier	Noble	2
Roturier	Roturier	22

Clearly (as far as this sample is concerned) nobles were giving way to *roturiers*. The same sample can also be used to trace the evolution of the residence patterns of the wealthiest landowners of the communes concerned:

Table 1.8

Address of the wealthiest landowner at the time of:		
First cadastral survey	1890	Number of communes
Resident	Absent	6
Resident	Resident	24
Absent	Resident	10
Absent	Absent	7

Rather more surprisingly, this table seems to suggest that major land-owners were *increasingly* resident – and this appears to be equally true of nobles as of *roturiers*.[107]

Another way to measure the evolution of noble property would be a comparative study of the cadastral survey of the first half of the nine-teenth century with that of 1913.[108] This however is a desperately laborious task, and I have only been able to complete it for one *arrondissement* out of five: the *Sarladais*. The following table compares the status of the three most heavily taxed landowners in each commune:[109]

Table 1.9

Nobles among the top three landowners	Number of communes where this was the case	
	1800–1850	*1913*
1st, 2nd & 3rd	3	2
1st & 2nd	8	6
1st & 3rd	5	4
1st	27	23
2nd & 3rd	1	3
2nd	17	4
3rd	5	2
None	59	81
TOTAL	125	125

There is evidently a decline in the noble element, but it is not as severe as one might have expected. It is clear that even if the nobility of the Dordogne was suffering in all the ways described above, it was also proving remarkably resistant. Some families had died out or sold out; a few had become impoverished. Most, however, retained an important position on the land at least right up until the First World War.

Such is, furthermore, my conclusion for rural France as a whole. The French nobility, at least in so far as its economic base was concerned, survived the nineteenth century remarkably well. In the Calvados, the Loir-et-Cher, the Pas-de-Calais or the Dordogne – and, I am sure, else-where in rural France – the nobility kept the greater part of its lands, and to a very considerable extent continued to reside thereon. In both ownership and residence, in fact, it succeeded much better than the rural bourgeoisie – which (though there is no space to show it here) simply disappeared, selling off its lands to an enriched peasantry, investing in Russian bonds, and setting up gaily in town. The nobility, on the contrary, refused to sell, and by and large stayed put.

Did this retention of its economic base in the land mean that the French nobility also retained its social and political influence? I want to look first at its political influence – at national, departmental and communal level.

Influence in national politics is most simply measured by election to legislative bodies. The most complete figures for the Bourbon Restoration and the early July Monarchy are given by Thomas Beck; the following table is a summary of his findings (all figures are percentages):[110]

Table 1.10

Election of:	Titled nobility	Non-titled nobility	Imperial nobility	Near nobility	Bourgeois
1815 (Aug.)	36	9	12	28	15
1816	25	9	18	27	21
1824	39	12	9	25	16
1827	32	12	13	22	21
1830	28	10	15	22	25
1830 (Oct.)	13	6	12	24	44
1831	11	3	13	24	49
1834	13	6	13	24	45

Rather different figures, arrived at by rather different definitions are given by the Higounets, and by Louis Girard and his collaborators:[111]

Table 1.11

Chamber of:	Nobility of Ancien Régime	Imperial nobility	More recent nobility	Doubtful nobility	Clearly bourgeois
1827–30	41	10	–	14	35
1831	12	12	–	9	66
1837–39	16.2	12	4.2	2.6	65

(All figures are percentages)

Whichever set of figures one takes,[112] it is clear that the lowering of the *cens* in 1831 (from 300 to 200 francs in direct taxes), and above all the political discredit suffered by the nobility from its association with the fallen Bourbons, had severely affected its influence at a national level. It is also clear, however, that once the initial shock of 1830 had receded, nobles began to recover their old position. By 1846, more than a quarter of those elected were Ancien Régime aristocrats (plus nearly a fifth of imperial nobles).[113] This was not quite back to the Restoration situation, but it was not far from it; the only real difference was that there was less correlation between noble status and political attitude.[114]

Thus the nobility survived the lowering of the *cens* without undue difficulty. It could also, in favourable circumstances, survive universal (manhood) suffrage. One third of the deputies elected in 1869 had at least a *particule*.[115] In 1871 — admittedly under the extraordinary conditions of the end of the Franco-Prussian war — the figure was unchanged.[116] It was only with the definitive advent of the Third Republic that the noble element among national legislators began an irreversible decline: 23 per cent in 1893, 9.4 per cent in 1910 (the first time below 10 per cent), 10 per cent in 1919, and 5.3 per cent in 1968.[117]

The nobility thus managed to hang on to much of its influence in national politics (despite a setback in 1830 from which it never fully recovered), at least until the days of the mature Republic. For its influence at departmental level, the simplest — though admittedly unsatisfactory — indicator is the membership of the *conseils généraux*. Tudesq (with his very loose definition of 'noble') has calculated that in 1840, in France as a whole, the *conseils généraux* contained 245 titled nobles (or belonging to titled families), and 169 with no title but with a *particule*; together, they made up 17 per cent of all councillors. By 1847, there were 528 such nobles or pseudo-nobles in the councils.[118] Louis Girard and his collaborators have calculated that after the universal suffrage elections of September 1848 the percentage of nobles (defined by the *particule*) had *risen* to 25 per cent, and that by 1870 it was 27.6 per cent.[119] Nobody has done a national analysis for the Third Republic, but the Dordogne figures suggest that the representation of the Ancien Régime nobility in the *conseil général* pursued a steady decline, and that pseudo-nobles began to follow the same evolution towards the end of the century. All in all, the analysis of the *conseils généraux* suggests that the evolution of the political influence of the nobility at departmental level was not that dissimilar from its evolution in national politics.

What about local (communal or parish) level? Most historians haven't bothered overmuch about the presence of nobles in the *mairies*. In the arch-reactionary arrondissement of Château-Gontier (Mayenne), in 1821, 23 out of 73 *maires* were former seigneurs or their descendants — sometimes because there wasn't anyone else capable of the job.[120] In the Loiret, in 1854, 28 *maires* out of 348 were noble (no definition given).[121] In the Manche, noble *maires* (defined by the *particule*) evolved from 24 in 1833 to 34 in 1834, and 58 in 1871.[122] In the Dordogne, the percentage of noble *maires* (strictly defined) was as follows:[123]

$$1821 : 23$$
$$1841 : 12$$
$$1861 : 12$$

There are no figures that I know of for the Third Republic. What there is for earlier regimes suggests that nobles were less concerned with this form of local influence than one might have expected – even in favourable areas like the Manche, let alone in the hostile territory of the Loiret.[124]

Two areas in which one might expect to come across noble activity, less strictly 'political' than those dealt with so far, are the church and the army – or more specifically, the episcopate and the officer corps. So far as the episcopate of the Restoration is concerned, such expectations were fulfilled: 78 out of the 98 nominated to bishoprics were of noble birth.[125] Thereafter, however, the pattern rapidly changed: only 12 of 77 nominees under Louis-Philippe were noble[126] – although in 1840 exactly half of the 80 bishops *in situ* were still noble, including 28 ex-*émigrés*.[127] Of the 167 bishops of the period 1870–1883, only 21 (12.6 per cent) were noble as against 90 (53.3 per cent) *enfants du peuple*, and 56 (36 per cent) from the bourgeoisie.[128] It appears in fact that, despite the increasing fervour that many legitimists manifested for the Church, fewer and fewer nobles were prepared to join the secular clergy. This may have been partly because, as one disgruntled catholic noble remarked, 'les fils des croisés n'ont plus rien de croisé que les bras',[129] but it was largely the consequence of an internal evolution of clerical attitudes too complex to evoke here. Whatever the reason, however, the sharp decline of a noble presence in the episcopate is an undoubted fact.

And the army? Was it really such a noble preserve? The recent *grande thèse* of William Serman suggests not. In particular, he has calculated the percentage of those commissioned as sub-lieutenants who came from the nobility, giving us the following table:[130]

Table 1.12

% from:	1825	1835	1840	1850	1855	1865
old nobility	24	16	4	6	5	7
imperial nobility	3	4	1	–	–	–

After the Restoration (and a short hangover in its immediate aftermath), the officer corps evidently recruited almost entirely from the *roture*. This has traditionally been seen as the consequence of the nobles' *abstention boudeuse* after 1830, but Serman shows quite convincingly that the nobility gave up the army not so much out of principle as because the privileged access to the officer corps offered to nobles by the Bourbons was done away with.[131] As a consequence, the origins of 6,474 officers active between 1848 and 1870 were as shown in Table 1.13.[132] (Compare Table 1.13 with Prussian officers of 1860, of whom 86 per cent

Table 1.13

	%
Old nobility	6.1
Imperial nobility	1.0
Recent nobility	0.6
Noble pretentions	4.4
Roture	87.9

were noble – and still 52 per cent in 1913.)[133] It is true that the upper echelons had a more generous sprinkling of aristocrats, as the next table (for 1870) shows.[134]

Table 1.14

	Ancien Régime nobility	Imperial and later nobility
Captains	4	1
Colonels	12	5
Generals of brigade	20	15
Generals of division	26	13

In 1876, 33 per cent of a sample of brigade generals were noble, and 39 per cent of divisional generals.[135] It is also true that noble officers continued to give the army its social tone: there took place what has been called in another context a 'feudalization of the bourgeoisie'.[136] But the army was clearly not a noble preserve – not even for the imperial nobility; it had not been since the fall of the Bourbons.

The picture so far is one of a nobility which survived the Revolution fairly easily, and which kept much of its economic base in the land throughout the next hundred years. It was however much less able to conserve its political influence, whether in the realm of formal politics (at any level), or in other traditional areas of noble influence such as the church and the army. The decline of that influence was by no means universal or linear, and the picture needs to be carefully nuanced in many ways. Overall, however, it is one of decline. The final part of this paper will be devoted to asking why such a decline took place. If the economic base did not disappear, the causes of the decline must be looked for elsewhere.

One simple blanket explanation is that even if the absolute wealth of the nobility did not decline, it certainly did so in *relative* terms. This thesis was classically formulated by Jean Lhomme:[137]

Jusque vers la Révolution et l'Empire, la fortune avait une source traditionnelle: la terre. Les propriétaires se trouvaient représenter non seulement *les riches*, mais encore présque *les seuls riches* . . . Or voici que, précisément vers 1830, sa richesse [celle de l'aristocratie] est en train de subir une diminution à la fois absolue et relative. Une diminution *absolue* . . . Tous les observateurs de l'époque signalent la faiblesse technique de l'agriculture, et spécialement dans les grands domaines, ceux de l'aristocratie foncière. La richesse foncière subit d'autre part une diminution *relative*, et celle-ci est même plus remarquable que celle-là. Dès 1830, les revenus tirés de la terre ne sont plus les seuls importants. A côté d'eux, les revenus tirés de l'industrie, de la banque, et, plus généralement, des 'affaires', viennent d'apparaître . . . Il est bien caractéristique que ces revenus et les fortunes qui en découlent n'appartiennent guère à l'aristocratie. Ce sont là les modes d'enrichissement qui sont au contraire typiques d'une autre classe: la grande bourgeoisie.

Even if this formulation is evidently excessive (particularly in its selection of 1830 as the crucial date in economic development) it is still clear that non-landed wealth in the nineteenth century was increasing faster than landed wealth could hope to do. Lévy-Leboyer has estimated that whereas between 1810 and 1840 agriculture accounted for 66.5 per cent of total production (excluding services), between 1850 and 1880 that figure fell to 54 per cent and to 42.3 per cent in 1890–1910.[138] Guy Palmade produces the following more limited but interesting figures:[139]

Table 1.15

	Revenus (en millions de francs) tirés de:	
	la propriété foncière (bâtie et non-bâtie)	les valeurs et avoirs meubles
1878	3600	< 2500
1903	4072	4044
1911	4700	5300

Clearly landed wealth was becoming relatively less important, even if it was increasing in absolute terms — which suggests that the nobility, with its wealth preponderantly in land, was suffering relative impoverishment. Old prejudices about *dérogeance* prevented them from branching out into new fields of economic endeavour, such that they were condemned to an increasingly backwoods existence. David Higgs is thus led to a conclusion which seems to agree with much of what precedes in this paper:

It was not the Revolution which destroyed the power of the nobility either in its confiscations or in the laws governing inheritance, but the reluctance of the nobility to enter into competition in new fields of activity.[140]

This thesis is seductively simple, but there are a lot of problems with it. In the first place (and less importantly), it was not entirely true that nobles neglected new fields of activity. Cadastral surveys (concerned uniquely with land and buildings) and censitary lists (based on a fiscal system that taxed land to a quite disproportionate extent) can give a very misleading impression. So can even the study of inheritance through the archives of the *enregistrement*, because nobles tended to transfer their *valeurs mobilières* via dowry rather than by bequest.[141] Yet even a sampling of the *mutations par décès* suggests to Tudesq that the nobility held proportionately as many *actions* as the bourgeoisie, and he documents the important rôle played by nobles in metallurgy, mining, insurance and numerous other fields (half the *conseil des manufactures* of Saint Gobain in 1830 was — at least in Tudesq's terms — noble). He is thus led to conclude:

> En dépit de sa prédilection, au moins théorique, pour une société agraire, la noblesse n'est pas absente des grandes affaires: s'il est incontestable qu'elle donne une impulsion moindre au mouvement industriel, il n'est nullement prouvé que sa part dans le financement de l'industrialisation soit proportionnellement moindre, compte tenu de sa faiblesse numérique.[142]

Even if this conclusion rests to a certain extent on a loose definition of the nobility, it is nevertheless striking.

In any case, it is far from clear that social groups that were much more successful in maintaining their social and political influence made any great contribution to economic development. Robert Locke has argued at length, and convincingly, that even if the legitimists of the 1870s (with their strong noble element) were cut off from the mainstream of economic modernisation, much the same could be said for their orleanist (and preponderantly *roturier*) opponents.[143] Michel Denis has found the same for the Orleanists of the Mayenne.[144] Even republicans, the ultimately successful political group of the nineteenth century, can scarcely be said to have represented the forces of a modern economy: to a considerable extent they spoke for backward and rural France, through the mouths of doctors and lawyers. This did not prevent them from establishing an unshakeable hold on national politics, and on much of local politics. So the nobility's (partial) abstention from new forms of economic activity will scarcely explain why their social and political influence was on the decline.

The second − and even more compelling − reason for rejecting such an explanation is that the France in which the nobility lived remained, at least until 1914 and probably until after the Second World War, a predominantly *rural* country. Agricultural production as a proportion of total production (excluding services) did not fall below half until some time about the turn of the century (see the Lévy-Leboyer figures quoted above). The urban population did not officially pass 50 per cent of the whole until the 1931 census[145] − and that was certainly an overestimate, for technical reasons; the rural population, in an everyday sense of the term, probably remained a majority until the Fourth Republic. In such a world, a concentration on landed wealth could not really be a source of social and political weakness. It was certainly not so in backward and rural areas like the Dordogne, where the proportion of the male adult population working in agriculture in 1901 was still 67.3 per cent (72.6 per cent in 1851),[146] and the rural population (technically defined, and thus underestimated) was 84.5 per cent.[147] Yet the nobility of the Dordogne had progressively lost its influence − to judge at least by its declining rôle in the *conseil général* (see p. 26), and by the following table of the social origin of deputies elected by the Dordogne:[148]

Table 1.16

%	With particule	Ancien Régime nobility
Restoration	76.5	64.7
July Monarchy	50.0	31.8
Second Republic	0	0
Second Empire	42.9	0
1871	40.0	10.0
1876–89	12.5	0

The Dordogne at least had not undergone any economic change that could possibly explain a change of such magnitude. The suffrage, of course, *had* changed; but that is not a sufficient explanation by itself.

The explanation is in fact to be sought (in considerable part at least) at a political level. The July Monarchy was less favourable to nobles than was the Bourbon Restoration, and the Republic was not favourable at all. Neither of these stances had anything to do with the economic bases of the régimes concerned: it was a purely *political* evolution. What one needs to know, therefore, is how and why the July Monarchy and the Republic were able to make political capital out of opposition to the nobility. There has been a great deal written on the widespread anti-noble reaction produced by the supposed excesses of the *ultra* nobles under the Restoration, and so I will take that simple explanation as read (even though I suspect it is too simple to be wholly adequate). What I want to concentrate on here is how the Republic managed to instil and exploit in its peasant supporters (in some areas at least) a hatred of anything noble.

In certain areas, in the early part of the nineteenth century, that hatred was as yet a thing of the future: deference of a fairly genuine kind does seem to have existed. The comte de Comminges recalled of the Haute-Garonne of that time that 'les usages gardaient encore une sorte de couleur féodale'. Of his father, he added:

> Les paysans lui étaient très attachés, quoiqu'il les traitait comme des nègres. Malheur à qui ne lui parlait pas chapeau bas, un revers de canne avait bientôt fait voler le couvre-chef récalcitrant. A cette époque, ces façons étaient supportées tout naturellement.

Tudesq, who quotes these memoirs, concludes that

> dans les pays du Massif Central et de l'Ouest . . . la suprématie sociale de la noblesse restait partout (à l'exception de quelques rares villes) naturelle et incontestée des masses populaires.[149]

In the West, that deference seems to have survived throughout the nineteenth century.[150] Elsewhere, it was more or less rapidly undermined. For the Var, Maurice Agulhon has attempted to explain this evolution in terms of a complex of essentially economic conflicts between peasants and wealthy landowners, particularly owners of forests — who were often nobles.[151] There must be a lot in this, but it has also be be remembered (as Agulhon himself points out) that the enemy of the people might equally well be the state — particularly after the *code forestier* of 1827 — and that noble landowners were in fact more likely to tolerate ancient *droits d'usage* than were either representatives of the state or newer, non-noble landowners of a more liberal economic persuasion. The analysis in terms of forest (and other communal) conflicts, while certainly crucial in explaining the radicalism of the Var peasantry in 1851, needs supplementing by an analysis of later developments — particularly of the increasing shortage of agricultural labour. The *Société d'Agriculture* of Draguignan explained what was happening in the Var to the agricultural enquiry of 1866:

> La difficulté des rapports entre les ouvriers et les propriétaires provient surtout de la certitude que l'insuffisance des bras donne aux premiers

de se placer toujours lucrativement, quels que soient leurs antécédents et leur mérite comme travailleurs.[152]

This suggests that the original deference had been largely a function of economic subjection, but it may have been sincerely felt all the same. However that may be, the point here is that both the communal conflicts of the early nineteenth century and the improving bargaining position of agricultural labourers under the Second Empire combined to eradicate entirely the deference that had made of the Var a legitimist fief in 1815; henceforth, it would always be the *Var rouge*. Other departments did not become as radical as the Var, but similar processes were probably at work to undermine deferential attitudes.

Republicans were therefore increasingly able to turn popular animosity against the nobility. However, the fact that economic developments helped to make this propaganda exercise effective does not mean that the republican arguments were economically justified. Basically, republicans presented the nobles (and the clergy) as the chief material enemies of the peasantry. Now, it is true, as we have seen, that nobles owned a lot of land. But they clearly owned less land than did non-noble landowners – many of whom were republicans. When M. Honoré Secrestat bought up (in 1880) the old seigneurial property of Lardimalie, he immediately established himself as the permanent and solidly republican *maire* of the commune;[153] similarly, a M. Simonnet, *ancien négociant*, who had purchased the château of Vendoire and disposed of 150,000 francs in revenue, was considered by the sub-prefect in 1878 a 'devoted republican'.[154] It would be easy to multiply these examples. Republican landowners were certainly exploiting the peasantry on a wider scale – and perhaps even more intensively – than was the nobility.

Furthermore, the real enemy of the peasant – at least in the first half of the nineteenth century – was not the great landowner (whether noble or bourgeois); but the *usurer*. The Rigou of Balzac's *Les Paysans* was in no way a figment of the novelist's imagination; men like him existed in at least every canton of rural France. They were usually men of humble origins. Between 1845 and 1855, in the arrondissement of Brive (Corrèze), 18 persons accused of usury included 6 *cultivateurs*, 9 artisans or merchants, and 3 oddments.[155] Of 70 persons accused of the same crime in the arrondissment of Sarlat (Dordogne), in the fifty years after the law of 1807, the professional breakdown is as follows:[156]

Cultivateurs	23
Propriétaires	6
Sans profession	8

Marchands	5
Artisans et petits commerçants	11
Agent d'affaires	1
Hommes de loi (huissiers, notaires, etc.)	7
Médecins	2
Capitaine et retraite	1
Sans indication	6

These were the real exploiters of the peasantry. As the prefect reported in 1812: 'Il serait difficile de dépeindre avec des couleurs assez fortes le mal que cet odieux trafic fait au départment'.[157] The problem was endemic until the 1850s, when a combination of judicial repression, ecclesiastical thunderbolts, and above all the enrichment of the peasantry with the accompanying development of a cash economy, finally contrived to 'mettre bas le fléau de l'usure'. But well into the Second Empire, in all of rural France but particularly in the south, usurious rates of interest were the major way in which surplus value was extracted from the peasantry. This was the real form of exploitation, and not the rents or share-cropping of the great landowner. It was carried out, not by the nobility, but by men who started off humbly. Vincent Courrège left the Hautes-Pyrénées in 1782 at the age of fourteen to work in Spain as a baker's boy; he died in 1848 worth 230,000 francs, having made his way up as a cattle-merchant and a supplier of the revolutionary and napoleonic armies, to become a usurer on a grand scale. Thomas Fau, worth 1,800 francs at the time of his marriage, worked his way up by usury to become a 'véritable seigneur féodal [qui] contraignait ses débiteurs, passés à l'état de serfs, à acquitter toute une série de redevances'.[158]

What I am suggesting is that when republican propaganda turned the animosity of peasants against the nobility — against the original *seigneurs féodaux* — it was in fact blinding the peasant to his real enemies. In the first half of the century, the most dangerous enemy was the usurer. Later, it is clearly true that landowners who rented land or let it out for share-cropping were, in a technical sense, exploiting the peasantry. But such landowners were as, or more, likely to be bourgeois than noble, and it is even possible that the former were more *âpres au gain* than the relatively easy-going, paternalist and often charitable noble proprietor.

The classic republican propaganda technique for rallying peasant support against the nobility was to brandish the spectre of the restoration of seigneurial dues and tithes, and in general of the supposed seigneurial powers of the Ancien Régime. This worked like a charm in many areas, particularly in the Dordogne. In late 1789 and 1790 (i.e. later than the

Great Fear) the Périgord had been the scene of an intensely passionate anti-seigneurial movement. If the persons of the nobility – and even their châteaux – were spared, the campaign against the emblems of seigneurialism, such as *girouettes* and *bancs d'église*, made the depth of popular resentment absolutely clear.[159] That resentment was so strong that it dominated the peasant mentality of the Dordogne for the following century, and beyond. It meant easy pickings for the republican propagandists. In 1849 – when the Dordogne was one of the sixteen departments to give an absolute majority to Ledru-Rollin's democratic socialists – *montagnard* propaganda owed much of its success (if the *procureur-général* and a local journalist are to be believed) to the claim that a victory for the party of order would bring back feudal dues and privileges, the tithe and the corvée.[160] Peasants on the banks of the Dordogne were convinced that the marquis de Gourgues, one of the party of order candidates, kept in his château 100 yokes, to which – in the event of a victory for his party – the peasants would be attached to plough the fields of the former *grand seigneur*.[161] In 1877, according to the prefect, propaganda against the candidate of the *16 mai* was on the following lines:

Si M. Raynaud est élu:
- la guerre éclatera immédiatement
- les curés seront maîtres du gouvernement
- les nobles seront rétablis avec les dîmes et les rentes.

Une enquête établirait (the prefect continued) que non seulement ces bruits ont été colportés et accrédités par des agents, mais qu'ils ont été acceptés comme vérité par la masse de la population des campagnes, qui en ont été effrayés et ont voté contre M. Raynaud.[162]

The same kind of propaganda appears to have been effective elsewhere – at least if one is to judge from the confidence which republicans placed in it. The most typical example comes from the West – Siegfried's 'forteresse ultime de l'esprit contre-révolutionnaire'.[163] For the 1885 elections, a republican poster in the Mayenne attacked the five legitimist candidates along the most classic lines:

Vous êtes tous les cinq des chouans, traîtres à la patrie, à la nation, à la France . . . Ce que vous voulez c'est le retour à cet exécrable et vieux régime où les privilèges, le bon plaisir, l'arbitraire et la toute-puissance d'un Roy et de ses courtisans et courtisanes gouvernaient la France et d'où la justice et l'équité étaient bannies. C'est le retour à ce bon vieux temps où le noble et le seignéur de chaque pays disposait

à son gré des biens et de la vie du paysan . . . Osez donc nier que le
noble avait le droit à la dîme . . . à la taille et à la corvée; que le paysan
devait la nuit gauler les étangs du château pour que le sommeil de la
châtelaine ou de la courtisane du château ne fût pas troublé par le
coassement des grenouilles; que le noble avait le droit de jambage, ce
droit infâme de se vautrer dans le lit nuptial du tenancier, la première
nuit de ses noces . . .[164]

There is every possibility that the author actually believed in this classic
republican image of the Ancien Régime, and in the legitimists' intention
to re-establish it. But there is of course little evidence for either — particularly for the latter. It is true that landowners of the 1790s had found
various ways of getting round the abolition of seigneurial dues and tithes
(largely by a compensatory increase in rents or in the owner's share of the
crop), and that a form of tithe lasted in the south-west until into the
twentieth century.[165] But this was a *dîme bourgeoise*, exacted by
republicans and non-nobles quite as much as by legitimists and aristocrats.
There was no chance at all of a return to the situation evoked by republican
propaganda — all the more because that situation was largely mythical
in the first place. Yet peasants continued to believe it, and republicans
continued to exploit that belief. In 1910, in the industrialised Pas-de-
Calais, a republican candidate denounced his adversary as 'le candidat
de la dîme et de la corvée.[166] In the election campagin of the Popular
Front in the Dordogne in 1936, the moderate candidates were presented
as 'l'homme du château', ready to re-establish 'le temps des seigneurs'.[167]

This kind of propaganda succeeded, not because it corresponded to a
real threat, nor because it promised to remedy a genuine exploitation,
but because it appealed to a distorted and impassioned folk-memory. In
doing so, it diverted the attention of peasants from more real and pressing
enemies: in particular, from usurers and from non-noble landowners —
both of whom could easily be republican. Republicanism thus helped,
in effect, to perpetuate the uneven distribution of wealth in the French
countryside, by directing the hatreds of the poor against a figment of the
imagination.

That is, at any rate, a partial explanation for the decline of the social
and political influence of the nobility. It was the victim of a folk-memory,
skilfully exploited by political enemies. This is evidently only a part of
the story: republican propaganda had other anti-noble themes, in particular, noble *accaparements* and *pactes de famine*,[168] and noble lack of
patriotism[169] — which were equally ill-grounded in fact. The clerical issue
— nobles being disproportionately and often ardently catholic — was also

clearly crucial. All of these themes, skilfully manipulated, helped republicans to discredit the nobles and undermine their social and political influence. It was this political offensive, much more than an absolute or even relative economic decline, which accounts for the erosion of that influence. There was no economic necessity about it;[170] the nobles simply lost the battle for the hearts and minds of Frenchmen.

It will not do, however, to overestimate the decline of noble influence and power, even a hundred years after the night of 4 August. Nobles did lose out at national and departmental level. At a local level, however, where they held onto their lands, they could still wield extraordinary power at the end of the nineteenth century. The following story should be a salutary warning against forgetting that fact.[171] In 1892, a very old noble family near Sarlat (Dordogne) was making an inventory of its silverware, and discovered a plate missing; it was found fairly easily, in the box of one of the domestic servants. Instead of informing the police (the agents of a hated government), the lord set up in the great hall of the château, in the presence of all the family and of the assembled servants, a court of seigneurial justice. The unfortunate domestic appeared before this court, which found him guilty, and sentenced him . . . to death. He was hung in the park of the châteux; the police were told that he had been caught *en flagrant délit* and had committed suicide. That was in 1892. . . .

Notes

1 P. Goubert, *Beauvais et le Beauvaisis, de 1600 à 1730* (Paris, 1960), pp. 206–21.
2 For the preceding details, see A.-J. Tudesq, 'Les survivances de l'Ancien Régime: la noblesse dans la société française de la première moitié du XIXe siècle', in D. Roche et C. E. Labrousse (eds), *Ordres et Classes* (Paris and The Hague, 1973), pp. 200–1.
3 See, for example, M. Denis, *Les Royalistes de la Mayenne et le monde moderne (XIXe-XXe siècles)* (Paris, 1977), p. 42.
4 S. W. Serman, *Le Corps des officiers français sous la deuxième République et le Second Empire . . .* (Lille, 1978), vol. I, p. 522.
5 T. Zeldin, *France, 1848-1945*, vol. I: *Ambition, Love and Politics* (Oxford, 1973), pp. 403–4. Zeldin does not mention Giscard, but for some scabrous details on his family tree, see E. Beau de Loménie, *Les Responsabilités des dynasties bourgeoises*, 2e éd. (Paris, 1963), vol. I, pp. 298 and 333, and Pol Bruno, *La Saga des Giscard* (Paris, 1980).
6 L. Girard, A. Prost, R. Gossez, *Les Conseillers généraux en 1870* (Paris, 1967), p. 116. For similar justifications, see A. Guillemain, 'Patrimoine foncier et pouvoir, nobiliaire: la noblesse de la Manche sous la Monarchie de Juillet', *Études Rurales* (July–December, 1976), no. 63-64, p. 117; A.-J. Tudesq, op. cit., p. 202, and *Les Grands Notables en France (1840-1849): étude historique d'une psychologie sociale* (Paris, 1964), vol. I. p. 161.
7 G. Désert, *Une Société rurale au XIXe siècle. Les paysans du Calvados, 1815-1895* (Lille, 1975), vol. I, p. 199 (n. 1); J. Bécarud, 'Noblesse et représentation

parlementaire: les députés nobles de 1871 à 1968', *Revue Française de Science Politique*, 1973, p. 977; F. Bédarida, 'L'Armée et la République: les opinions politiques des officiers français en 1876-78', *Revue Historique*, vol. CCXXII (1964), p. 150.

8 A. Froidefond de Boulazac, *Armorial de la Noblesse du Périgord*, 2 vols. (Périgeux, 1891; repr. Marseilles, 1976). This work is roundly and justly abused by the authoritative E. de Sereville et F. de Saint Simon, *Dictionnaire de la noblesse française* (Paris, 1975), p. 1024 on the grounds that it mixes up noble and bourgeois families, that its sources are unreliable, and that its system of classification is arbitrary. Careful use can however overcome these very real defects. It is supplemented by le comte de Saint Saud, *Additions et Corrections à l'Armorial du Périgord* (Périgueux, 1930).

9 Sereville et Saint Simon (op. cit., p. 16) reject this definition. But their own definition is at least equally inadequate, if not tautological.

10 Lists from the annual *Calendrier de la Dordogne.*

11 Anyone familiar with the parish registers of the Ancien Régime will know that it was not uncommon even for peasants to have a *particule*. See E. le Roy, *Recherches sur l'origine et le valeur des particules des noms dans l'ancien comté de Montignac en Périgord* (Bordeaux, 1889).

12 A.-J. Tudesq, *Les Grands Notables en France (1840-1849) . . .*, op. cit., vol. I, pp. 8-9.

13 We know that the 1830 revolution contained a strong Bonapartist element. See D. Pinkney, *The French Revolution of 1830* (Princeton University Press, 1972), esp. chs. 8 and 9.

14 e.g. A.-J. Tudesq, 'Les survivances . . .', op. cit., p. 123.

15 A. Guillemain, op. cit., pp. 127-9.

16 A.-J. Tudesq, 'Les survivances . . .', op. cit., pp. 206-7. See also A. Guillemain, op. cit., p. 129, and R. Locke, *French Legitimists and the Politics of the Moral Order in the Early Third Republic* (Princeton University Press, 1974), pp. 68-9. The same phenomenon was evident in the Dordogne (although I have not yet attempted to quantify it), as can be seen from the genealogical studies of the comte de Saint Saud: *Généalogies périgourdines* (Bergerac, 1898); *Généalogies périgourdines (2e série)* (Bergerac, 1925); *Essais généalogiques périgourdins* (Paris, 1934); and *Nouveaux Essais généalogiques périgourdins* (Paris, 1942).

17 L. Girard et al., *La Chambre des Députés en 1837-1839: composition, activité, vocabulaire* (Paris, 1976), p. 20.

18 D. Higgs, 'Politics and Landownership among the French nobility after the Revolution', *European Studies Review*, vol. I, no. 2 (April, 1971), p. 116.

19 A. Guillemain, op. cit., p. 119. It is not clear whether the electoral list concerned was drawn up after the new electoral law, lowering the *cens* from 300 to 200 francs in direct taxes, came into effect. 'Nobility' is defined by the particule.

20 Tudesq never found these. The 1839/40 lists lurk, for some mysterious reason, among the archives of the *sous-préfecture* at Nontron: Arch. Dép. Dordogne, 2Z 61. One of the 7 arrondissements (Périgueux II) is missing. The 1829 list survives, even more obscurely, in the communal archives of Hautefort: Arch. Dép. Dordogne, E-supplément, Hautefort.

21 R. Locke, op. cit., ch. 2.

22 Ibid., p. 172.

23 A.-J. Tudesq, *Les conseillers généraux en France au temps de Guizot, 1840-1848* (Paris, 1967), p. 166; also 'Les survivances . . .', op. cit., p. 207.

24 M. Denis, op. cit., p. 27.

25 Ibid., p. 35.

26 P.-B. Higounet, 'La composition de la Chambre des Députés de 1827 à 1831', *Revue Historique*, vol. CCXXXIX (1968), p. 376.

27 Ibid., pp. 356-7.
28 Arch. Dép. Dordogne, 4K 23.
29 *Gazette de France*, 3 September 1836.
30 Arch. Dép. Dordogne, 1M 71.
31 Arch. Dép. Dordogne, 3M 146.
32 This is the thesis of R. Price, 'Legitimist opposition to the Revolution of 1830 in the French provinces', *Historical Journal*, vol. XVII, no. 4 (1974), pp. 755-78; perhaps he overdoes it. I would like to thank him for tolerating this criticism, and for making many helpful suggestions for this paper.
33 D. Greer, *The Incidence of the Terror during the French Revolution: A Statistical Interpretation,* 2nd edition (Harvard University Press, 1966), p. 163.
34 'Liste des périgourdins les plus connus condamnés à mort par le tribunal révolutionnaire, guillotinés à Périgueux ou à Paris et ailleurs', *Chroniqueur du Périgord et du Limousin*: 1855, pp. 57-61; 1856, pp. 1-2. This list is much more exhaustive than that of *Le Tribunal révolutionnaire et criminel de la Dordogne. Documents . . . classés . . . par les commis greffiers du tribunal civil de Périgueux* (Périgueux, 1880-1).
35 J. Vidalenc, *Les émigrés français, 1789-1825* (Caen, 1963), pp. 377-8.
36 D. Greer, *The Incidence of Emigration during the French Revolution* (Harvard University Press, 1951), pp. 109-11.
37 *Liste des noms, surnoms et ci-devant état et grade des émigrés des neufs districts du département de la Dordogne* (Périgueux, 1793), repr. in *Le Chroniqueur du Périgord et du Limousin*, 1856, pp. 82-9. Like all the other lists, this one gives so little detail that my calculation of the percentage of nobles may be seriously awry.
38 J. Vidalenc, op. cit., p. 377.
39 D. Greer, *The Incidence of Emigration . . .*, op. cit., p. 109.
40 A. Gain, *La Restoration et les biens des émigrés*, 2 vols (Nancy, 1928), vol. II, p. 178.
41 Ibid., pp. 211-14. The denominator for these percentages includes ecclesiastics. Gain's calculations, based on the *milliard*, produce a very much higher percentage of nobles than do Greer's, based on contemporary lists – e.g. 26.9 per cent for the Doubs, as against 11.8 per cent, and an estimated majority in the country, as against 17 per cent. It seems likely that nobles, being richer, were more likely than their fellow-*émigrés* to qualify for the indemnity of 1825.
42 Ministère des Finances, *États détaillés des liquidations faites par la commission d'indemnité . . . en exécution de la loi de 27 avril 1825 au profit des anciens propriétaires . . . de biens-fonds confisqués ou aliénés révolutionnairement* (Paris, 1826-1830), 10 vols. (The unique copy of the last volume is in the library of the Ministry of Finance.) 32 of the 405 were ecclesiastics; they are included in the calculations.
43 R. Forster, 'The survival of the nobility during the French Revolution', *Past and Present*, no. 37 (July, 1967), pp. 74-5.
44 A. Gain, op. cit., vol. II, pp. 417-30.
45 P. Massé, *Varennes et ses maîtres: un domaine rural, de l'Ancien Régime à la Monarchie de Juillet (1779-1842)* (Paris, 1956).
46 R. Forster, op. cit., p. 82.
47 D. Higgs, op. cit., p. 110.
48 M. Agulhon, *Le Vie sociale en Provence intérieure au lendemain de la Révolution* (Paris, 1970), pp. 257-9.
49 C. Brelot, *La Noblesse en Franche-Comté de 1789 à 1808* (Besançon, 1972), pp. 122, 146-7, 165.
50 P. Bois, *Paysans de l'Ouest: des structures économiques et sociales aux options*

politiques depuis l'époque révolutionnaire dans la Sarthe (Le Mans, 1960), pp. 319–21.

51 Ibid., p. 675.

52 M. Denis, *Les Royalistes de la Mayenne et le monde moderne (XIXe–XXe siècles)* (Paris, 1977), pp. 157–63.

53 Arch. Dép. Dordogne, Q117*.

54 Arch. Dép. Dordogne: 63P 634 (*matrice cadastrale*, St. Aubin d'Eymet); 2Z 61 (*listes censitaires*).

55 G. Rocal, *De Brumaire à Waterloo en Périgord* (Angoulême, n.d.), vol. I, p. 53.

56 Communication from Mme Lafaye. See also comte de Saint Saud, *Généalogies périgourdines (2e série)*, op. cit., p. 265. Claude Brelot gives other examples, op. cit., pp. 124 and 138.

57 Arch. Dép. Dordogne: 63P 445 (*matrice cadastrale*, Meyrals); 2Z 61 (*listes censitaires*).

58 Arch. Dép. Dordogne, 63P 367 (*matrice cadastrale*, Jumilhac). For slightly contradictory versions of this story, see O. Wolff, *Ouvrard . . .* (London, 1962), ch. 10, and M. Secondat, *Eugène le Roy, connu et méconnu . . .* (Périgueux, 1978), pp. 190–1. Claude Brelot has documented another method, very widespread in the Franche-Comté, of saving the lands of *émigrés*: the laws of 9 floréal an III and 20 floréal an IV, which allowed the parents of émigrés to arrange with the state a *partage de présuccession* (op. cit., pp. 122–3).

59 H. Corneille, 'Archives de Puyguilhem, près Villars', *Bulletin de la Société Historique et Archéologique du Périgord*, vol. 67 (1940), pp. 216–20.

60 Arch. Diocèse Périgueux, C 37.

61 See in particular H. Labroue, *La Mission du conventionnel Lakanal dans la Dordogne en l'an II (oct. 1793–août 1794)* (Paris, 1911); also D. Greer *The Incidence of the Terror . . .*, op. cit., pp. 161–3.

62 J. Vidalenc, op. cit., pp. 377–8. The Dordogne is fifth in the original list of émigrés, tenth in the lists based on the *milliard*, and seventeenth in population.

63 The cadastral survey was set in motion by Napoleon; it was not completed, in many departments, until the later years of the July Monarchy. In the Dordogne, it took from 1810 till 1846.

64 G. Dupeux, *Aspects de l'histoire sociale et politique du Loir-et-Cher, 1848–1914* (Paris and The Hague, 1962), pp. 102–3, 107–8.

65 R. H. Hubschner, *L'Agriculture et la société rurale dans le Pas-de-Calais du milieu du XIXe siècle à 1914* 2 vols, (Arras, 1979), vol. I, pp. 102–3.

66 G. Garrier, *Paysans du Beaujolais et du Lyonnais, 1800–1970*, 2 vols, (Grenoble, 1973), vol. I, pp. 138–9.

67 G. Désert, *Une société rurale au XIXe siècle*, op. cit., pp. 198–9.

68 Arch. Dép. Dordogne, sous-série 63P (which consists of all the *matrices cadastrales*, with the exception of a small number of lacunae).

69 A.-J. Tudesq, *Les Grands Notables . . .* , op. cit., vol. I, p. 186. (On p. 430, slightly different figures are given for the >10,000 bracket: 39 nobles, out of 58.) In a later publication ('Les survivances . . . ', op. cit., p. 208) Tudesq calculates that of 521 *censitaires* paying >5,000 francs, 238 were nobles and 78 *'à prétention nobiliaire'* – a total of 61 per cent.

70 'Les survivances . . . ', op. cit., pp. 208–9.

71 G. Désert, op. cit., vol. I, p. 201; G. Garrier, op. cit., vol. I, p. 137; Y.-M. Hilaire; *Une Chrétienté au XIXe siècle? . . .* (Lille, 1977), vol. I, p. 47; R. H. Hubschner; op. cit., vol. I, p. 104; J. Vidalenc, *Le Département de l'Eure sous la monarchie constitutionnelle (1814–1848)* (Paris, 1952), p. 376 (n.1); G. Dupeux, op. cit., p. 143.

72. See note 20 for references. Remember that the list for Périgueux II (4 cantons) is missing.

73 Dupeux finds that a significant proportion of the wealthier nobility of the Loir-et-Cher was not locally 'active', in that it chose to have its *domicile politique* elsewhere (op. cit., pp. 106–7). This appears to have been much less the case in the Dordogne, which may help to explain why the nobility figures based on the *listes censitaires* are relatively high.

74 Nouvelles Acquisitions Françaises 22284.

75 Taken from Statistique de la France . . ., *Territoire et Population* (Paris, 1837), pp. 213–14.

76 It seems likely that the Dordogne nobles, although not themselves poor, were not quite as well off as some of their counterparts elsewhere. This would explain why the department is more to the forefront in a simple head count than in calculations where the extent or value of their lands is involved.

77 G. Dupeux, *La Société Française, 1789–1960* (Paris, 1964), p. 118 (available as *French Society 1789–1970* [London, 1976]).

78 G. Désert, op. cit., vol. I, p. 204.

79 Arch. Diocèse Périgueux, C 37.

80 Arch. Dép. Dordogne, 8J 37 (letter of 23.1.1828).

81 M. Secondat, op. cit., pp. 134–8. It is true that the girl in question was not herself of aristocratic birth.

82 E. le Roy, *Carnet de Notes* . . . (Périgueux, 1970), p. 96; G. Guillaume *Eugène le Roy, romancier périgourdin (1836–1907)* (Bordeaux, 1929), pp. 77–8. Neither source states clearly that the girl whose presence thus stimulated this anecdote was Charlotte de Lostanges, but the circumstantial evidence is strong.

83 Most of this story is based on oral evidence, but local people at any rate believe it to be true.

84 P. Vigier, *Essai sur la répartition de la propriété foncière dans la région alpine. Son évolution des origines du cadastre à la fin du Second Empire* (Paris, 1963), pp. 194–200. For 27 of the 47 cantons of the Dordogne, we possess the electoral lists for the end of the Restoration (1829), and the beginning (1833/4), middle (1839/40) and end (1846) of the July Monarchy: Arch. Dép. Dordogne 2Z 61; E – supplément, Belvès, Pazayac, Léguillac de l'Auche et Razac de Saussignac; Arch. Ville Périgueux, série K, no. 2, vol. I. For these 27 cantons, the number of electors (of all kinds) paying more than 1,000 francs evolved from 132 in 1829, through 113 (1833/4) and 146 (1839/40), to 145 in 1846; at the same time, the number of electors in the lower brackets increased much faster. I have not yet analysed the role of specifically noble property in this evolution.

85 M. Denis, op. cit., pp. 27–32.

86 G. Désert, op. cit., vol. III, p. 1082. (15.8 per cent if one family residing on the border of the department is excluded.)

87 Ibid., p. 1083. This figure is a bit exaggerated, because Désert has classed as *'forains'* all those residing outside the *bureau de perception* – usually smaller than a canton.

88 Ibid., p. 1084.

89 G. Dupeux, 'Aspects de l'histoire politique du Loir-et-Cher, 1848–1914', op. cit., pp. 102, 575.

90 Ibid., p. 576.

91 R. Hubschner, op. cit., vol. II, pp. 715–16.

92 Ministère de l'Agriculture, de la Commerce et des Travaux Publics, *Enquête agricole, 2e série: enquêtes départementales, 16e circonscription* (Paris, 1867), p. 180.

93 R. Pijassou, *Regards sur la révolution agricole en Dordogne* (Périgueux, 1967), p. 16.

94 Arch. diocèse Périgueux, D 9.

95 C. Brelot, op. cit., p. 120.

96   A.-J. Tudesq, *Les Grands Notables* . . . , op. cit., vol. I, pp. 103–7.

97   On the failure to reintroduce a *droit d'ainesse* – important, but for which there is no space here – see R. Forster, op. cit., pp. 83–4, and M. Denis, op. cit., p. 339. Balzac was obsessed by it – see (inter alia) *Le Curé de village* (Paris, ed. Libres de Poche, 1965), p. 282, et passim.

98   The fate of some of the families who became extinct in the course of the nineteenth century can be traced in the genealogies of the comte de Saint Saud (see note 16 for references). It seems that the failure to marry, and the failure to have children when married, were at least partly to blame.

99   See J. Goumet, *Autour du château d'Hautefort, 1789–1890* (Périgueux, 1972), chs. XI and XII; E. Secondat, *Eugène le Roy* . . . , op. cit., pp. 46, 92–4, 376 et passim.

100 See A. Froidefond de Boulazac, *Armorial de la Noblesse du Périgord*, op. cit., vol. I, pp. 105–6.

101 Quoted by A. Gain, op. cit., vol. II, p. 419 (n.4).

102 Bibliothèque Nationale, Fonds Périgord, vol. 104, f. 638. It is true that according to the malicious pen of comte Horace de Viel-Castel, the lady in question was no more than an ex-cook, married *in extremis* by M. de Taillefer. (*Mémoires . . . sur le règne de Napoléon III*, vol. I, [Paris, 1883] p. 73.)

103 G. Lavergne, *Histoire de Périgueux* (Périgueux, 1945), pp. 139–41; R. Fournier de Laurière, *Les Grands Travaux de voirie à Périgueux du XIXe siècle* (Sarlat, 1938).

104 Arch. Diocèse Périgueux, unclassified: registre des confréries (at the end of the register).

105 Arch. Diocèse Périgueux: two unclassified notebooks, kept in the library.

106 Arch. Dép. Dordogne, sous-série 47P.

107 It is possible that a local address in the 1890 rolls sometimes had a different significance from one in the *matrice cadastrale*.

108 The matrices of the 1913 *cadastre* form the continuation of the sub-series 63P in the departmental archives.

109 I have been forced to adopt a rather more lax definition of nobility for 1913, inasmuch as many names with a *particule* are evidently newcomers to the region (probably the husbands of noble ladies of the Périgord), such that the position of their ancestors in 1789 is not clear. Communes where the *matrice* from either cadastral survey is missing are not included.

110 T. D. Beck, *French Legislators 1800–1834: A Study in Quantitative History* (University of California Press, 1974), Appendix C. The categories are not wholly satisfactory – see his page 147.

111 L. Girard et al., *La Chambre des Députés en 1837–1839* . . . (Paris, 1976), p. 19; P.-B. Higounet, 'La composition de la Chambre des Députés de 1827 à 1831, *Revue Historique*, vol. CCXXXIX (April–June, 1968), pp. 369 and 376. 'Doubtful' nobility means with a *particule*. Both these authors reject the figures given by J. Bécarud, 'La noblesse dans les chambres, 1815–1848', *Revue Internationale d'Histoire Politique et Constitutionnelle* (July–September, 1953), pp. 189–205.

112 For a brief discussion of their differences, see Beck, p. 129 (n.9).

113 P.-B. Higounet, op. cit., p. 368.

114 Ibid., p. 369.

115 L. Girard, A. Prost, R. Gossez, *Les conseillers généraux en 1870* (Paris, 1967), p. 117.

116 J. Bécarud, 'Noblesse et représentation parlementaire: les députés nobles de 1871 à 1968', *Revue Française de Science politique* (1973), p. 976.

117 Op. cit., p. 976 and 990–1; G. Dupeux, *La société française, 1789–1960*, op. cit., p. 188.

118 A.-J. Tudesq, *Les conseillers généraux en France* . . . , op. cit., pp. 162 and 168.

119 L. Girard et al., *Les conseillers généraux en 1870*, op. cit., p. 118.

120 M. Denis, op. cit., p. 135.

121 C. Marcilhacy, *Le diocèse d'Orléans au milieu du XIXe siècle* (Paris, 1964), p. 111.

122 A. Guillemain, 'Patrimoine foncier et pouvoir nobiliaire . . .' (op. cit.), p. 123. (No total for the number of communes in the department is given.)

123 From the annual *Calendrier de la Dordogne*. I hope some day to finish the calculations for 1881 and 1901.

124 The legislation on the election or selection of *maires* changed a number of times. In particular, the law of 21.3.1831 stipulated that they had to be selected from the elected *conseil municipal*, which was not previously the case. See F. Ponteil, *Les institutions de la France de 1814 à 1870* (Paris, 1966), pp. 156 et seq.

125 C. Pouthas, 'Le clergé sous la monarchie constitutionnelle, 1814–1848', *Revue d'Histoire de l'Eglise de France*, vol. XXIX, (1943), pp. 19–53.

126 Ibid.

127 A.-J. Tudesq. *Les Grands Notables* . . . , op. cit., pp. 188–9.

128 J. Gadille, *La Pensée et l'action politique des évêques français au début de la IIIe République, 1870/1883*, 2 vols. (Paris, 1967), vol. I, p. 27.

129 A. de Pontmartin, quoted by A. Mathet, 'Rapport sur les vocations sacerdotales dans les collèges catholiques . . .', '*L'Enseignement Chrétien* (suppl. au no. du 1er nov., 1899), p. 14.

130 W. S. Serman, *Le Corps des officiers français sous la Deuxième République et le Second Empire: aristocratie et démocratie dans l'armée au milieu du XIXe siècle*, 2 vols. (Lille, 1978), vol. I, p. 496.

131 Ibid., pp. 496–507.

132 Ibid., p. 634.

133 K. Demeter, *The German Officer-Corps in Society and State, 1650–1945* (London, 1965), p. 28.

134 'Les généraux français de 1870', *Revue de Défense Nationale*, vol. 26 (1970), p. 1326.

135 F. Bédarida, 'L'Armée et la République: les opinions politiques des officiers français en 1876–78', *Revue Historique*, vol. CCXXII (1964), p. 150.

136 W. S. Serman, op. cit., pp. 516–35; L. Muncy, *The Junker in Prussian Administration under William II, 1888–1914* (Providence, R.I., 1944).

137 J. Lhomme, *La Grande Bourgeoisie au pouvoir (1830–1880): essai sur l'histoire sociale de la France* (Paris, 1960), pp. 39–40. (It will be apparent from the foregoing that I do not entirely agree with his formulation about a decline in *absolute* wealth either.)

138 M. Lévy-Leboyer, 'La croissance économique en France au XIXe siècle: résultats préliminaires', *Annales E.S.C.* (July–August, 1968), p. 800.

139 G. Palmade, *Capitalisme et capitalistes français au XIXe siècle* (Paris, 1961), p. 204.

140 D. Higgs, op. cit., p. 123.

141 G. Dupeux, *Aspects de l'histoire sociale et politique du Loir-et-Cher, 1848–1914*, op. cit., pp. 143–4.

142 A.-J. Tudesq, '. . . La noblesse dans la société française de la première moitié du XIXe siècle', op. cit., p. 212. See also *Les Grands Notables* . . ., op. cit., p. 435.

143 R. Locke, *French Legitimists* . . ., op. cit., ch. 3.

144 M. Denis, op. cit., p. 242–3.

145 J.-C. Toutain, *La Population de la France de 1700 à 1959*, Cahiers de l'I.S.E.A., *Histoire quantitative de l'économie française*, no. 3 (Paris, 1963), pp. 54–5. (Toutain's column headings are inverted.)

146 Ministère du Commerce, de l'Industrie, des Postes et des Télégraphes . . . ,
     *Résultats statistiques du recensement général de la population effectué le
     24 mars 1901* (Paris, 1906), vol. III, p. 552; Statistique de la France, 2e série,
     T. II, *Territoire et Population* (Paris, 1855), pp. 182-3.
147 I.N.S.E.E., *Population par commune de 1876 à 1962: département de la Dor-
     dogne* (Bordeaux, 1964), p. 8.
148 The *Calendrier de la Dordogne* for 1900 has a convenient list of all past deputies,
     pp. 50-1.
149 A.-J. Tudesq, *Les Grands Notables* . . . , op. cit., vol. I, p. 122.
150 This is one of the themes of Michel Denis, op. cit. It is also evoked with great
     skill by Jean d'Ormesson, *Au plaisir de Dieu* (Paris, 1974) – see, for example,
     pp. 28-30.
151 M. Agulhon, *La République au village* (Paris, 1970), esp. pp. 42-92.
152 Quoted by E. Constant, *Le département du Var sous le Second Empire et au
     début de la Troisième République*, Thèse pour le Doctorat-ès-Lettres, Université
     de Provence-Aix (1977), pp. 458-9. Other organisations of agricultural nota-
     bilities made similar remarks (loc. cit.). The phenomenon has been lucidly
     analysed in an as yet unpublished paper by Roger Price, 'Labour supply and
     social relationships in the French countryside during the Second Empire'.
153 Arch. Dép. Dordogne: 3M 175, 189, 203, 227.
154 Arch. Dép. Dordogne: 3M 173.
155 A. Corbin, *Archaïsme et Modernité en Limousin au XIXe siècle, 1845-1880*,
     2 vols. (Paris, 1975), vol. I, p. 170 – and see pp. 163-70 for the best local study
     of usury that I know of. See also G. Désert, op. cit., vol. II, pp. 510-15; P.
     Vigier, *La Seconde République dans la région alpine: étude politique et sociale*,
     2 vols. (Paris, 1963), vol. I, pp. 38-40; J.-F. Soulet, 'Usure et usuriers dans les
     Pyrénées au XIXe siècle, *Annales du Midi*, vol. 90, nos. 138-9 (1978), pp.
     435-47.
156 Arch. Dép. Dordogne 3U 1 (registres des jugements du tribunal correctionnel
     de Sarlat. Lacunae: 1807-9, 1825-43, 1847-9). It is of course possible that
     userers higher in the social scale (specially notaries) managed to avoid inculpation.
157 Arch. Nat F 1C III Dordogne 7 (rapport du premier trimestre, 1812 – et passim).
158 J.-F. Soulet, op. cit., p. 141.
159 G. Bussière, *Études historiques sur la Révolution en Périgord*, 3 vols. (Bordeaux,
     1877-1885-1903), vol. III, livre 2e: 'La fin de la féodalité – esp. p. 409; P.
     Caron, 'Le mouvement antiseigneurial de 1790 dans le Sarladais et le Quercy',
     Bulletin d'Histoire économique de la Révolution (1912), pp. 353-86; J. Boutier,
     'Les révoltes paysannes en Aquitaine (décembre 1789-mars 1790)', *Annales
     E.S.C.* (July-August 1979), pp. 760-86.
160 A. Siegfried, *Tableau politique de la France de l'Ouest sous la Troisième Répub-
     lique* (Paris, 1913), p. 73.
161 Arch. Nat. BB 30 359; G. Rocal, *1848 en Dordogne*, 2 vols. (Paris, 1933),
     vol. II, p. 232.
162 Arch. Nat. BB 359.
163 Arch. Dép. Dordogne 3M 60. See also (for the same phenomenon in 1868)
     A. Soboul, 'Survivances féodales dans la société rurale du XIXe siècle', *Annales
     E.S.C.* (Sept.-Oct. 1958), repr. in A. Soboul, *Problèmes paysans de la Révolu-
     tion, 1789-1848* (Paris, 1976), pp. 164-5.
164 Quoted by M. Denis, op. cit., p. 475.
165 See A. Soboul, op. cit., and M. Denis, op. cit., p. 167.
166 Y.-M. Hilaire, *Une Chrétienté au XIXe siècle?* . . . , op. cit., p. 811 (and p. 511),
     for 1877).
167 Quoted by J.-Y. Lachaudru, *Le Front Populaire en Dordogne*, Travail d'Étude
     et de Recherche (Bordeaux, 1971), p. 72.

168 This was also a theme employed by Louis-Philippe's administrators – see M. Denis, op. cit., pp. 210, 274, 276, 305 (n.82). I very much doubt whether there was any truth in it, despite G. Désert, op. cit., pp. 490–4.

169 In 1870, it was widely believed that the nobles and curés were in league with the Prussians – see J. M. Villefranche, *Curés et Prussiens*, 2e éd. (Bourg, 1877). It was a major theme of the famous 'meurtre d'Hautefaye', when a peasant mob in the north of the Dordogne lynched a local noble and burnt him alive. See J.-L. Galet, *Meurtre à Hautefaye* (Périgueux, 1970); E. Secondat, op. cit., pp. 172–3; and the forthcoming book (and perhaps film) currently being prepared by Georges Marbeck. In 1914, it was claimed in the Haut-Nontronnais that Wilhelm II had installed himself in a château in the region, from which he sallied forth at night, and in the morning the sandy driveway bore the traces of his footsteps (G. Rocal, *Croquants du Périgord* [Paris, n.d.], p. 124).

170 Unless perhaps one sees it as the long-term consequence of the relations of production under the Ancien Régime.

171 This story was told to me more or less under the seal of the confessional; readers are requested not to reproduce it in any written form.

2 The baccalaureate and its role in the recruitment and formation of French elites in the nineteenth century*

PAUL GERBOD
University of Paris-Nord

In spite of the heritage of the French Revolution and of the Declaration of the Rights of Man and Citizen, elites — prominent individuals in the fields of politics, administration, the economy and culture — exerted an undeniable if not exclusive influence within French society during the last century. If we are to understand their nature and the forms which their influence took, it is necessary to examine closely their modes of recruitment (birth, wealth or talent?) as well as their technical and cultural education and training. What we find is that selection processes operating through school and university began in the nineteenth century to compete with the more traditional advantages of birth and wealth. In this context, it is important to look at the role played by the baccalaureate — which was not only the official certificate marking the completion of secondary education but also the lowest level of higher education — in the recruitment and formation of elites.

How rigorous was the baccalaureate as a mode of selection?

The baccalaureate existed in the French university system before the Revolution of 1789, and was re-established in 1809 within the framework of the Napoleonic university and higher education reforms (in law, theology, arts and sciences).[1] The arts baccalaureate (*baccalauréat ès lettres*) soon came to be thought of as a secondary school leaving certificate for the *classe de philosophie* (the equivalent of the upper sixth form) and as indicating the level of grades necessary for going on to study for first and higher degrees — *licence* and doctorate — in the faculties of the state university system. It even succeeded in the bourgeois society of the last century in taking on an unexpected and growing significance, as the yardstick of career success and thus of social mobility upwards into the ruling classes.[2]

    Of course access to the arts baccalaureate came only at the end of

* translated by Philip G. Cerny

studies at the secondary level. These could have been pursued by private tutoring, but in fact they tended overwhelmingly to take place either in state schools (lycées or royal colleges and communal colleges) or in private establishments (academies, boarding schools and small seminaries). In the last century secondary schooling was itself still the privilege of a minority of children. In 1809 51,085 students were enrolled in the various secondary establishments; in 1854 they had risen to 119,560 and to just 176,796 by 1910. Over a century, then, the secondary school population only increased by a factor of 3.5. It must be noted that these statistical estimates include older students still doing primary classes in both public and private secondary schools (25 to 30 per cent of the total) but do not take into account female students until 1881 (in 1900 lycées and colleges for girls in the state sector had only 15,500 students).[3]

The importance of social and cultural advantages is even more apparent when one considers the figures for the proportion of the 10–19 age group (boys only) attending school and the relationship between the number of pupils and the total population between 1809 and 1910. The following table shows how the situation evolved:[4]

Year	Enrolment rate (per 10,000 school-age children)	No. of pupils per 10,000 total population
1809	167	17
1820	162	16
1830	209	21
1854	375	33
1876	483	41
1884	478	42
1898	500	42
1910	470	38

Secondary schooling represented a process which was both relatively long (at least seven years from the first form – the *sixième* – to the *classe de philosophie*) and costly in that it did not lead directly to well-paid job opportunities. Among children from modest backgrounds only those who were thought extremely gifted and who could win a scholarship could embark on this road alongside the heirs of the bourgeoisie. Of course this is a very broad claim, and it will be useful to look more closely at the nuances of the situation over the course of the century.

Thus in the royal colleges and lycées the percentage of scholarship students, which had been as high as 43 per cent in 1810, soon diminished, going down to 16.6 per cent in 1830, 11 per cent in 1850 and as low as 7 per cent in 1880. By 1890 this proportion had still not risen above about 10 per cent. In the communal colleges the number of *boursiers* was even lower: just one per thousand in 1809, 0.5 per cent in 1830 and 4.1 per cent in 1882. In girls' schools, which also gave scholarships, only 6 per cent were *boursières* in 1900. What is more, under the Empire scholarships were not given to the poorest or brightest children but to the sons of civil servants and military officers (who belonged therefore to the bourgeoisie). Under the July Monarchy (1830–48), the situation had become scandalous: scholarships for secondary education were all too often given out for electoral purposes to the children of the *notables* who made up the electorate of the *Monarchie censitaire* (which was based on a wealth qualification). Even under the Third Republic, this traditional 'fiddle' was far from having disappeared: in 1890 60 per cent of the *bourses* were given out to the children of civil servants and only 20 per cent went to those of 'modest' background (farmers and farmworkers, artisans, and industrial workers). It would also seem to have been the case that some scholarships were available in private church schools, but the extent of this practice and its change over time as a proportion of students are unknown. In the smaller seminaries, alongside paying students of noble or bourgeois background there was also a certain number of scholarship students who were taken on with a view to their eventual entry into the priesthood, as witnessed by the more modest class backgrounds of much of the clergy in the nineteenth century.[5]

Even after 1880 children of lower-class backgrounds did not enter the lycées and colleges; they tended to leave with just their primary school leaving certificates, unless they went on to study in the *écoles primaires supérieures* or the *écoles normales primaires*. On the other hand secondary education did open up rather more for the children of the petty bourgeoisie with backgrounds in commerce, the lower ranks of the civil service and primary school teaching (sons and daughters of schoolteachers and white-collar workers in the post office, the railways, etc.). In the public establishments (lycées and colleges) of the Seine department in 1879, the children of professional men, of state employees and of those with an independent income from property represented more than half of the school population. The *embourgeoisement* of the clientele was even more highly accentuated in the private schools than in the state sector.

This socio-cultural selection process was exacerbated further by the high dropout rate for both intellectual and disciplinary reasons. In the first half of the century between 12 and 20 per cent of pupils dropped out between the *sixième* and the *classe de philosophie* in the royal colleges. In the 1860s the rate went up to 20–25 per cent; ten years later it rose steeply to 47–50 per cent (just a third between the *sixième* and the *classe de rhétorique* or lower sixth form); and by the end of the century it had reached 55-60 per cent. The dropout rate was even higher in the communal colleges, where it was already on the order of 60 per cent in the 1870s (in the classics sections) and 70 per cent in the 1880s. The situation was yet worse in the mathematics sections (in 1887, where there had been 4,156 pupils in the first year only about a hundred were left in the last). There is no statistical information available on dropout rates in private schools.

But for those students who did manage to stay the course up to the *classes de philosophie*, there remained the hurdle of the arts baccalaureate (and, for a smaller number, the science baccalaureate). And, from the 1830s onwards, this examination — the first stage of a system of examinations based on elimination of those who did not reach a particular standard (*concours*) — tended to become more difficult. A pass rate of more than 60 per cent turned into a failure rate of higher than 50 per cent. Between 1840 and 1900, while the number of candidates was growing from year to year (from 7,000 to 20,000), the pass rate varied between 39 and 46 per cent for all of the baccalaureates taken as a whole (*lettres*, sciences, and later 'modern studies'). In sciences the success rate seems always to have been below 40 per cent (between 34 and 39 per cent).

In these circumstances, the number of *bacheliers* each year between 1820 and 1909 rose from 3,000 (3,068 in 1820) to around 7,000 (7,225 in 1909). This increase was primarily linked to the growing number of science *bacheliers* (119 in 1850 and 2,570 in 1909), for in *lettres* there were 3,059 in 1820 and only 4,638 in 1909. The title of *bachelier* thus remained a rare qualification in French society as a whole. In 1820 10 young French people received their baccalaureates for every 100,000 of the population, and only 18 by 1909. As a proportion of the total cohort of 19-year-old males (i.e. about 300,000), the percentage of *bacheliers* varied between 1 per cent and 2.4 per cent from 1820 to 1909. But even if there were only a few thousand baccalaureates given out each year, over the whole century (1809-1909) the impact was considerable; the total number of baccalaureates in arts and sciences was 440,000 (312,630 *lettres*, 127,000 science and modern studies). The holders of these diplomas were to be found in increasing numbers in the entering classes of the *grandes écoles* and in the faculties of the state university system, not to mention in both public and private sector management, for the baccalaureate had become no more and no less than an indispensable step on the road to eventual admission into the elites of the country.[6]

The baccalaureate as badge of intellectual ability and certificate of bourgeois culture

Even though the baccalaureate came only as the culmination of a variety of selection processes and remained a rare and sought-after qualification in the nineteenth century, it is important to look closely at the examination process itself and at its intellectual and social significance.

From the 1840s onwards the baccalaureate was the object of impassioned attacks from certain quarters. Defenders of private education denounced the examination as one of the most unjust features of the state monopoly in the university sector; others stressed the formal character of the studies which it endorsed, rewarding 'lightweight rhetoricians' ('*rhéteurs au petit pied*'), puffed up with pretensions, and ready and waiting to serve the demagoguery of socialism. Parents of pupils attacked the severity of the juries, while in their annual reports the deans of faculties multiplied their criticisms of incapable, ill-prepared and uncultured candidates.[7] For its part the academic bureaucracy waged a continuous campaign against the practice resorted to by some better-off pupils of hiring proxies, translators and ghost-writers to do their work and to sit their examinations for them.[8] Between 1820 and 1850 one can identify no fewer than seventy ordinances, decrees, regulations, circulars and ministerial instructions relating to the baccalaureate.[9]

Despite these legislative and regulatory measures the baccalaureate continued to arouse criticism during the second half of the century. Modifications introduced in 1864 and 1874 in its administration did not assuage the discontent, which had become chronic. In 1885 the Ministry of Public Instruction launched an extensive enquiry in the faculties and secondary schools with a view to proposing reforms to this 'cornerstone of French secondary education': 306 of these establishments provided precise and often rather long replies. Again in 1898–9 at the time of the great parliamentary enquiry on the subject of the 'malaise of secondary education', the problem of the baccalaureate was discussed several times and treated in depth during the course of the committee's work.[10]

When dealing with as controversial a question as this, it is useful to make a certain number of observations with regard to the nature of the baccalaureate itself. In the first place, it became indispensable after 1820 to be a *bachelier* in order to embark on university courses (particularly in law and medicine) and to enter a variety – growing all the time – of posts in public administration; it also progressively became a prerequisite for access to what were then called the '*écoles spéciales du gouvernement*' (now called the *grandes écoles*), such as the École Polytechnique and the

École Normale Supérieure. During the course of the century a number of other baccalaureates were set up alongside the arts baccalaureate (in 1859 one can identify five types of science baccalaureate), especially in mathematics education and later in modern studies; furthermore, after 1874 the baccalaureate was divided into two parts, the first part being taken at the end of the *classe de première* (also *rhétorique*), equivalent to the lower sixth form.

As well as this structural diversification of an examination which gradually came to authenticate different types of secondary education, the forms by which it was controlled changed too. Up to 1830 the examination itself consisted of a discussion of about three-quarters of an hour between the candidate and the members of a jury concerning the subjects studied in philosophy, rhetoric and humanities classes; in 1830 an eliminatory written test was introduced (a dissertation in French or a Latin translation) and in 1840 the written test became a compulsory Latin translation; in 1852 it comprised a Latin translation and a composition in Latin or French. The oral examinations (which now lasted an hour) included *explications de texte* from Latin and Greek and oral questions on various problems from the curriculum. Comparable changes were introduced in the other baccalaureates (science and mathematics).

As these structural changes were taking place – imposed, in fact, by the teaching profession – the main characteristics of the *baccalauréat ès lettres* became more and more precise. Firstly, the examination rewarded a certain kind of ability to reason (the object of the Latin translation) and to express oneself (the aim of the Latin or French essay). The oral tests were supposed to bring out the candidate's appreciation of the nature and dimensions of a humanist culture built upon Latin, French and even Greek literature, history, geography and philosophy, as well as to make it possible to judge such qualities as thoughtfulness, quickness of mind and oral expression.

Results were frequently rather far removed from the objectives implied in the nature of the tests themselves. Even before 1850 many of the juries (made up of university teachers) deplored the mediocrity of the majority of candidates and emphasised the indulgence which the judges were called upon to show time after time. Between the 1840s and the 1860s, the rather too precise setting out of the problems on the syllabus (up to 500 questions) contributed to the advent of the age of study manuals for those taking the baccalaureate and the success of cramming schools ('*boîtes à bachot*'); the baccalaureate became a memory test, the result of mechanical cramming and without great cultural or intellectual value. ['*Bachotage*', the word for cramming, stems from the slang for baccalaureate. *Trans.*] In the 1880s, in spite of a number of structural improvements (a less constricting syllabus, separation into two parts, etc.), progress was scarcely discernable. According to a national survey concerning the arts baccalaureate, the proportion of excellent candidates was only 8.17 per cent, while mediocre candidates comprised nearly 70 per cent of the total. At that time the university authorities generally recognised that the baccalaureate was not a sufficient guarantee of the ability to get a good start on, and successfully to complete, a course in higher education, and the first moves were made towards instituting a transitional year (called an *année de propédeutique*) which would lead to a *certificat d'année préparatoire*.

The career prospects of *bacheliers*

From the beginning the baccalaureate constituted a university entrance qualification; it progressively became a prerequisite for studying towards the entrance examinations of the *grandes écoles*; and it also allowed direct entry into supernumerary posts in the civil service. But it was not indispensable for becoming well known in literature, arts and politics. What sorts of careers, then, did nineteenth-century *bacheliers* in fact go into?

The *grandes écoles*, at that time called *écoles spéciales du gouvernement*, were limited for most of the century to the following: the École Polytechnique, the École Navale, and the École Forestière in Nancy, to which must be added the École Centrale des Arts et Manufactures and the École Normale Supérieure in the Rue d'Ulm. (The École des Mines and the École des Ponts et Chausées mainly provided specialised service courses for students at the École Polytechnique at this time.) At the end of the century other *grandes écoles* appeared such as the École Normale de Sèvres, the Hautes Études Commerciales, the École Libre des Sciences Politiques and various engineering schools such as the Institut Industriel du Nord and the École des Ingénieurs de Marseilles. At about 1840 there were around a thousand students studying for the competitive entrance examinations (*concours*) of the *grandes écoles* in the lycées, the royal colleges and the communal colleges. In the 1880s and 1890s this figure had nearly tripled (to 2,900) if state and private schools are taken together (e.g. the École Sainte-Geneviève in the Rue des Postes, run by Jesuits since 1857). But at that time the number of places made available through *concours* in the various schools was only 800. Candidates who failed could always do a *licence* in arts, sciences or law in the universities. Furthermore, admission to the *grandes écoles* was no guarantee of an illustrious future: many *normaliens* in arts and in sciences, after having achieved the title of *agrégé*, finished their careers as *professeurs de lycée* (senior secondary school teachers); similarly, many of the Polytechnique's old boys were to be found as officers in the artillery or engineer corps. At the beginning of this century, public opinion was shocked to find engineers trained at the École Centrale out of work or in low-status occupations.[11]

A rather higher number of *bacheliers* entered the university faculties, although this took different forms in different disciplines. For example, from the time of the Restoration onwards the Catholic faculties of theology found it difficult to attract students. Aspiring clerics received their secondary education in small seminaries and then went on to the larger seminaries to study theology;[12] thus the theology faculties were closed in 1885. The *Facultés des Lettres* and the *Facultés des Sciences* did not really have proper students before the 1880s, when the first university scholarships were introduced; their staff gave public lectures, along with a few '*conférences fermées*' for those rare students who actually aspired to a *licence* or an *agrégation*.[13] In contrast, by 1890 these faculties already had 3,100 full-time students and by 1914 this figure had risen to nearly 14,000.[14] It is true that the *licence* in arts or sciences was not much use except for becoming a boarding school master, a professor or a form master (*régent*) in a state secondary school. On the other hand it was a prerequisite for a university student who wished to enter for the *agrégation*, but the competition from students of the École Normale Supérieure was stiff and the chances of success by non-*normaliens* pretty marginal, especially outside Paris.[15]

In fact, only the faculties of law, medicine and pharmacy led into the professions. They also had the most students. In the first part of the century their overall enrolment averaged around 8,000–9,000 per year; thus between 2,000 and 2,500 *bacheliers* entered first-year courses in law or medicine every year. In the second half of the century student numbers grew more rapidly: from around 10,000 law and medical students in the 1850s they rose to more than 20,000 at the turn of the century; first-year enrolments went from 2,700 to 5,100 in 1900. But by the beginning of the present century it becomes more important to take into account the number of arts and science students, at least after the 1880s when their numbers rose from the region of 3,700 around 1890 to nearly 12,000 in 1910.

Between 1820 and 1850 an estimated 50–60 per cent of new *bacheliers* went on to study law, and about 45 per cent of these lasted the course and received their law degrees; about 25 per cent went on to study medicine, and nearly half of these became doctors. After 1850 a certain number of changes took place in these career patterns. The proportion opting to study law dropped to around 30 per cent and medicine to about 18 per cent. On the other hand the percentage of those who successfully completed a *licence en droit* or a *doctorat en médecine* hardly varied (49 and 53 per cent respectively). However, in relation to the student population as a whole, the proportion who received their *licences* (in *lettres*, sciences and law) or who became medical doctors decreased sharply: it was about 15 per cent in the 1830s–1850s and 14 per cent between 1860 and 1890; but it was not more than 10 per cent just after the turn of the century.

Indeed at this time access to the professions seems to have been more difficult; the term 'intellectual proletariat' was applied to doctors without patients and lawyers without clients.[16] The future of those who obtained their baccalaureates tended to become more insecure for the same reasons. The certification of elites by means of examinations and *concours* – and notably by means of the *baccalauréat ès lettres* – became a more and more hazardous process.

Nonetheless, the baccalaureate – as the highest level of secondary education and the lowest of higher education – remains one of the important elements in the recruitment and training of French elites in the nineteenth century. It did not, in fact, test any real level of intellectual ability or attainment; rather its primary function was to legitimate and sanction a certain form of culture, that of the decent and virtuous '*honnête homme*', capable of holding his own in bourgeois society and of being recognised and respected within it. Many successful personalities in the world of the arts, however, never obtained this '*brevet de bourgeoisie*', although they could not help but be marked by the imprint of that particular form of humanist culture in the lycées and colleges even if they turned a deaf ear to it or rejected it outright. There is no doubt that the twentieth century has been more eclectic and liberal in its recognition of elites, reducing the baccalaureate to a less important and more contingent role.

Notes

1 In the distant past the church was a means of upward social mobility for children of modest background; but from the seventeenth century and particularly the eighteenth century onwards, writers, artists and intellectuals contributed to the constitution of a new bourgeoisie – the bourgeoisie of 'talents': cf. Paul Benichou, *Le sacre de l'écrivain: Essai sur l'avénement d'un pouvoir spirituel laïque dans la France moderne* (Paris, 1973). In the nineteenth century, in the context of a

society which had emerged from the Revolution and the Empire, the baccalaureate was given a legal status as the means of access into the *catégories dirigeantes* (see the Statute of 13 September 1820 and the Circular of 19 September: '. . . dorénavant, le grade de bachelier va ouvrir l'entrée à toutes les professions civiles et devenir pour la société une garantie essentielle de la capacité de ceux qu'elle admettra à la servir . . .').

2 Cf. J. B. Piobetta, *Le baccalauréat*, thesis in *lettres* (Paris, 1937) and Octave Gréard, *Éducation et instruction en l'enseignement supérieur* (Paris, n.d.). pp. 151 ff.

3 Edmond Gobot, *La barrière et le niveau* (Paris, first edition 1925; originally written before the First World War).

4 These statistics are drawn from successive ministerial enquiries into secondary and higher education published between 1842 and 1900 (in the series Lf 242, Bibliothèque Nationale). Numbers in private education are more difficult to estimate; nonetheless some useful indices can be found in the enquiries cited above (cf. also the enquiry of 1854 in the *Bulletin administratif* of the Ministère de l'Instruction Publique). Note that before 1850 private school students had to have done courses in state schools in order to sit the baccalaureate; students who had received private tutoring had to produce a *'certificat d'études domestiques'*.

5 In the book in which he deals with recruitment to the clergy in the Diocese of Besançon from the nineteenth to the twentieth century, Abbé Huot-Pleureoux provides useful information on the social origins of seminarians (in this rural diocese, about 70–80 per cent of seminarians came from peasant backgrounds; in contrast, less than 8 per cent came from the bourgeoisie).

6 In volume 21 of the series *Enquêtes et documents relatifs à l'enseignement supérieur* there appears the annual account of diplomas awarded by the various faculties of the state university system (between 1795 and 1885). This account can be completed after 1885 thanks to the ministerial enquiries of 1898 and the *Annuaire statistique de la France*, which began publication in 1878.

7 The literature hostile to the baccalaureate was varied and significant. It is referred to in Louis Grimaud, *Histoire de la liberté de l'enseignement en France – Restauration et Monarchie de Juillet*, and in Paul Gerbod, *La condition universitaire en France au 19e siècle*, especially the analysis on pp. 252–3 of F. Bastiat, *Baccalauréat et socialisme* (1850).

8 In the first part of the century specialised reviews like *le Lycée, la Revue Spéciale de l'Instruction Publique* and *la Revue de l'Instruction Publique* published extracts of the annual reports of the deans of the *facultés des lettres* on the various sittings of the baccalaureate; the same is true for the period 1850–80. After 1885 it is possible to consult the annual reports of the deans and university councils included in the series of *Enquêtes et documents relatifs à l'enseignement supérieur*.

9 Texts relating to the baccalaureate were collected and published in the appendices to the work of J. B. Piobetta, op. cit.

10 There is an analysis of the reports in Gréard, op. cit., and they are published in *Enquêtes et documents relatives à l'enseignement supérieur*, vol. 18 passim.

11 In the *Annuaire de la Jeunesse*, published by the Librairie Vuibert from 1881 onwards, can be found a breakdown of the various *grandes écoles* and faculties (including admissions criteria, syllabi and job opportunities after graduation).

12 In the 1880s large and small seminaries together had no more than 9,000–10,000 students (in the 1830s, following the ordinances of 1828, numbers in small seminaries rose to 20,000). Between 1860 and 1885 the annual number of ordinations into the priesthood ranged between 1,200 and 1,600.

13 Louis Liard in *L'enseignement supérieur en France* (1894), vol. 2 on arts and science faculties.

14 According to the annual account of diplomas awarded by the faculties (vol. 21, *Enquêtes et documents* . . .), the annual number of *licences* in arts rose from 20 (1820) to 215 (1880), and in science from 9 to 221.

15 Statistical references relating to the *concours d'agrégation* are taken from the series of statistics on secondary education published in 1834, 1868, 1878, 1887 and 1898.

16 Particularly Henry Berenger in *La Conscience nationale* (Paris, 1897) and *Le Proletariat intellectuel* (1901).

3 Women and elites from the nineteenth to the twentieth century*

FRANÇOISE MAYEUR
University of Lille 3

The title I have chosen is preferable to the original title of my paper: 'Why were women excluded from the elites in the nineteenth century?' which in reality amounts to an overly categorical answer to the question of the relationship between women and the elites and is liable, at least in part, to bypass a genuine analysis of the problem. Moreover, it is problematic to speak of elites in the plural when referring to a century which preferred vaguer and more varied expressions: 'the upper classes', 'the wealthy classes', 'men of exceptional merit'. A century ago elite was above all singular and designated the best in every respect. At the same time there is an abundant literature on the recruiting mechanisms, the renewal and the safeguarding of the 'best' elements in society and on the functions they performed.

The somewhat ill-defined notion of elites as well as the wealth of reflection to which they have given rise constitute the point of departure for this paper which addresses three main problems:

(1) An inventory of female elites in the nineteenth century will allow us to note the most obvious areas of exclusion. This will demand an enquiry into the reasons behind these exclusions which will in turn bring out the social role played by the specific type of education dispensed to women.
(2) By examining the evolution of the situation since the early nineteenth century and above all in the last two decades, we can catch a glimpse of the modification of these reasons and the way in which change has come about.
(3) We will then be in a position to ask certain questions about what has been achieved as well as about types of resistance to genuine integration.

From the outset, a basic point needs stressing: the problem of whether

*Translated by Jolyon Howorth

or not women were integrated into the elites ceases to be a problem if women are considered not as isolated individuals but as integral factors in broader social units which could not exist without them: families, lines, classes or rather social milieux. In other words, units in which women are generally agreed to have a well-defined function. Seen in this light the integration or exclusion of women is no longer an issue. They belong quite naturally to the elite by birthright or by marriage, the latter being most often the logical consequence of the former. It is much less common for women to be integrated into the elite through their profession or their creative activity. And it is this latter question which needs close scrutiny for therein lies one of the keys to an understanding of nineteenth century society.

It is a truism to state that elites need to be conscious of their status as such. It is also true that a collection of brilliant individuals is sufficient to make up an elite. To this extent, there are scarcely any women who belong to French elites as a result of personal merit.

The most indisputable female elite, the most noticeable and the most obvious, is therefore one whose members combine upper-class birth with personal qualities which confer upon them eminence in the social role which such birth assigns to them. These are the perfect *femmes du monde*, accomplished in the art of running a salon, at a time when salons were an important feature of intellectual and social life. These women knew how to produce a good social mix, to steer conversations and even, at times, the speakers themselves in a certain direction.

In the salons of liberal Catholicism there were Mme Swetchine, Mme Craven, Mme de Forbin d'Oppède. These women could also be prominent leaders of charity like Mme Mallet who belonged to Protestant high society. The daughter of the industrialist Oberkampf, the wife of a banker, she gave moral support to day-care centres and hospices and wielded considerable influence over her nephew Salvandy who was Louis-Philippe's Education Minister.

In the religious world, there was a genuine female elite: prominent nuns and founders of religious orders like Madeleine-Sophie Barat or Mother Javouhey or even founders of charitable organisations like Pauline Jaricot. The qualities displayed by these great ladies do not at first glance reflect that feminine specificity to which the century ostensibly adhered. Their Catholic biographers, while insinuating from time to time that such features were not the essence of womanhood, nevertheless wax complacently lyrical about the vast culture of Mother Eugénie Milleret or Mme Barat. To make their creations survive, they all had to exercise energy and heroism and a good many of them showed evidence of great intellectual gifts. But in this case we are talking about women who were often seen only with hindsight as belonging to the Church elite.

The world of art also had its female elite. Without mentioning the world of entertainment which witnessed some lasting but difficult female triumphs, or what is referred to as the world of 'fine art', the world of literature was, in the nineteenth century, the refuge for women with a creative urge. Abundant scorn has been heaped on the 'bluestockings', those female pedants with a craving to write and to broadcast their knowledge. The elite of writers and pamphleteers is nevertheless relatively well endowed with women whose talent or even genius was generally recognised. George Sand is only the most brilliant of them.

It is precisely this world of art and creation which invites the closest scrutiny as to the price which most women paid for membership. A female novelist or essayist was frequently banished to the margins of society, rather like artists, unless she restricted herself to moralisation or insignificance, or unless she made a brilliant marriage, like Delphine de Giradin. Occasionally she would marginalise herself through public display of 'relaxed' behaviour. This was the case with both Daniel Stern and George Sand. The use throughout the century of male pseudonyms by female authors is highly revealing. What conditions were necessary for literary talent no longer to be considered as abnormal in a woman? The female novel, it seems, was required to respect social conventions. George Sand's 'berrichon' period, coming after the scandals of her private life, was destined for instant success. Books touching in one way or another on education or childhood seemed to be the special reserve of women. Mme Campan, Mme Guizot and the Countess of Ségur — but also a host of less well-known writers like Joséphine de Gaulle — illustrate the extent to which, in the nineteenth century, women colonised educational literature. They were part of a long tradition going back to Mme de Maintenon and the fénelonian Mme Leprince de Beaumont.

And so we arrive at the only professional field, beside manual or domestic skills, into which the nineteenth century woman was regularly admitted and in which she could excel without provoking a scandal or being regarded as a brilliant exception: teaching and education. Paris and the major cities were familiar with a type of woman who, while earning her own living, enjoyed a solid reputation: the *maîtresse d'institution*. [Impossible to translate easily, this term designates the head or director of a rather select educational establishment for young ladies. *Trans.*] The best among them, blessed with a faithful clientele from the upper reaches of society, were showered with respect and esteem by the families and by the former pupils. They could reach a relatively high standard of living.

Their influence did not, of course, spread beyond a limited sphere. But these women nevertheless bear witness to the fact that it was possible for a woman to enter a certain elite while exercising a profession and indeed because of this profession.

Artists, writers, *maîtresses d'institution*: women hardly had any other possibility for being integrated into an elite unless they already belonged through family connections. Many of these active women in any case owed some of their social influence to their social origins. If such and such a *maîtresse d'institution* acquired real celebrity in the art of training young ladies, it was because she knew the milieu from the inside. Many female writers already belonged to an elite through their husband or their parents and through the upbringing they had received. Mme Campau was born at court, and a woman like Juliette Adam added to her own talents her husband's name as well as her father's. Otherwise an extraordinary degree of tenacity and a genuinely exceptional talent was necessary if a woman were to succeed. If she lacked wealth or birth a woman needed a network of friends and protectors: one thinks of Mathilde Salomon who was the *protégée* of the republicans and was appointed director of the Collège Sévigné, or Marie Pape-Carpentier who was supported by Mme Mallet in training the first female hospice directors.

Women were of course prohibited from exercising most professions. These prohibitions stemmed from different factors. First, there was the social and judicial status of women. The *Code Civil* had represented the consecration of a hierarchised society in which the husband was the master. Nineteenth-century French society considered that a woman was naturally inclined to dependency — first on her parents if she were unmarried, then on her husband. A woman could not handle her own property affairs, buy, sell or run a business without her husband's authorisation. This prohibition disappeared if the marriage was dissolved. At a time when divorce did not exist (it was only re-established in 1884) and separation was socially unacceptable. there was virtually only one way out of this bondage: widowhood. Legal amendments which modified the juridical inferiority of married women were gradually introduced around the turn of the century and generally dealt with the problems of female wage-earners. They culminated in the 1938 law which, in theory, did away with all legal restrictions for women. It is therefore not surprising that women should be absent from the commanding heights of the nineteenth century economy — that no woman was in charge of any major economic, industrial or commercial firm. Nor did any woman dare to enter the exclusively male preserve of economic or juridical theory. The education received by women in no way prepared them for this type of speculation.

Another prohibition for women was the world of politics. Excluded from the vote until 1945, they were also, of course, ineligible for election. The inclusion of three women (Cécile Brunschwig, Irène Joliot-Curie, Suzanne Lacore) as junior ministers in the Popular Front Government of 1936 was purely symbolic. Journalism and trade-union activism did in fact allow a few women to make their voices gradually heard outside the rather intimate circles of feminism. The 1848 explosion was too short and finished too badly to allow women to emerge from the confused activity of the clubs as a serious militant elite. Most often they sorely lacked any serious training. Towards the end of the century, the patronage of certain republican milieux and one wing of freemasonry, in particular the entourage of Léon Bourgeois, helped generate a political feminism among whose leading lights was Maria Deraisme. The republicans were not without their female representatives: Louise Cruppi, Mme Jules Siegfried, Mme Avril de Ste-Croix. Among the lay sections of the bourgeoisie, a new figure emerged – the free-thinking charitable lady energetically launching initiatives, making lecture tours, writing articles. But she nevertheless remained outside of politics proper: both the law and moral convention tended to keep women clear of the dirt of the political arena. The main reason was no doubt the fear that the female vote would go to the clerical right.

If women were denied access to the economic and political spheres, their situation was no better in that of public administration. There were in fact women civil servants in the nineteenth century and the state welcomed them since they were paid less than men. But they were given only the most routine, insignificant posts. It was inconceivable that women should aspire to the spheres of decision-making.

So many areas of exclusion can be explained by the lack of adequate education and by the peculiar orientation which girls' schooling was given. But that is to beg the question. Why were they given this schooling? What does it tell us about morals, manners and states of mind? Not only the entire French bourgeoisie but also the popular classes agreed that girls and boys should have radically different destinies and that their schooling should be similarly divergent. Right up to the twentieth century, in every social category except for that of industrial workers, girls were brought up essentially for domesticity. The upper classes merely gave their daughters a more refined version of the basic domestic education.

The young woman of the nineteenth century was trained in piety, the running of a household, the command of servants, the conducting of a salon. She learned all sorts of expressive arts: dance, piano, painting, embroidery. In the best families she also acquired a solid knowledge of French language and literature, history and some proficiency in foreign languages. Truly learned women were few and far between. The Duchesse de Broglie, for instance, the daughter of Germaine de Staël and the wife of Louis-Philippe's minister, wrote to a friend that she felt her own knowledge inadequate to educate her own children. Two basic subjects in secondary education which were passports to elite status were denied to women: Latin and philosophy. By this means, young women were unable to sit the *baccalauréat* which was the only route to higher education. Other subjects were either absent or extremely rare: science in general and especially mathematics and the physical sciences. These were precisely the subjects which, after the humanities, allowed the brothers of these same young women to apply for the École Polytechnique or the École Centrale, the elite engineering schools which furnished the future leaders of the French economy. The only argument in favour of this ostracism was a sentimental one: science would 'dessicate' the minds of young women. In fact, science was considered useless since the education of women in the upper classes was regarded as strictly disinterested whereas men studied science in order to apply it in their engineering schools.

General consensus therefore strove in various ways to prevent women from embarking on careers which would lead to responsibility or power either in the public or the private sector. And, lacking a classical secondary education, they were similarly disbarred from a liberal profession. Theoretically a pharmaceutical training had been a possibility ever since the revolutionary period. Yet the nineteenth century saw precious few women pharmacists. In the 1860s the Empress Eugenie had the medical profession opened up to women, but there were very few women doctors until after the turn of the century. It was only much later (1900) that women were allowed to enter the Law Faculty and be called to the bar. The first woman to pass the *baccalauréat*, Julie Daubié, only did so (in 1861) in the teeth of administrative obstacles and with the silence of the law. There was no subsequent tidal wave of women pouring into the University: the type of secondary education they received as well as the prevalent moral code were more than adequate as barriers. The first women to enter the French University were foreigners.

In 1867 the Minister, Victor Duruy, and in 1880 the Republic itself put together a programme of secondary education for women. But they made it clear that the aim of this programme was none other than a preparation for marriage and family responsibilities. Although conceived in different terms from the educational programme for men, secondary education for women nevertheless represented, at the beginning of the twentieth century, a sphere of change. Young women began to pass the *baccalauréat* and go to university. Even before the First World War, they were beginning to enter the liberal professions, and they were to be found in higher posts than ever before in the civil service. Nevertheless, the École Libre des Sciences Politiques, which trained the elite of the *grands corps* and the upper civil service, refused entry to women until 1919. The war had begun to demonstrate the absurdity of the ostracism which victimised women, because women were of necessity employed in managerial posts, and were usually very successful.

Up until the Second World War women civil servants were the victims of various forms of discrimination. They could be charged with drafting administrative documents or could even become section heads. But their promotion was slow and their numbers voluntarily limited. On the other hand they continued to colonise the liberal professions in ever growing numbers.

In principle all this was to change with the Liberation. The law of 19 October 1946 abolished all discrimination between men and women for access to posts in the civil service. Michel Debré, in founding the ENA, opened it up to women, a measure which would certainly never have been passed if the normal consultation procedures had been respected. Women nevertheless continued to be excluded from certain competitive civil service exams, usually on the grounds of their not having carried out military service. They were in any case a small minority in the A grade of the civil service (planning and administration) even though, in the overall statistics, the large numbers of women in secondary education tended to conceal this phenomenon [teachers being classed as civil servants in France. *Ed.*].

A good illustration of this is provided by the administrative grades of the Department of Education, one of the first departments to grant equal pay and conditions of service for equal qualifications (in 1927 and 1931). Like all other departments, this one proved reluctant to feminise its senior posts. At the Ministry itself, even in 1981, no woman has ever occupied a post of *directeur.* Only three women have ever been appointed as *recteur.* There are very few women *inspecteurs généraux.* Even the universities are reticent: there have only been two women deans and in nine years only two women presidents.

In the private sector, if women have easy access to the liberal professions, and to the middle-rank positions in management, they hardly ever make it to the elite positions. The opening up of the École Polytechnique at the start of the 1970s, the feminisation of HEC and of the Instituts d'Administration des Entreprises are developments which are too recent to allow any statistical analysis of their consequences.

Thirty years after the founding of ENA, it can be seen that although women are comfortably ensconced in the *Conseil d'État,* the *Cour des Comptes* and ambassadorial posts are still masculine preserves. The same is true of the prefectoral administration, with very few exceptions. There is in any case not one woman Prefect. A study carried out in the 1970s of lists of elites, such as *Who's Who,* shows women to represent only 2 per cent of the total.

At the end of the survey one has to conclude by saying that, overall, women as individuals are subject to numerous forms of exclusion. Indeed these very areas of exclusion serve to define – negatively – the elites which are most clearly seen as such. Wherever women have the greatest difficulty in penetrating one can be sure that such an area is seen as essential both for the power it confers and for the advantages which go with it. One is therefore obliged to ponder on the long-term fate of the sectors which are subject to rapid feminisation. Will they not, at least initially, through the process of feminisation, lose the prestige which they originally possessed?

Another point is that the education system, originally the main factor of exclusion, was to become in part (and only in part) a means whereby women could become integrated. Why was this process not taken even further when co-education became generalised? Girls had entered secondary education *en masse.* They were in a majority in long-term programmes. There were more passes in the *baccalauréat* among women than among men. But the various sections of the *baccalauréat* were what counted. Deeply engrained habits ensured that girls were oriented towards the literary section whereas, at least nowadays, it is the scientific section which opens the doors to the *grandes écoles* and thereby to the elites. Girls only constitute one third of the candidates for Section C (maths and physics) which is considered to be the most selective and which leads to the best jobs.

If the education system itself plays a restrictive role, family attitudes towards education also play their part. These attitudes are linked to traditions which can be influenced by educators. Families do not have the same educational strategy for girls as for boys and sacrifices of time and money will more rarely be made for girls, even for those of equal ability to their male counterparts. The least prestigious jobs, easy to take on and easy to give up in the event of marriage, seem to be preferable. The obstacles to the promotion of women in the educational system do not come so much from the system itself, where women generally perform better than men, as from a conflict of motivation within the family and the persistence of 'essentialist' stereotypes (women are more suited for arts than for sciences; they are more fragile). The more or less overt opposition of the ensconced male elites to any thought of influence-sharing also has a big role to play, as does the inertia of the institutions which are always slow to conform to the letter of the law.

It must nevertheless be noted that the accession of women to command posts, to the *grands corps*, to the elites of every type, is increasing, albeit in an erratic way from sector to sector. But it is not worsening. One can even make out a strong acceleration of the trend over the last twenty years. But this progress always takes place in the same way: a slow (or rapid) erosion at the base of the pyramid.

There nevertheless remains the most difficult element to quantify, the one which has existed much longer than the individual, egalitarian conquest by women of certain posts, functions and situations. And that is the latent or at least indirect power which women exercise through and over the men they are in contact with, and their often considerable influence in the cultural sphere. This is a form of power which defies numbers, which must be added to the conquests of recent years and suggests extreme caution before concluding that women are in fact excluded from the elites.

4 The École Normale Supérieure and elite formation and selection during the Third Republic[1]

JEAN-FRANÇOIS SIRINELLI*

University of Paris X – Nanterre

The successive directors of the École Normale Supérieure under the Third Republic often used the word 'elite' in their assessments of the School. In 1880, for example, Numa-Denis Fustel de Coulanges wrote that his school 'was fitted only for an elite', and that 'the sort of work which is done there is appropriate only for intelligent minds which possess rare and delicate qualities'.[2] Georges Perrot, his successor, asserted in 1895 – on the occasion of the centenary of the School in the rue d'Ulm – that

> Democracy needs an elite, which represents the only sort of superiority recognised in such a society – the superiority of the mind. It is our duty to recruit that elite, or, more modestly speaking, to work to provide it with some of the elements which will serve to make it up,[3]

and he specified in 1898, in evidence to the parliamentary commission of enquiry which was looking into secondary education:

> Today, we are still recruiting our candidates from rural areas and from the working classes – the bedrock of democratic society, where so much treasure is stored up in the way of human energy, and where so many forces are ready to burst forth and need only to be developed . . .[4]

A quarter of a century later, the then director, Gustave Lanson, explained to the readers of the *Revue des Deux Mondes*:

> It is hard to understand just what the École Normale Supérieure is, what kind of role it has played in the life of the nation, and what role it will be called upon to play in the future, unless it is seen in the context of a set of institutions the purpose of which is to ensure the recruitment and formation of the elite.[5]

There is a striking continuity between these statements over the decades. To analyse its meaning and significance, it is of course necessary to begin

* Translated by Philip G. Cerny

by locating these phrases in the context of the ideology of the Third Republic — based, with regard to state instruction, on 'merit' and on a selection process which was supposed to transcend social cleavages. In this context, the École Normale Supérieure is simply the highest expression of the pattern of elite selection and advancement characteristic of the school system in general. However, we shall only touch upon this problem here; rather, this chapter will focus on two other approaches to the relations between the ENS and the 'elite'.

Access of ENS graduates to elite positions

The first of these approaches can be summarised quite simply: did the School in the rue d'Ulm really provide a part of the 'elite' of the Third Republic? There can be only one answer to this question: Yes. Although 'Normale' only produced around thirty arts and twenty science graduates each year, it played a fundamental role in the realms of politics, the universities and, to an even greater extent, culture and science.

Célestin Bouglé, who was also a director of the ENS, recalls that the publisher Bernard Grasset wanted to put a publicity wrapper around Albert Thibaudet's *La République des professeurs* with the slogan: 'France is run by Normale Ltd'.[6] Indeed, many leaders of the large left-wing parties in the 1920s were ex-*normaliens*: Léon Blum, Paul Painlevé,[7] Edouard Herriot,[8] Yvon Delbos and many others. And in the same period the right-wing press began to stress the theme that the École Normale Supérieure had become a sort of training school for left-wing *cadres* — a theme which would be taken up and amplified a few years later by Hubert Bourgin in his book *De Jaurès à Léon Blum: l'École Normale et la politique.*[9] On the other hand, it must be added that one of the leading lights of French right-wing politics in the '20s was a sort of *normalien*, André Tardieu, who got top marks in the 1895 ENS entrance examination — although he withdrew before beginning the course.[10]

Furthermore, *normaliens* held important positions in the university system. At first glance this may not seem surprising, since the School was supposed to lead to a career in teaching. But the reality was even more striking; the few dozen students welcomed each year in the rue d'Ulm were later to be found at the highest levels of the university system. Between 1894 and 1903, for example, they appropriated 33.1 per cent of the places on the pass list for the *agrégations littéraires* for themselves.[11] Even more to the point, they often got the top marks: thus in 1902, for example — and this was not atypical — the four highest-ranking places on the agregation in History and Geography was carried off by *normaliens*, among whom were the future Socialist leader Albert Thomas (ranked first) and the historian Lucien Febvre. The proportion of *normaliens* was even higher among holders of chairs in higher education, notably at the Sorbonne. In 1935, *normaliens* occupied 53.6 per cent of the arts posts in that establishment, including thirteen of the seventeen chairs in History.[12]

The proportion of *normaliens* elected to the Institut was also striking. Certain graduating classes in arts from the École Normale Supérieure have also been celebrated for the number of their members which the Institut has included in its ranks. For example, exactly one-third of the famous class of 1878 — which included such names as Jaurès and Bergson — was later to be found in the various establishments of the Quai Conti: two in the Académie Française (A. Baudrillart and H. Bergson), four in the Académie des Inscriptions et Belles Lettres, one in the Académie des Sciences Morales et Politiques and another at the Académie des Beaux-Arts. And of the 93 arts graduates from 1876 to 1879, 22 were admitted to the Institut.[13] This phenomenon was amplified further in the interwar period: between 1920 and 1930, of the twenty-three new members of the Académie Française, eight were *normaliens* — 34.8 per cent of the total.

Sources of recruitment to the ENS

Thus the École Normale Supérieure played a fundamental role in certain sectors during the Third Republic. There is another major problem, however, which calls for another approach and which we will concentrate on here: Did the ENS really recruit its students from the '*couches profondes de la démocratie ouvrière ou rurale*'? Was it a factor of social mobility, a lock through which numerous young men of modest or poor background passed before reaching the shores where the 'elite' reigned? Or was it just an institution for the heirs of the privileged (the *héritiers*), an instrument of social reproduction? The answer, as we shall see, is a complex one and requires qualification as well as the examination of rather different sorts of evidence from that considered above.

A study completed in 1934 by the Centre de Documentation Sociale of the School provides some precise data on the occupations of the parents of arts students at the rue d'Ulm between 1927 and 1933.[14] It can be summarised in Table 4.1.

This table suggests some immediate observations. On the one hand, out of the 214 students of the seven graduating classes studied, 71, or 33.1 per cent, were the children of teachers in secondary or higher education

Table 4.1

Professions exercées par les parents des élèves	Reçus							Total 1927–1933	%
	1927	1928	1929	1930	1931	1932	1933		
Professeurs	3	2	1	7	6	5	6	30	14
Instituteurs	5	6	–	5	8	4	–	28	13
Autres universitaires (Administration)	3	2	7	–	–	1	–	13	6
Autres fonctionnaires	6	1	–	3	3	–	1	14	6.5
Officiers	1	2	3	2	1	1	1	11	5.1
Ingénieurs, architectes	–	2	2	–	–	1	1	6	2.8
Industriels	3	–	–	2	1	1	2	9	4.2
Médecins, pharmaciens	–	2	1	–	3	–	1	7	3.2
Notaires	2	–	–	1	1	–	–	4	1.8
Avocats, avoués	–	1	–	–	–	–	–	1	0.5
Banquiers, assureurs	–	1	1	–	1	–	1	4	1.8
Agriculteurs	–	1	–	–	–	2	1	4	1.8
Commerçants	5	4	4	6	2	5	4	30	14
Employés PTT, chemins de fer	1	–	1	3	–	5	4	14	6.5
Autres employés	1	2	3	2	1	3	6	18	8.4
Artistes	–	–	1	–	–	–	–	1	0.5
Pasteurs protestants	1	1	–	–	1	–	1	4	1.8
Ouvriers, contremaîtres	–	1	3	–	–	–	1	5	2.3
Professions indéterminées	–	–	2	1	3	4	1	11	5.1
Total	31	28	29	32	31	32	31	214	

(*professeurs*), primary teachers (*instituteurs*) or other university graduates, etc. (*autres universitaires*). At this time, however, there were only around 130,000–140,000 members of the teaching profession as a whole, i.e. less than one per cent of the active population. On the other hand, the category of primary school teachers includes 28 of the 214 parents, i.e. 13 per cent. We can add to this most of those in the 'other university (administration)' category; a detailed analysis of the files shows, in fact, that at least two-thirds of this category consisted of administrators in primary and 'higher primary' teaching. Thus 9 of the 13 '*autres universitaires*' can be included with the 28 primary teachers, bringing the total of those working in primary and 'higher primary' education to 37, or 17.2 per cent of the whole. During this period, then, one *normalien* out of every six had parents from the world of primary school teaching. It must finally be emphasised that the children of all civil servants represented half of the total student numbers; in effect, if the 71 children of teachers are added to the 14 *autres fonctionnaries*, the 11 military officers and the 10 white-collar employees of the Post and Telecommunications service (PTT),[15] 106 of the 214 had parents employed by the state (49.5 per cent).[16]

These figures provide us with a profile of ENS students halfway through the interwar period – the last two decades of the Third Republic: half were children of civil servants, a third were children of teachers of one sort or another, and a sixth were children of primary school teachers or administrators. But this observation suggests a further question: How does this profile compare with that of aspirants who at about the same time were studying for the rue d'Ulm's entrance examinations (in classes called *khâgnes*)? Was the social composition of the student body different from, or a faithful microcosm of, that of the *khâgneux*? A study of the social origins of the latter[17] gives the following results:

Table 4.2

Parents' occupation	Normaliens (littéraires) (1927–1933)	Khâgneux (1920–1930)
Civil servants	49.5 per cent	50 per cent
Teachers (all)	33.1	35.7
Primary and 'higher primary' teachers	17.2	20.4

The young people who passed the entrance examinations (*concours*) thus had broadly the same social characteristics as the pool of applicants. Of course it must be stressed that the modalities of the process of discrimination between different occupational categories over time in the selection of the students of the School in the 1920s were not to be sought in the functioning of the examination system itself, which was restricted to the global reproduction of the main traits of the clientele of the pre- paratory classes in *lettres*.

Furthermore, even though a reading of Table 4.1 indicates that these main traits did not reflect the occupational distribution of the active population in France in the 1920s and that one cannot speak of widespread recruitment from the '*démocratie ouvrière ou rurale*'[18] — despite some notable exceptions which we will return to later — it was of course the case that both the *khâgnes* and the ENS itself flowed from the secondary school system; therefore the only truly fruitful analytical course would be to compare their recruitment with that of the lycées and colleges in the 1920s. Such a comparison shows[19] that the middle and lower-middle classes were better represented in the *khâgnes* than in secondary edu- cation.[20]

Thus it is difficult to label the École Normale Supérieure a simple instrument of 'reproduction' or a school of *héritiers*. The studies carried out by Pierre Bourdieu and Jean-Claude Passeron cannot be directly transposed backwards into the situation of the '20s: their data on the ENS concerns the period 1961–2 and their results — very different from the situation of the 1920s[21] — make the work of these two sociologists rather time-bound, and their conclusions cannot be applied to other periods without careful qualification because of significant changes in the statistical data.[22] And despite the fact that for an entire school of sociology the educational system is seen as an instrument of reproduc- tion which perpetuates a form of social organisation which profits only the dominant classes, it is crucial, when looking at the 1920s — and what- ever the hypothesis being tested — scrupulously to avoid any anachronism. On the one hand, as we have seen, it is very tempting to project con- clusions drawn from a period a half-century later backwards into a different historical and sociological context from the one studied. On the other hand, as we shall see, it will be important to locate any such research in a longer-term perspective over several generations; indeed, our perception of the situation is significantly modified by such an approach, at least for the period studied here.

The ENS and long-term social mobility

It seems basic to us, in fact, if we are to study the relationships between the school and university system, on the one hand, and social organisation, on the other, to ground our analysis on data covering three generations at least. The problem appears in a very different light, especially with regard to the *khâgneux* and the *normaliens*.

But in order to do this successfully, the researcher is faced with the classic problem of anyone trying to wade through administrative archives: they do not, in fact, make it possible to go back more than two generations (i.e. father's occupation). If one wishes to go back further in reconstructing genealogies, it is necessary to find alternative archives, especially direct oral testimony, which make it possible to measure family situations. The questionnaire sent to 250 *khâgneux* of the 1920s, mentioned earlier, included a question on grandparents' occupation. The replies, although fragmentary, are revealing.

We have already noted that in the 1920s, 50 per cent of *khâgneux* were the children of civil servants and 35.7 per cent of teachers. The children of farmers, on the other hand, represented only 3 per cent of the total.[23] But if one looks at the paternal grandparents of the same group, the following distribution appears:

Table 4.3

Occupation	Fonctionnaires	Enseignants	Agriculteurs
Father's	50 per cent	35.7	3
Grandfather's	50	23.3	30

The proportion of civil servants was apparently unchanged. But a more precise analysis reveals that lower civil servants were much more numerous among the grandparents of *khâgneux* than among their parents. This is the first indicator of upward social mobility between the two generations. The proportion of teachers, which shows a much greater degree of contrast than that of civil servants, leads to the same conclusions. And the proportion of farmers confirms the above observations and reinforces them. Globally, then, the grandparents of these *khâgneux* were cultivators or minor civil servants. Their children – the parents of the *khâgneux* – had lost their links with the land and largely entered the middle classes. In order to illustrate this upward social mobility over three generations, let us take two examples of politicians who attended the ENS in the Third Republic forty years apart.

Great-grandson of a manual worker, a grandson of a corporal and a dressmaker, Édouard Herriot was the son of an officer promoted from the ranks and who had been brought up in the barracks.[24] In 1887, the future Radical leader was in the *classe de rhétorique* in the lycée of La Roche-sur-Yon. His father wanted him to study for the military academy at Saint-Cyr. When the Inspector General Charles Clachant came to the school, he was given the task of expounding a passage from *Pro Milone*. From that moment, everything fell into place: 'When I had finished my presentation, M. Glachant offered me a scholarship to the Collège Saint-Barbe in order to study for the École Normale Supérieure . . .'.[25] And a few months later, Édouard Herriot moved to Paris, to the Collège Sainte-Barbe and the Lycée Louis-le-Grand. In 1891, he passed the *concours* for the rue d'Ulm.

This story is revealing in more ways than one. First of all, it is very similar to that of the 'discovery' of Jean Jaurès at the Lycée de Castres by the Inspector General Deltour. Thanks to the latter, who had been impressed by Jean Jaurès's gift for Latin, the future Socialist spokesman was also directed towards Paris, to the Collège Sainte-Barbe and Louis-le-Grand, and came top of the entrance examinations in 1878. The similarity between the stories does not end there, and highlights the role played by the classics and the humanities in the selection process operated by the Third Republic regime[26] on several generations of scholarship students who would make up a considerable proportion of the political personnel and the intelligentsia of twentieth-century French history. Finally, there is another striking parallel. A more detailed study shows, in effect, that the outline of an apology and justification for the education system of the Third Republic can be read into both cases: in each case we are faced with a defence and illustration of upward social mobility into the 'elite' through the schools. This was seen as true by Herriot himself; his story, often quoted — but always with reference to *Jadis* — was taken originally (almost word for word) from another work by the Mayor of Lyon written twenty years before his memoirs and entitled *Pourquoi je suis radical-socialiste*,[27] the second chapter of which was itself entitled . . . 'Études'.[28]

The children of primary school teachers, as we have seen, represented a not inconsiderable part of the *normaliens* of the Third Republic. A study of their itineraries also shows frequent changes over several generations. The first stage involves the children of peasants ascending through the primary school and the *école primaire supérieure* to primary school teacher training colleges (*écoles normales d'instituteurs*). For the next generation, the children of *instituteurs* frequently got as far as the baccalaureate and went on to higher education. The case of Georges Pompidou,[29] who entered the ENS in 1931, is revealing in this respect. Jantou Pompidou, the paternal grandfather of the future President of the Republic, was head farmhand on the family farm in the canton of Maurs in the south of the Cantal department. Two of his three children became peasants in their turn. The third, Léon Pompidou, was noticed by the primary school teacher in Maurs, M. Joie,[30] who pushed him to enter for scholarship competitions. Having been successful, he was able to continue his studies, to spend two years in the *école primaire supérieure* in Murat and to get top marks on the entrance examination to the *école normale* at Aurillac. Appointed a primary teacher at Murat, he met the daughter of a cloth merchant from Montboudif who had just been appointed to a primary teaching post herself. They were married in 1910, and Georges Pompidou was born in July 1911. This son of two primary schoolteachers had a brilliant school record which took him to the École Normale Supérieure: as a student at the lycée in Albi, he walked off in 1927 with the first prize for Greek translation in the Concours Général;[31] from that point onward, his path was cut out for him; he did the *khâgne* first in Toulouse and then at Louis-le-Grand,[32] came eighth on the ENS entrance examinations in 1931, and later came first in the *agrégation des lettres* in 1934.

Conclusion

Other than a few exceptional trajectories, it was rare for the children of workers or farmers to go through *khâgne* and to enter the École Normale Supérieure. However, that establishment undoubtedly constituted a ladder of upward social mobility for a few gifted *lycéens* from the middle and lower-middle classes.[33] And the fact that primary school teachers and post office workers, for example, might hope to send their children to one of the most prestigious *grandes écoles* no doubt reinforced their image of French society as being fluid, with social mobility always remaining within the realm of possibility. This notion was perhaps to a modest extent one of the strengths of the Third Republic regime; at the very least, it was one of the symbols of the consensus which ensured its solidity and longevity. Indeed, the 'Republican synthesis' described by Stanley Hoffmann developed, if only indirectly, through the *khâgnes* and the École Normale Supérieure.

Notes

1   The majority of the material in this chapter is taken from the first part, as yet unpublished, of a thesis for the Doctorat d'État which the author is preparing

on *Khâgneux et normaliens d'une guerre à l'autre*. The first part of the thesis examines the *khâgnes* – preparatory classes for the ENS – including their composition, their spatial distribution, their recruitment and their teaching staff; the second part analyses the itineraries of *khâgneux* from the 1920s during the period 1929–45. Among them were, among others, Jean-Paul Sartre, Paul Nizan, Raymond Aron, Maurice Merleau-Ponty, Simone Weil, Robert Brasillach, Léopold Sédar Senghor and Georges Pompidou. It should be pointed out that we are here dealing only with the literary (arts or humanities) section of the École Normale Supérieure of the rue d'Ulm, and not the smaller science section.

2   Letter of 18.9.1880 to the Minister of Public Instruction (National Archives 61 AJ 169).

3   *Le Centenaire de l'École Normale, 1795–1895* (Paris, 1895), p. xlv.

4   Chamber of Deputies, 7th Legislature, 1899 Session, *Enquête sur l'enseignement secondaire: Procès-verbaux des dépositions*, presented by M. Ribot, President of the Commission de l'Enseignement (Paris, Imprimerie de la Chambre des députés, 1899), vol. I, p. 139.

5   Gustave Lanson, 'L'Ecole Normale Supérieure', *Revue des Deux Mondes* (1 February, 1926), p. 512.

6   *Bulletin de la Société des Amis de l'École Normale Supérieure*, no. 13 (July, 1928), p. 21: *'C'est Normale et Cie, qui mène la France.'*

7   Who belonged – unlike the other names cited in this chapter – to the scientific section of the School.

8   The other protagonist of the 'War of the Édouards' within the Radical Party, Édouard Daladier, twice failed the entrance examinations for the ENS in 1903 and 1904 (Archives Nationales 61 AJ 17). As a student in a *khâgne* in Lyon, his *professeur de lettres* was none other than . . .Edouard Herriot.

9   (Paris, 1938)

10   Archives Nationales 61 AJ 13 and 61 AJ 16. Of course, the use of the term *normalien* here applied to André Tardieu is wrong, because he never entered the School except to take the oral part of the *concours d'entrée*; furthermore, he never figured in the 1895 class list.

11   Figures arrived at by comparing ENS class lists and those of the results of the *agrégations littéraires* between 1894 and 1903.

12   Source: biographical notices of titular professors as of 1 January 1935, in A. Guigue, *La Faculté des lettres de l'Université de Paris depuis sa fondation (1808–1935)* (Paris, 1935), pp. 241–359.

13   Without taking into account the *normaliens* from the scientific sections, who, at certain times, represented more than half of the members of the fifth Academy of the Institut – the Académie des Sciences.

14   This study was reproduced in *L'École Normale Supérieure: D'où elle vient? Où elle va?* (Paris, 1934), p. 107. We have of course checked the validity of this table using the same sources as the authors did, i.e. the registration files for the ENS entrance examinations (cf., for 1927–1933, Arch. Nat. 61 AJ 254 à 61 AJ 260).

15   A breakdown of the information on file makes it possible to identify the sub-categories of the heading *'employès PTT, chemins de fer'*.

16   [It must be remembered that these are overlapping categories: teachers in the state school and university system as a whole are normally classified as civil servants in France. *Trans.*] In the Census of March 1926, 'public services' represented 1,059,000 members of the active population, including the armed forces, i.e. 4.9 per cent of the 21,394,088 men and women in the whole active population of France (from Statistique générale de la France, *Résultats statistiques du recensement général de la population effectué le 7 Mars 1926*, vol. I,

part 3: 'Population active, 'établissements' (Paris, Imprimerie nationale, 1931), pp. 7 and 8.

17   Study based on a retrospective survey carried out by the mailing of a questionnaire to 250 former *khâgneux* from the '20s. For the question on social origins, 98 replies can be used. The figures in the following table have been confirmed by a statistical examination of the student file of the Lycée Louis-le-Grand, which admitted more than a third of candidates to the ENS.

18   Table 4.1 shows 4.1 per cent as having been the children of peasants and workers (respectively 1.8 and 2.3 per cent). In the March 1926 census, these two categories represented 63 per cent of the total working population (cf. Statistique générale de la France, loc. cit.).

19   Without going into detail here, note that this comparison is based on three sources: recruitment to the Lycée Louis-le-Grand in 1929–30 according to an enquiry by the headmaster (Archives Louis le Grand), the social composition of the 2,072 students of the lycée in Bordeaux in 1925–26 (according to the *Revue Universitaire*, no. 1 (1926), p. 274, which was based on a report presented by an academy inspector at a meeting of the Conseil académique de Bordeaux), and that of Parisian and provincial candidates for the baccalaureate in the session of June–July 1932 (Archives Nationales 61 AJ 166).

20   The sources mentioned in the foregoing note indicate, however, that in these secondary establishments, the middle and lower–middle classes (*classes moyennes*) were already widely represented even before free places had been introduced.

21   Thus, in 1961–62, 51 per cent of the parents of students at the Écoles Normales Supérieures in Sèvres and in the rue d'Ulm belonged to the category of 'liberal professions and higher executives', while 9 per cent came from industrial and merchant backgrounds ('*patrons de l'industrie et du commerce*'): P. Bourdieu and J.-C. Passeron, *Les Héritiers: Les étudiants et la culture* (Paris, 1964), pp. 22–3. Table I, for the period 1927–33, suggested very different social origins.

22   Another example of the gap between the situation in the early 1960s studied by the authors of *Les Héritiers* and the period of our research: Bourdieu's and Passeron's work showed that in 1963, out of the eighteen first prizes in the Concours Général, 'fifteen were sons and daughters of higher executives or of professional men and three were sons of shopkeepers (ibid., p. 69). Prizewinners in the Concours Général under the Third Republic came from totally different backgrounds: thus, at the end of the nineteenth century (1890–6), scholarship students took 64 per cent of the top places. *L'enquête sur l'enseignement secondaire: Rapports adressés à la Commission parlementaire de l'enseignement* (Paris, 1899), pp. 138–9.

23   Figures calculated from the statistics cited in note 17.

24   Cf. M. Soulié, *La Vie politique d'Édouard Herriot* (Paris, 1962), p. 1, and P. O. Lapie, *Herriot* (Paris, 1967), p. 30.

25   E. Herriot, *Jadis*, vol. I (Paris, 1948), p. 38.

26   A selection process often carried out by the Inspectors General of Public Instruction during their tours of provincial schools. These higher civil servants sometimes distinguished young people from even more modest backgrounds than Édouard Herriot, and, in such cases, upward social mobility took place in just one generation.

27   (Paris, 1928)

28   Ibid., pp. 24–39.

29   Cf. Merry Bromberger, *Le Destin secret de Georges Pompidou* (Paris, 1965), pp. 14–36; and Pierre Rouanet, *Pompidou* (Paris, 1969), pp. 30–5.

30   Alongside the Inspector General, the primary school teacher was the other 'discoverer' of talent under the Third Republic. Sometimes such a 'discovery'

took the happy chosen one right into the rue d'Ulm in just one generation: thus Charles Péguy, whose mother repaired cane-bottomed chairs for a living, was noticed by M. Naudy, as told in *L'Argent*. Having obtained a scholarship, he was able to go to the lycée in Orleans in order to study for the ENS *concours*.

31   *Revue Universitaire*, no. 2 (1927), p. 271. The second prize went to René Billières from the lycée in Tarbes, son of a local government clerk and a primary school teacher; he also went to the ENS and, several decades later, became Minister of National Education.

32   Where he became friends with the future President of the Republic of Senegal, Léopold Sédar Senghor.

33   It is vital to point out here that the middle and lower-middle classes [a category – *classes moyennes* – which in French does not usually include the upper-middle and upper classes, as it frequently does in English – *Trans.*] had virtually no other channels by which to enter the 'elite' of the higher civil service under the Third Republic. In 1901 the members of the Conseil d'État and the Cour des Comptes, the Finance Inspectors, the *directeurs* in ministries, the Prefects, high-ranking Generals in the armed forces and the Inspectors General of the *corps* of Mines or Roads and Bridges, had been recruited to the extent of only 10.7 per cent from the lower-middle classes or the urban and rural working classes ('*la petite bourgeoisie ou les classes populaires*'); see Christophe Charle, 'Le recruitement des hauts fonctionnaires en 1901', *Annales E.S.C.*, vol. 35, no. 2 (March–April, 1980), p. 383.

PART II   REPRODUCTION

5   A changing of the guard? Old and new elites at the Liberation*

JEAN-PIERRE RIOUX
Institut d'Histoire du Temps Présent
Centre National de Recherche Scientifique

Does the study of particular historical events have a place in the analysis of elites? This account covers a period with strict chronological limits — the Liberation of France in 1944 and its aftermath — and therefore runs certain risks. It highlights the conjunctural, the transitory, even — as certain of the actors in the drama of 1944 liked to proclaim — the revolutionary elements within the mass of information about elites, whereas, by definition, the subject matter should be treated in terms of structure, the long term, gradual change and patterns of inheritance. Nonetheless, I hope to show that a historical study of the events of this period can shed light on certain crucial characteristics of the elite structure of France.

I. The obsession with 'new elites' before the Liberation

As we shall see, the various actors at the time of the Liberation confronted the problems of the period with vigour and passion. But if we are to understand both their enthusiasm and their disillusionment, we must go back and examine the ten or fifteen tumultuous years leading up to the Liberation, years during which a number of groups reopened the vexed question of elites and made an appointment with the future.

The upheaveals of the Thirties

The strains and crises of the 1930s which form the background to this study came together in a shock wave which shattered the old social and political contract of the Third Republic which had accommodated both the newer social categories and the propertied elites. Today we can clearly distinguish the component parts of this upheaval.[1] The Great War was a bloodbath for the bourgeois and intellectual elites; the drop in the birthrate made their renewal highly problematic. A divided bourgeoisie, hit by

*Translated by Philip G. Cerny

the crisis of the franc and the undermining of fixed incomes, lost a large part of the privileges which it derived from wealth and position. The middle and lower-middle classes were destabilised by falling incomes and the decline of the Radical Party. The Popular Front created favourable conditions for the emergence of working-class counterelites. And international tension, culminating in the 'spirit of Munich', deepened the crisis of confidence felt by those groups which had considered themselves the 'natural' elites of the country.

In the midst of this social turmoil, small groups of individuals came together, mainly young people, often friends, to start up reviews, to observe these changes and to discuss their ramifications. They brought together intellectuals, white-collar workers, civil servants, trade unionists, and even some employers. These minority groups, marginalised and isolated from the mainstream political forces of the day, did not attempt to adopt a unified approach, but rather concentrated on a critique of routine choices and received wisdom. A veritable ideological *bric-à-brac* — nationalism, personalism, spiritualism, planning — infected them and, in the long run, divided them. But, from *Ordre Nouveau* to *Nouveaux Cahiers,* and from *Esprit* to *Révolution Constructive,* they shared a keenness for concrete analysis of society and a belief that qualified people must stand up and be counted — *les clercs ne doivent plus trahir.*[2] Thus equipped, they reached a number of new and interesting conclusions.

It is vital, they argued, to distinguish clearly between *elites* in the plural and *the elite* in the singular. Certainly the 1930s were characterised by virulent critiques of the traditional elite: the 'bourgeois dynasties' or the '200 families', self-centred and immobile, were said to block all attempts at renewal, and condemned the republican middle classes, with which they had been allied since 1871, to impotence and disarray. The old elite of blood, of land, of money or of intelligence — with its selection procedures and its privileged patterns of reproduction — had created deep cleavages in society, and these groups of young people rejected the historical fatalism which was implicit in the notion of an elite cut off from the rest of the social order.

On the contrary, they asserted, to advance the notion of a plurality of elites was to recognise that no single class should rule by vocation. To admit that elites exist *within* each social category and each ideological or spiritual family, and to struggle to prevent these elites from turning into a single ruling class — i.e. to block any further *embourgeoisement* which would result from their becoming detached from their category of origin — would be to increase social mobility and to achieve 'a sort of equilibrium or egalitarian tension between all classes'.[3] This attitude was more sociological than ideological, being based on the presupposition that society exists prior to the state. It achieved a singular success in the Christian milieux of the Confédération Française des Travailleurs Chrétiens and the specialised groups which grew out of Action Catholique and the popular education movement — organisations which recruited and nurtured new *cadres* after 1940. And it found an echo among all of those who sought to define and to enlarge the scope of liberty, caught between the dominant ideologies of Fascism and Communism.

Its ambition was to replace the republican elite as prescribed by Alain — the elite of power, knowledge and progress — with elites dedicated to service and to the good of the community. This ambition expressed certain reflections about the nature of democracy. The advancement of the masses, that great aim of the twentieth century, was seen as being compatible with the emergence of leadership structures within social groups; these structures would help to raise the consciousness of group members and to place their particular aspirations and interests at the service of the community. This idea is at the heart, for example, of the personalism of Mounier.[4] But affirmation of the rights of the community cannot be separated from a critical stance towards the liberal state.

The theme of the reform of the state was certainly widely discussed, and even politicians such as André Tardieu or Léon Blum suggested solutions. The critique put forward by our young musketeers was, however, more lively, and their aims for the future more far-reaching. The traditional state, limited to providing for public order, was seen as being on its deathbed, incapable of facing up to the economic and social tasks which were demanded by the crises of the century — a fragile plaything in the hands of the moneyed oligarchies. This was the dawn of the all-embracing welfare state — *L'État-Providence*; of the state as arbiter of the class struggle (remember the obsession with the compulsory arbitration of disputes at the time of the Popular Front!); and of the state as the common denominator of forces, which, without it, were incapable of coalescing and burying their mutual hatred. The new state would also be stronger and more democratic; it would favour the emergence of new elites which would cross-fertilise and blossom in the name of the general interest. All in all, they described what they saw as the new characteristics of a state which would no longer attempt to repress society and to reduce it to the requirements of the state itself; rather it would become, in Bertrand de Jouvenel's words, a state in 'permanent revolution', at the service of a society which was *itself* organising the basis for a better life. Only this could ensure the passing of the elitist *imperium* and the development of a democracy which would emancipate its component groups.

From this vision they drew several diverse and contradictory solutions: a move towards more comprehensive state planning, as espoused by the Socialist Party (SFIO) and the Confédération Générale du Travail, the largest trade union; a form of liberalism adjusted and adapted by Keynesian technocrats; and corporatism. Only a detailed tracing of the career trajectories of a large number of individuals would allow the analyst to describe the nuances of these various developments and to avoid the pitfall of over-schematisation. It should be remembered that Léon Blum himself, who had been so horrified by the blunt proposals of the '*néos*' (disciples of H. de Man), later provided a eulogistic preface to James Burnham's *The Managerial Revolution* in 1947; and that a certain supporter of planning from the CGT could move on to a successful career in the Vichy regime, while another who was involved in drawing up the '9th of July Plan' was still to be found in the top ranks of the state hierarchy in 1945 after a career in the Resistance!

But the core of this account is the foresight which motivated these young intellectuals, civil servants and managers. As Auguste Detoeuf summed up in the *Nouveaux Cahiers* of June 1938: 'many of our current misfortunes come from the fact that people no longer know where their leaders are, and much of the disorder comes from the fact that there *are* no more leaders. Of course, there are those who have authority. But that is not the same thing.' It matters little that they did not know the works of Pareto, Mosca or Weber, or that they had only vaguely skimmed Marx and often preferred Nietzsche or even Baden-Powell; they nonetheless discovered in a more empirical fashion the ways in which elites functioned, and the aspirations for their renewal, which would appear later in the theories of Karl Mannheim and C. Wright Mills. It matters little that few listened to them and that they were extremely isolated; their ideas became dominant after 1940.

Vichy and the Resistance

It might seem, with hindsight, as if the world conflict (and civil war) which overwhelmed France had dictated the adoption of some of the solutions previously advanced by the 'non-conformists of the Thirties'. This was not the doing of the declared collaborators, whose obeissance to the concepts of race, *Volk* and party which had come from across the Rhine freed them from giving any thought to the problem of specifically French elites. But both at Vichy and in the Resistance there was a clear line of continuity with the prewar period.

The regime established by Marshal Pétain was in fact quite straight-forwardly reactionary. Its aim was to restore the old social hierarchies, to bring about the rebirth of 'the true elites which the previous regime has tried for years to destroy and which will in the future constitute the *cadres* which will be necessary for the development of the well-being and the dignity of all' – in other words, to erase the legacy of the Revolution of 1789 – according to a declaration of October 1940. This determination to install the old discredited elites in the command posts of state and society itself became a crucial factor in the rejection of the National Revolution by French public opinion.[5] Nonetheless, it cannot be denied that the circumstances of the time demanded new solutions and new men. Any social history of the personnel of the Vichy regime (as yet unwritten) will doubtless demonstrate this fact, whether it examines the Conseil National or the Comité de Rassemblement pour la Révolution Nationale, the Legion or the École des Cadres at Uriage,[6] the youth movements or the Organisation Committees. One cannot help but be struck by the way that the group which de Moysset called the 'young cyclists' – as opposed to the 'old Romans'[7] – immediately flocked to Vichy. What sweet revenge for the dissidents of the Thirties! Examples include planning-oriented trade unionists like Belin, higher civil servants and dynamic executives from the private sector like Pucheu and Lehideaux, Bichelonne and Barnaud. Given the general financial penury of the time, an elite based on technocratic competence exercised power in the Délégation Générale de l'Équipement, planners converted employers, and top-ranking officials attempted to initiate a thoroughgoing reform of the administration.[8] From this point of view, Vichy was indeed a time of experimentation for the new elites – and they would also prove necessary for the recovery of the country after the Liberation, despite the lack of any formal continuity between the two periods.

Similarly, the Resistance hatched new elites – sometimes from the same brood. The writings of Marc Bloch in *L'étrange defaite* come to mind, ferocious and sad – or those of Léon Blum in *À l'échelle humaine*, inveighing against bourgeois elites, *notabilités* and the parliamentarians of the Third Republic, accused of being deserters, ready to rally to the Marshal. 'My country is like a small boat abandoned by the winds', wrote Louis Aragon. From this starting point, a handful of Frenchmen (only 1–2 per cent of the population prior to 1944, it must be remembered) made their elitism respectable by their patriotic participation in the Resistance. There was, firstly, the elite composed of the meagre bands of General de Gaulle's *compagnons* in London; and, secondly, the elite made up of the earliest leaders and organisers of the Resistance networks and movements in France itself in the winter of 1940–1. These groups included many who had been marginal to political life, ill at ease under the Third

Republic — as well as Christians, and those Communists who cared little about following the letter of the fluctuating tactical directives of the Comintern. They believed spontaneously that by defending France they would carry off the honour of representing her once victory had been achieved.[9]

This early Resistance, which represented only a minority in a country which had long remained silent, could not however become too exclusively dependent upon the advancement of renascent elites. First among its values was patriotism *per se*, which alone, it was believed, could rebuild a sense of national unity around the movement; this spirit would best be achieved not through elitism but through defining a new democratic spirit which would emerge from direct contact with the people. Furthermore, as Stanley Hoffmann has remarked, it was too moralistic, too disparate and too pressed by the urgency of the struggle to confront the real question: how were the new elites effectively to sink their roots deep into society and politics?[10]

Indeed, this self-sacrificing *avant-garde* could only legitimise its ambitions to bring together all of the French people (excluding traitors, of course) — and thus begin to answer this question — by paying close and detailed attention to ensuring the transfer of the power of the state into the hands of its best disciplines. In the view of de Gaulle and Resistance leader Jean Moulin, it would be necessary to develop a sense of the state which would prevail 'over and above' all of the structures and all of the activities of the internal Resistance — a state power under the authority of which France would rally. Thus it was the sense of the state which alone could broaden the painfully constructed unity of the Resistance into the unanimity of the nation, and which could weld back together a country worn out and dismembered by its defeat and humiliation: thus an elite born of patriotism would be transformed into an elite of public service. From this point onwards the question became one not merely of hunting the enemy but also of ensuring that the country, once liberated, was spared 'the dread of nothingness' and of preserving the continuity of the Republic.

It is clear at this stage that the word 'elites' can become singularly expandible and that the voices of former dissident groups came to be submerged in the notion of the general interest. Thus we find that the militants of the various political parties which were also participating in the Resistance were coming in in greater and greater numbers alongside the heroes of the original movements. These parties were tough-minded and more powerful than the other groups, having been strengthened through taking part in both the underground struggle and the governmental activities of Free France in London and Algiers; they had developed a greater capacity for providing the basic structures of a functioning democratic process and for representing a wide range of interests and groups. Despite what has been said to the contrary, de Gaulle increasingly threw his influence behind them in order to reinforce his own position with the Allies, for example by installing a number of Radicals and liberals on the National Council for the Resistance (CNR) and negotiating a firm agreement with the Communist Party (PCF).

At the same time, the Comité Générale d'Études – a sort of clandestine Conseil d'État – was in the process of selecting future officials to run the administration in the liberated areas; in doing so, they demonstrated a solid sense of the need for continuity of personnel.[11] René Courtin, too, was very careful in his report on economic policy to specify that the restarting of production would be undertaken with the assistance of all *cadres* of good will. And even the CNR itself, in its 'Programme' of 15 March 1944, did not propose any systematic purge of all those who had held posts previously. Among the men of the past, therefore, all those who 'had not given up on France' were to have their place among the higher echelons of the country during reconstruction. In the first great speech setting out his programme at the Palais de Chaillot on 12 September 1944, de Gaulle stressed this felicitous continuity:

'We see assembled here, *as well as* the representatives of the *grands corps* of the state, men from all sorts of backgrounds and of all shades of opinion who have placed themselves in the front rank of those who are carrying on the fight. Now is it not crystal clear that the entire French elite is inspired by the same burning passion (*flamme*) and the same sense of right reason?

Thus the realism of *raison d'État* triumphed in the end: passion and reason – *flamme et raison* – converged, and the elite was made one. But this clearly did not mean that such a policy of amalgamation had dampened the enthusiasm of those who wished to advance the cause of new elites. On the left wing of the SFIO and in the conglomeration of Resistance groups, which were groping towards a new form of working-class movement ('*travaillisme*'), the theme of bringing about a renewal of elites through a systematic immersion in the mass of ordinary people was not abandoned.[12] Clandestine study groups put forward a number of proposals which were derived directly from the experiences of the Thirties. One of these groups called itself the Thebans – *Thébaïde* – and had gone underground deep in the Isère department; it was led by a graduate of the Uriage School, Gilbert Gadoffre. In their writings we find easily recognisable themes: an elite which is defined by its excellence, and no longer by its function; and elites which no longer identify with a ruling class but which express the manifold needs of all social categories. Among these would be found working-class elites, elites within social organisations, governmental elites and civilising elites: such propositions provide a summary of the development of such concepts since 1930.[13] They dominated the everyday activity of a great many members of the Resistance, who prepared themselves to put their ideas into practice when the great day arrived. But, along with the test of facts, came the hour of truth.

The test of facts

In what ways, then, did hopes for the renewal of elites succeed after the Liberation? Although the question seems clear enough, it is a complex problem to approach. Of course it is easy enough to identify the factors which favoured greater social mobility: the right had gone to ground, the left – representing the hopes of more ordinary people – had triumphed, and the winning of votes for women had changed the old rules of the democratic game; at the same time, the demographic renewal which came with the postwar baby boom, along with new aspirations for a better life following the defeat of Fascism, sustained the dynamism of the reconstruction process. But on the other side of the coin, the weight of the constraints and the pressing needs of the times always threatened to put the brakes on.[14] It must be admitted that our examination of the concentric arenas in which this renewal was taking place – from the most obvious to the most problematic – can only be a very general one in the absence of any in-depth social history of the period. Here and there, a shaft of light pierces the shadow. But it must be stressed that a systematic prosopography of elites would be necessary if we were to test properly – to qualify or falsify – the various observations which follow.

The renewal of elites

First of all, it can be fairly safely asserted that national political elites were characterised by a large degree of turnover from 1945 onwards. This renewal had two salient aspects – ideological and sociological.[15] All of the work in this field confirms the point: the membership of Parliament, the holders of ministerial office and those who held high-level advisory positions in the *cabinets* of the Fourth Republic and, to an even greater extent, of the Provisional Government, all exhibited a high degree of turnover. The situation in Parliament was particularly astounding, where 80 per cent of those elected in 1945–6 came directly from the Resistance and in the period to 1958 two out of every three deputies were veterans of the underground. Within the political parties and groups which predominated in the period up to 1952 the turnover was also great: within a Communist Party which had miraculously revived after its collapse in 1939–40, swollen by the addition of younger elements, and which did share power for a time before the hardening of the lines of the Cold War in 1947; within a new party, the Mouvement Républicain Populaire (MRP), which facilitated the entry of Christians into the heart of the Republican system; and not least among those organisations which developed directly out of the Resistance, the Union Démocratique et Sociale de la Résistance (UDSR – the party of François Mitterrand) and, of course, the Gaullists. In contrast, it can be seen that the only forces in decline – the SFIO and the right – are precisely the ones which had not been capable of renewing their *cadres*.

However, this seemingly brutal changeover reflected the culmination of long-term social trends: the Liberation really only accelerated a long process of the maturing of the petty and middle bourgeoisie, members of which had been increasing their representation in Parliament and in government ministries over the preceding half century. With the PCF having assured itself of a monopoly over the recruitment of working-class leaders through both its party posts and its public officeholders, and with rural elites having been compromised by their salient role in both the Third Republic and the Vichy regime, a great influx of personnel – especially after the Communist Party's move into opposition in 1947 – facilitated the capture of the political system by these new elites of the centre and the non-Communist left.

But the novelty of the period is more of an ideological nature. The Resistance – that accident in the history of political attitudes and social forces – became the primordial point of reference, the criterion for determining the legitimacy of the new political elites, and, over the years, the certificate of civic respectability which would permit their officeholders to win re-election. At the same time, it became the infallible sign by which members of these elites recognised each other – whatever political family they happened to belong to. After all, an elite is made up primarily of those who define themselves as the best, and who are able to maintain that conviction – a perennial law of history which is confirmed by the behaviour of the Resistance fighters once installed in power. After the *Républic des ducs* and the *République des camarades* came the *République des résistants*: and the French, flabby and wet, acquiesced. The personnel had changed, but the notion of an *élite d'excellence* was never seriously challenged.

Other arenas in which innovation was taking place included social hierarchies and communications. Several factors combined to reinforce the aspirations of the 'non-conformists' of the Thirties. The urgent need to increase production and the demands of reconstruction and economic growth had become so fully internalised by the masses as to open the way for the emergence of new elites of foremen and supervisors. The need for new forms and structures of communication and culture, after four years of silence, brought new creative and managerial talent into the media. The middle classes and the peasants — who had suffered from their organisational impotence during the inter-war period — now aspired to become more efficient and modern. Thus the rise of these new elites reflected the emergence of powerful new demands in society itself.

The first arena in which these demands were felt was trade unionism. New union elites controlled a movement which was more powerful, better structured and incessantly subjected to demands by the state for its collaboration in the national task of reconstruction. It can easily be seen — subject, again, to qualifications concerning the need for a systematic study of individual career profiles — that there was a *levée en masse* of new men, young for the most part, equipped with solid Resistance credentials, within the trade unions and even within certain craft occupations regarded as vital to the future of the country (miners, for example, were included in the national elite in all official pronouncements). The dimensions of the social 'New Deal' of the Liberation even carried it into the internal structures of business enterprises and other socio-economic decision-making processes through the elected members of the new factory committees (*comités d'entreprise*), shop stewards, the managers of the Social Security and Family Allowance funds, and members of arbitration committees, of the Modernisation Committees of the Planning Commissariat, and of the Economic and Social Council. From the traditional bastions of the blue-collar and white-collar working classes, the movement spread to the middle classes, through the white-collar staffs union (the Confédération Générale des Cadres — CGC) and the Confédération Générale des Petites et Moyennes Entreprises (PME — the small business pressure group), to the employers and even to the peasants — whose 'silent revolution' soon got underway under the organisational umbrella of the FNSEA (the Fédération Nationale des Syndicats des Exploitants Agricoles — National Federation of Farmers' Unions) and the CNJA (the Centre National des Jeunes Agriculteurs, which specifically set out to organise the modernising elite of younger farmers). Everywhere the thrust to increase production and living standards had brought new personnel into positions of responsibility by the beginning of the 1950s.

In much the same way we can see how the ideals of the Resistance came to dominate the means of communication and culture. The tone was set by the symbolic installation of a member of the Resistance, Jean Guignebert, in the same offices in the Rue de Lille where the prewar Office de Publicité Générale had poured out its propaganda and where now a General Secretariat for Information would attempt to impose moral standards within the communications media — after an extensive purge of staff and the rapid promotion of younger employees. The size of newspaper readership and radio audiences in the post-war Liberation period was greater than ever before, and new men proposed to undertake a profound re-education of the people. At the same time one saw the emergence of the notion of a 'right to culture', transmitted by members of the Resistance who had come down from the heights of the Vercors and had founded the organisation known as 'People and Culture', orchestrated by Jean Guehenno in the Ministry of National Education and disseminated soon afterwards through the Théâtre National Populaire under Jean Vilar. And the mandarins — the intellectuals who predicted the dawn of a golden age radiating out from the sunlit square of Saint-Germain-des-Près — greeted with tears in their eyes that great uplifting of the masses under the firm guidance of noble bands of dedicated educators of the people and of those who would use their wisdom in the service of virtuous authority.

But behind this moral *magisterium* of intoxicated intellectuals, behind the great aspiration to achieve the necessary social discipline to defeat adversity and to act as the midwife of a modern age, the newly-emerging power of the *État-Providence* was clearly beginning to take shape. In the same way as *raison d'État* largely controlled the evolution of new elites under the Resistance, so the innovative spirit of the Reconstruction — which got its dynamism from the public authorities — encouraged new forms of social hierarchy and installed new men in them. This process can be observed in the huge growth of state elites: the number of civil servants grew from 840,000 in 1936 to 1,350,000 in 1956, with the most spectacular growth occurring precisely in those sectors most closely linked with the increase in state intervention — the Interior Ministry, transport, public works, labour and health. As the increased level of government employment became institutionalised and unionised, new decision-making structures developed: in the firms of the recently nationalised sector; in the Planning Commissariat; in the statistical service INSEE; and, of course, in the École Nationale d'Administration, which by the end of the 1950s would ensure the reproduction of these new administrative elites.

Is this to say that these years witnessed the rise of a self-conscious technocracy and of a group of welfare-state managers who really believed that public sector decision-makers had replaced the decadent elites of the prewar years? André Siegfried was convinced of this as early as 1956: 'An aristocracy of technical competence now manages France.'[16] But in the eyes of certain of these *administrateurs du mieux-être*,[17] any such 'caste' was too divided and still too isolated from political power, it would seem, to assume the social status of an elite. The Fifth Republic would set the matter straight. But let us simply say that during the early years of the Fourth Republic, new men achieved positions of power and responsibility, and that its potential force began to take shape. It was, perhaps, a kind of unfinished elite.

The continuity of practice

Thus a brief survey of political, administrative, trade union and 'cultural' personnel supports the conclusion that there was a fairly general renewal of the people in influential positions in these structures. But it does not answer the question as to whether the notion of an elite as such was transformed in any meaningful way by the victories of the Liberation and the Reconstruction. It is doubtful that, for example, the relations between voters and their elected representatives, between bureaucrats and clients, or between the intelligentsia and the masses, changed significantly. It is even possible to demonstrate point by point the other side of the coin — that the social rules of the game were not modified. Political life was restructured along the lines of previous practice: the internal life of the political parties scarcely differed from the patterns of the 1930s; individuals who had been disqualified because of their previous activities began to surface again in 1952 with the arrival at the Hôtel Matignon — the Prime Minister's residence — of a former member of the National Council of Vichy, Antoine Pinay; and the ex-members of the Resistance movement who filled the positions of power did not constitute a new elite. After 1947, when the Communists and the CGT were excluded from power and withdrew to their Cold War ghetto, the return of old conservatives and liberals, such as René Mayer and Paul Reynaud, diverted public investment towards the old business elites, while Marshall Plan aid contributed to putting the old capitalism back into the saddle and the nationalised sector was no longer in a position to control its future so easily. A largely Americanised mass culture swept away the active supporters of the 'right to culture'. Disillusionment on the part of the new men, and the return of the old elites in force, took place at the same time and within a few years the old Resistance dreams of purifying and reconstructing France had faded.

In trying to determine the reasons for this regression, the historian of elites can quickly suggest three sorts of answers. The most obvious is linked to the failure of the collective purges after 1944: whatever might have been said at the time among the pensioned-off remnants of the bankrupt right, the old elites had not been 'decapitated'. Even worse, the purges of individuals hit the 'little men' harder than the 'big'.[18] The civil service, business and the professions were systematically spared, and the old elites, largely retained in positions of authority, blocked the ascension of the new in the management of economic and social activity. Furthermore, it can be observed that the former members of the Resistance who were in positions of power were incapable of modifying the system of reproduction of elites; the democratisation of the teaching system advocated in the Langevin-Wallon plan fizzled out, the taxation system was scarcely touched and the inheritance laws were more sacrosanct than ever.

Finally it must be acknowledged that the slowing down of the purges and the inability to overturn the structures of society was linked to the existence of a huge mass of constraints in the economy and society — constraints which may provide the decisive explanation. Would it have been possible for state and society to survive without making concessions to retailers, distributors, manufacturers, peasants, etc.; without tolerating, for example, the gradual takeover of the Specialised Associations for agricultural production by the old elites of the Peasant Corporation of Vichy; or without giving government aid to employers? Could the country have been governed without trained personnel? Since revolution was not on the agenda — in spite of a long debate on its merits — the Liberation could only proceed imperceptibly towards a partial restoration of the old elites, which were the only ones capable of giving coherence to public action and heading the nation along the path of economic growth. At the same time, the increasing pace of economic expansion and the rapid growth in the Gross National Product, by spreading a bit more comfort through all sectors of society, made it possible to tolerate social immobilism rather better: although the France of the Resistance may have needed new elites, the France of the Renault 4 and of the consumer society (even among the working class) had little difficulty consoling itself for the fact that it was partly run by old managers.

Conclusions

There are lessons to be drawn even from this rather brief survey of a period which was short but eventful. The first of these concerns the role of short-term, conjunctural elements in the history of elites. The penetrating social observations made by a few restricted groups in the 1930s came to the fore in the patriotic upheaval of the Resistance; in 1944, as in 1793 or in 1871, the attempt to transform French elites began with reflections on intellectual and moral reform. Without the impetus which came from a handful of people of marginal social status, without individual successes which blazed the trail, and without certain ideological themes which could mobilise wider support, could society have emerged from the torpor which had kept existing elites in place? Without the historical accidents of 1938, 1940 and 1947, could the processes which ensured the turnover of elites have been able to function? Of course, although the Liberation created favourable conditions for the extensive turnover of elites, it did not lead to any continuous process of installing new elites in power. But without the shock of specific events, would anything have been achieved at all?

At the same time, an examination of conjunctural factors can throw light on a number of longer-term structural characteristics. Our second point, then, concerns the diversification and specialisation of elites: the experience of the post-1944 period in fact confirms the notion which had obsessed thinkers in the 1930s, as evidenced by the proliferation of different kinds of authority structures within various social groups. This, it could be argued, can be seen as a concrete demonstration of a law of twentieth-century French society — that initiatives and decisions tend to be taken more and more exclusively within certain specialised groups such as public sector managers, trade unions and middle-class pressure groups rather than by the old elites. The latter were too multifunctional and had become too sluggish, but their authority could not easily be broken by the forces of renewal. In this sense, it might perhaps be said that aspirations for a renewal of elites have led to the atomisation of society and the creation of new blockages.

In any case, a study of the postwar years shows that a new kind of actor entered the scene, at one and the same time the agent of social transformation *and* of the integration of old forces into new patterns of behaviour, able to arbitrate conflicts and control the tensions created by the new system — an actor whose role grew as the various forces of society cancelled each other out, and whose activity, however necessary, cooled the passion for social renewal. This actor was the state. Its salience raises an unavoidable question: whether the *État-Providence* of the 1950s and 1960s was forced into becoming a substitute for other social institutions and processes precisely because of the failure of the new elites to establish their ascendancy at the time of the Liberation?

Notes

1 See F. Braudel and E. Labrousse, *Histoire économique et sociale de la France*, vol. 4, part 2 (Paris, 1980); A. Sauvy, *Histoire économique et sociale de la France entre les deux guerres*, 4 vols. (Paris, 1965 et seq.); S. Hoffmann et al., *In Search of France* (Cambridge, Mass., 1963); J.-P. Azema and M. Winock, *La Troisième République* (Paris, 1978); D. Tartakowsky and C. Willard, *Histoire de la France contemporaine*, vol. V (1918-1940) (Paris, 1980).

2 They had all reflected upon *La Trahison des clercs*, by J. Benda, which had appeared in 1927. On these groups and these reviews, see J. Touchard, 'L'esprit des années 1930: une tentative de renouvellement de la pensée politique française', in *Tendances politiques dans la vie française depuis 1789* (Paris 1960); J.-L. Loubet del Bayle, *Les Non-conformistes des années 30* (Paris, 1969); and M. Winock, *Histoire politique de la revue 'Esprit' (1930-1950)* (Paris, 1975).

3 J. Lacroix, 'La promotion des masses', *Esprit* (January 1953), p. 33.

4 Personalism 'is an effort − and a technique − for the constant development within all social milieux of a spiritual elite able to exercise authority; at the same time it is a system of guarantees directed against the claims of power elites (which can be categorised, within the limits of time, place and political regime, into "elites" based on birth, wealth, function or intelligence) to ascribe to themselves the right to dominate others as the result of the influence which they derive from the services they perform.' E. Mounier, 'Manifeste au service du personnalisme', *Esprit* (October, 1936), p. 188.

5 See, for example, the failure of the Legion in the Vienne department analysed by J.-P. and M. Cointet in the *Revue d'histoire moderne et contemporaine* (October-December, 1973), pp. 595-618.

6 On this school − whose role was the subject of a lively polemical debate following the publication of B.-H. Lévy's *Idéologie française* (Paris, 1981) − see B. Comte, 'L'expérience d'Uriage', in *Eglises et chrétiens dans la IIe guerre mondiale* (Lyons, 1978), pp. 252-66.

7 See the best synthesis on the period, J.-P. Azéma, *De Munich à la Libération* (Paris, 1979), ch. 3.

8 See R. F. Kuisel, 'Vichy et planification économique', *Le Mouvement Social* (January-March, 1977), pp. 77-101.

9 This feeling was particularly strong in *Combat, Franc-Tireur* and *Défense de la France*. See H. Michel, *Les Courants de pensée de la Résistance* (Paris, 1963).

10 S. Hoffmann, op. cit., p. 64.

11 See D. de Bellescize, *Les Neuf Sages de la Résistance* (Paris, 1979).

12 See, for example, A. Ferrat, *La République à refaire* (Paris, 1945), with a preface by A. Philip. The same appeal to new elites appears in J. Maritain, *Christianisme et démocratie* (New York, 1943; reprinted Paris, 1945).

13 They were published in *Esprit* between February and May 1945 under the evocative title of 'La cristallisation des élites nouvelles'.

14 For the whole of this period see J.-P. Rioux, *La France de la Quatrième République*, vol. I, 'L'ardeur et la nécessité (1944-1952)' (Paris, 1980).

15 See J. Charlot, 'Les élites politiques en France de la IIIe à la Ve République', *Archives Européennes de Sociologie* (1973), pp. 78-92; R. Cayrol, J.-L. Parodi and C. Ysmal, *Le Député français* (Paris, 1973), and P. Birnbaum, *Les Sommets de l'Etat* (Paris, 1977). It remains to be seen whether an analysis of the origins of regional and local elites would support these conclusions.

16 *De la IVe à la Ve République* (Paris, 1958), p. 220.

17 See F. Bloch-Lainé, *Profession fonctionnaire* (Paris, 1976).

18 See J.-P. Rioux, 'L'épuration en France, 1944-45', *L'Histoire* (October, 1978), pp. 24-32.

6 The grandes écoles: selection, legitimation, perpetuation

MICHALINA VAUGHAN
University of Lancaster

It is hardly surprising that there should be no English appellation for *grandes écoles*. Not only are they idiosyncratic institutions, the product of a unique historical configuration conducive to 'a double-track, or parallel, system of higher education . . . the foundation on which rests the elite structure of French society'.[1] They are also rather less than explicitly delineated in their original milieu. 'What exactly defines a *grande école* has never been specified'.[2] The underlying concept remains elusive, unless it is approached from an evolutionary perspective, so as to investigate the meaning it has gradually acquired over time. In the absence of a formal definition, its scope can only be ascertained through its connotations. As a result the number of establishments which can claim the title of *grandes écoles* remains somewhat uncertain.[3] The assessment of their attributes entails drawing distinctions of degree rather than kind. All the difficulties involved in confronting reality with an ideal type[4] arise. This is a most unsatisfactory situation from the stance of Cartesian logic and hence the persistence of such indefiniteness may appear puzzling. Yet is is probably the fact that they were variations on a general theme rather than set in the same mould which enabled the *grandes écoles* to meet changing social needs, so that their network expanded in the nineteenth and twentieth centuries. This feature contrasts with the rigidity of other French educational institutions. It is tempting to relate it to the diversity of political influences which shaped the first *écoles spéciales* (as they were initially called) and of philosophical arguments later advanced to support imitations of this pattern. The complexity of their historical origins may well be a contributory factor to the persistence and to the adaptability of which they have proved capable.

Although *grandes écoles* are generally viewed as typical products of the Napoleonic educational system, some actually date back to the revolutionary era (École Polytechnique and École Normale Supérieure) and one to the *Ancien Régime* (École Nationale des Ponts et Chaussées). This fact is not of merely anecdotal interest, since it highlights a number of durable trends by reference to which the development of a particular approach to education can be characterised. The most striking is the provision of specialised advanced training for future civil servants. The close connection between state employment and social prestige clearly predated the Revolution. It is perhaps less widely known that the subordination of curricula to the needs of society as defined by the state was advocated, before Napoleon, by the Parliamentarians of the late eighteenth century. According to La Chalotais, the purpose of education was to be vocational: 'to successfully fill the different occupations in the State'.[5] Although the Revolution of 1789 was aimed at the destruction of absolutism, its educational ideology posited a complementarity between the fulfillment of individual potential and the service of the community, embodied in the state. *Polytechnique* and *Normale* were created to provide vocational training for entrants into the technical branches of the administration and into the teaching profession. They were intended to supply the government with trained specialists, selected by the most exacting intellectual criteria and subjected during the course to a strict discipline, modelled on the military and on the monastic pattern respectively.

The underlying contradiction between the republican postulate of state efficiency and the revolutionary ideal of social equality could only be resolved by legitimating educational disparity. Rather than to serve the needs of individuals for social integration and upward mobility, instruction was to be dispensed in unequal measure, so as to reward those who appeared most worthy of receiving it. The conjunction of aptitude and effort was construed as sufficient ground for meting out preferential treatment by granting access to *écoles spéciales*. According to Condorcet, 'one ought not to prefer only those who have demonstrated ability, but those who can be seen to have added effort to it'.[6] In the educational plan he submitted to the Legislative Assembly, he spelt out how the individualism inherent in enlightened philosophy led to the establishment of a meritocracy. By erecting intellectual fulfillment into a natural right, he subordinated the establishment of educational equality to the assertion of individual freedom, equated with the pursuit of excellence. It became an integral part of the republican tradition that inequalities of access to tuition were justified, provided equality of opportunity remained formally guaranteed by the systematic testing of individual merit. *Grandes écoles* conformed to this requirement, since it was through measured intellectual attainment that the standard for admission was reached and also that the rank-ordering of graduates was effected.

State service, vocationalism, selection — all the attributes associated with *grandes écoles* and systematically expanded under the imperial regime – had actually emerged before Napoleon's advent to power, albeit in a limited number of establishments. They corresponded accurately to his concern for the efficiency of the state machinery, to his ultilitarian and anti-intellectual view of education, and to his determination that the recruitment of elites should be institutionalised. Although he did not actually initiate the *grandes écoles*, he found in them instruments which were well suited to the pursuit of his design for endowing France with trained cadres. By the reform or re-formation of these establishments,[7] he systematically attempted to foster talents in order to reinforce the power both of the state and his own, to the extent that it depended on the competence and the dedication of those who served him. The over-riding goal of his policy was administrative efficiency, served both by meritocratic selection and by the subordination of curricula to centrally defined societal needs. 'To instruct is secondary, the main thing is to train and to do so according to the pattern which suits the State'.[8] A strong, politically motivated dislike of what he termed *idéologues* prompted Napoleon to emphasise specialist training at the expense of general education. This narrowly vocational approach was not only derived from practical considerations, but was inseparable from expectations of loyalty to his regime – of which generalists were presumed to be less capable. Typically, École Normale, recreated exclusively as a training centre for secondary teachers, was assigned the task of inculcating sound views to its pupils, who would then spread them in the newly founded *lycées*. Its curriculum was designed to sponsor a conservative philosophy through the study of the Latin and French classics. The belief that great literary works were not only formative for young minds, but actually prompted a respectful attitude towards authority may be debatable. Nevertheless Napoleon held it firmly: 'Above all, let us give some sound and strong reading material to the youth of the regime. Corneille, Bossuet, those are the masters it needs. That is great, sublime, and at the same time regular, peaceful, subordinated. They do not make revolutions; they do not inspire any . . .'.[9] Although in point of fact, *Normale* was to prove 'faithful to its revolutionary origins . . . [and] a centre of *esprit critique*',[10] it certainly contributed to fostering the classical bias characteristic of French secondary education throughout the nineteenth and the first half of the twentieth century.

The definition of vocationalism may have been controversial, as this example was intended to show, so that the training of specialists produced a surfeit of generalists and that civil servants turned out less 'respectful' than they were meant to be. Both *Polytechnique* and *Normale* evolved towards a very broad intellectual formation, covering mathematics and the physical sciences in the former, the humanities (for the majority) and the sciences (for a less respected minority) in the latter. However, both perpetuated the tradition whereby intellectual eminence was to be fostered among those who were destined for the civil service, even though their alumni were to be found also in other careers (particularly in industry in the case of *polytechniciens* and in the literary professions in that of *normaliens*). Above all, both remained uncompromisingly meritocratic and owed their prestige to their exclusiveness. The 'archetypal' *grande école*, Polytechnique, provided a pattern for the creation of École Centrale des Arts et Manufactures,[11] thus showing that − in addition to a broadly vocational curriculum − the most distinctive characteristic other establishments would seek to emulate was the entrance examination. The limitation of intakes achieved through the screening of applicants for entry emerged as the *differentia specifica*, whereby elite training establishments were those to which access was difficult, requiring a period of preliminary study at post-*baccalauréat* level. By contrast, the other institutions of higher learning, especially the faculties, practiced an open-door policy. Since − within the Imperial University − they had also been designed as vocational, providing training for the liberal professions, it is logical that the demarcation should have been drawn by reference to the criterion for admission (merely the possession of the *baccalauréat* or successfully negotiating another screening device).

The *concours* as a prerequisite for entry into specialised higher education is not just an attribute of *grandes écoles*. It may well be the central feature which reflects their dual intellectual origins, since it can ensure both meritocratic selection (of entrants) and elitist classification (of finalists). The apparently contradictory postulates of the two conflicting ideologies which contributed to shaping French education are thus reconciled. One focuses on the link between elite performance and state efficiency, justifying the exclusiveness of training establishments by reference to their utility. The other highlights the complementarity between individual achievement and membership of an elite, gained through the acquisition of educational qualifications. It is thus on grounds of morality rather than of expediency that selection is legitimated, since it differentiates between unequals (in accordance with the Aristotelian concept of equality). The latter view inspired educational planning during the revolutionary era, while the former underpinned Napoleon's policy. Despite their philosophical divergence, both could be invoked to justify the existence of the *concours* as an avenue to elite membership. Indeed the replacement of ascription by achievement orientation[12] served the needs of the state by promoting a meritocracy and satisfying authoritarian preoccupations with social control. It also satisfied the aspirations of individuals, by rewarding merit and thus complying with the republican emphasis on natural rights. The means by which elite recruitment through education was effected provided also a number of diverse arguments for legitimating its existence.

Such legitimation was undoubtedly essential for the recognition of the group selected and trained by *grandes écoles* as capable and worthy of exercising functions of leadership within the sphere of their expertise. The founder of elite theory, Gaetano Mosca, has called attention to the need for providing official confirmation before intellectual merit can be acknowledged in the wider society as an avenue to membership of what he called the 'political class' and what would now be known as the 'decision-makers'. While he realised that knowledge represented a novel social force in modern societies, he did not feel that its possession sufficed to establish a new elite of merit. 'Personal achievement . . . has this special trait that it does not impose itself of its own accord; it does not, as is the case with wealth or birth, become an active force by just existing, it becomes valuable only if it has already, in a more or less official way, found recognition'.[13] The *grandes écoles* secured such recognition for their alumni by giving them a training which had received the seal of state approval and by providing them with a qualification which was granted the ultimate consecration of access to state employment upon graduation.

Paradoxically, despite the well-established connection between *grandes écoles* and government service, it was only after a crisis in leadership had been revealed, by the defeat of 1870, and widely diagnosed that training for the *grands corps de l'État*, which fulfilled key administrative functions, was actually designed. Until then, the network of *grandes écoles* expanded as and when it was officially acknowledged that a particular activity required special training or that a given field warranted advanced study. For instance, the institution of École des Chartes under the Restoration coincided with the rediscovery of medieval history and art.[14] That of École Centrale — which was actually a private rather than a state establishment — was a response to early industrialisation and to the diffusion of Saint-Simonian technological philosophy. Specialised schools were created mainly to meet the needs of an expanding economy,[15] in accordance with the utilitarian approach characteristic of the *grande école* pattern. In addition to their specific vocational purpose, they were explicitly intended to produce an elite. '. . . The *grandes écoles*, where one entered by competitive examination, which became more and more difficult, established within the powerful but fluid divisions of birth and of fortune, a new social category, defined at once by its small size and by its merit.

It carried a name, the "elite".[16] This type of training certainly contributed not only to raising intellectual standards, but also to promoting social cohesion within the elite, through the solidarity born of a common educational experience. It simultaneously ensured the acceptability of this group by linking its privileged position to meritocratic tenets. Somewhat belatedly, the same approach was implemented to select and train top civil servants, diplomats, politicians 'and, if possible statesmen', so that France would have 'mechanics, technicians, experts in politics'.[17] Optimism about the accuracy of the social sciences, typical of the age, was added to a confidence in the efficacy of education inherited from the Enlightenment. This new scientism inspired the foundation of the École Libre des Sciences Morales et Politiques in 1872. From the outset, an overlap between politics and public administration, amounting to a confusion between the roles of political leader and high-ranking public servant, was noticeable in the programme of the *Sciences Po* (as the new school came to be called) and contributed to its appeal. So did its position outside the state educational network, as a private foundation, especially after the Dreyfus case had polarised anti-clericalism and anti-intellectualism. Conservative society, alienated from university circles and attracted by the concept of rule by trained experts (*gouvernement des capacités*), as an alternative to political representation, increasingly took over the civil service at its apex.

The existence of an administrative elite, whose establishment had been facilitated by centralisation, dated back to the *Ancien Régime*, to the *grands commis* of bourgeois descent with whom Louis XIV surrounded himself to weaken the nobility and to increase the personal power of the monarch.[18] Until the Third Republic, appointments to the *grands corps de l'État* had remained discretionary, thus perpetuating political control over administrative assignments. Then, in an attempt at depoliticisation, parallelling the British Northcote-Trevelyan report, recruitment by *concours* had been introduced and the newly founded *École Libre* came to monopolise the preparation to the main competitive examination, that which led up to posts in the great central administrative offices.[19] From then on top-ranking administrators owed their position to systematic testing rather than to preferment. This meritocratic recruitment enhanced their prestige as well as their ability to serve under successive political masters, for whose instability in a parliamentary democracy the permanence of administrative careers provided a compensatory device.

The *grands commis de la République* did not affront republican ideology insofar as their position was the reward of intellectual merit rather than inheritance or purchase of office. Inequalities of power could be justified by educational attainments — a less invidious ground to invoke in a democracy than either hereditary privilege or the acquisition of wealth. Yet the economic principles on which the civil service career was based had the indirect result of limiting recruitment to a certain level of income. Though the initial requirement of a private income as a guarantee of financial independence was relinquished at the beginning of the twentieth century, the low remunerations of entrants into administrative posts made economic self-sufficiency (whether due to birth, to marriage or preferably to both) necessary. Hence the administrative elite was virtually co-opted from among the Parisian bourgeoisie. It was from the same milieu that the top level of business management was also recruited, so that close links naturally existed between the public and private sectors. Modest administrative salaries discouraged the lower middle classes from aspiring to *grande école* education and civil service careers for their sons — a fact corroborated by the increase in their source of intake when scholarships to Polytechnique became more widely available between 1880 and 1914 than during the previous half-century.[20]

They were not such a disincentive to the more affluent; on the contrary, 'advanced education is used to legitimate wealth; an acquired class position is both consolidated and complemented through an advance in status and power'.[21] The possibility of restoring or rather increasing family fortunes by embarking on a second career upon retirement or after resignation from the civil service (the practice known as *pantouflage*) remained open. It was facilitated by the intellectual prestige inseparable from a *grande école* background and by the useful connections which it entailed. *Polytechniciens* found the industry particularly welcoming, due to the relevance of their qualifications and their *esprit de caste*. However, they had no monopoly of transfers to private posts — for instance, banking provided a refuge for *pantouflards* from the Ministry of Finance. Such examples could be multiplied. It suffices to say, however, that a similarity of social origin and intellectual background strengthened elite cohesion and that the *grandes écoles* contributed to enhancing this solidarity.

Towards the end of the nineteenth century, the undemocratic character of *grandes écoles* came in for a great deal of criticism, especially from the universities with which they had competed so successfully. The source of their intakes and the nature of their curricula were criticised as socially biased and intellectually elitist. Hence they were mainly denounced as divisive institutions: 'so long as the *grandes écoles* continued to function in accord with the principles of conservative pedagogy and on behalf of the *haute bourgeoisie* there would be an irreparable cleavage in the nation which would only be bridged when the *grandes écoles* accepted the modern curriculum and utilitarian and democratic axes of the *facultés*'.[22] Polytechnique, the most exclusive and enjoying the highest reputation of all *grandes écoles*, was predictably the main target. Its refusal, despite government pressure, to accept the *baccalauréat* as an entrance qualification, confirmed the crucial importance of the *concours* and resulted in a war of attrition which lasted from 1881 to 1914. Only the outbreak of World War I ended a crisis in which the inability of republican politicians to regulate educational institutions, entrenched in their position of privilege, became blatant. A contributory factor to this weakness was no doubt the increasing influence of the administrative cadres, trained in *grandes écoles*, an official policy.

The importance of *grandes écoles* for the selection and training of intellectual, administrative and technical elites can be illustrated by statistical data, insufficiently explored as yet, as well as by biographical evidence. Such an approach would show two trends: an increasingly close connection at decision-making levels between public administration and private enterprise and an almost complete monopolisation of the *grands corps* by the upper echelons of the Parisian bourgeoisie. Both trends became particularly marked between the wars and stimulated left-wing polemics against the 'two hundred families' alleged to be ruling the country. Yet the prestige of meritocratic selection remained high and even those who advocated an educational reform continued to pay tribute to intellectual superiority as the only acceptable ground for social differentiation. It is surely significant in this respect that, after the Liberation, the democratisation and modernisation of civil service training should have been based on the creation of the École Nationale d'Administration.

Though intended to destroy pre-war structures of geographic and social privilege, it was organised on the familiar *grande école* pattern. The *concours d'entrée* recovered its traditional role of a screening as well as a classificatory device, whereas *Sciences Po* had increasingly relied on social selection.[23] Attempts were made to diversify the intake and reduce the social bias inherent in a purely theoretical curriculum by adopting a more practical approach (*stage* in an administrative post as part of the course). Yet, despite these adaptations, the model on which ENA was designed was Polytechnique and consequently the principles on which it relied were meritocratic selection, vocational training and a commitment to state service on the part of its alumni. It would be uncontroversial and probably superfluous to assert that a new elite has in fact emerged in thirty years from among their ranks. The term *énarchie* has been coined to describe the group of ENA-trained technocrats and has occasionally been used to denounce their growing power not only in the *grands corps*, but in the successive governments of the Fifth Republic.[24] It is equally well known that little change has occurred in the social and geographical origins of higher civil servants, that any initial trend towards widening the basis of recruitment has been reversed since the late fifties.[25] It remains doubtful whether the entrenchment of the privileged, which necessarily includes making use of the best educational facilities available to buttress their social position, can be countered by reform. On this score the École Nationale d'Administration is vulnerable to the same criticisms as Polytechnique, indeed as any educational establishment offering a highly regarded training conducive to a position of authority – as an elite institution, it attracts the children of the elite.

Throughout this paper the focus has not been on issues of 'social arithmetic'. No attempt has been made to analyse the patterns of recruitment to *grandes écoles*, either to assess changes over time or to draw comparisons between schools.[26] Indeed it has been felt that the originality of *grandes écoles* derived from the type of selection they operated, the kind of training they provided and the unique connection between them and the French state. Even if the composition of intakes altered significantly over time or could be modified drastically as a result of far-reaching educational reform or government intervention, it is doubtful whether this would result in any marked modifications to the meritocratic ethos. It is as bastions of the meritocracy that the *grandes écoles* have been created, it is in this role that they have survived and it is as such that they remain attractive to the best endowed applicants. The durability of the early *écoles spéciales*, as well as the extent to which they have been imitated to organise training for technicians and administrators along similar lines, bear witness to the wide reliance on institutionalised training. It has been perceived by the rulers as a source of efficiency and accepted by the ruled as a form of legitimate differentiation.

Grandes écoles have endured and proliferated because they have fulfilled with distinction their manifest function: to produce an elite of knowledge, while performing no less effectively their latent function: to justify the position of this elite by guaranteeing its calibre. That they have contributed, both through their educative and through their legitimatory function, to increasing social stability might be described as an unintended consequence. To the revolutionaries who founded École Polytechnique and École Normale Supérieure the meritocratic contest was a fair means of discriminating between candidates; in their individualism, they failed to foresee entrenchment along class lines. To Napoleon, who reorganised both schools, the interest of the state dictated a meritocratic solution and ruled out any consideration of 'sectional' interests. 'Nationalism led to utilitarianism and utilitarianism to meritocracy'.[27]

Yet the cultural authoritarianism from which the definition of merit derived was such that the *concours* was bound to operate as a means of confirmation more than of selection *sensu stricto*, helping to perpetuate an elite and to justify its claims to intellectual superiority. Therefore the conservative function performed by *grandes écoles* is probably an inescapable consequence of their elitist character. After all, it is hardly their social bias which makes the *grandes écoles* distinctive. 'In all countries of the world . . . agencies for exerting social influence . . . good education, specialised training, high rank . . . are always readier of access to the rich than to the poor'.[28] Therefore it is by their historical origins that the *grandes écoles* are set apart and by the level of their cultural attainments that they should be assessed.

Notes

1   E. N. Suleiman, *Elites in French Society* (Princeton, 1978), p. 29.
2   F. K. Ringer, *Education and Society in Modern Europe* (Bloomington, Indiana, 1979), p. 124.
3   According to *Le Monde* (11.5.1978), approximately 150 establishments with about 35,000 students could claim to be *grandes écoles*. Another 20, mainly in business management, are known as such and train about 8,000 students.
4   On the concept of ideal type, cf. H. Gerth and C. W. Mills (eds), *From Max Weber* (London, 1970 edn), p. 59.
5   J. Delvaille, *La Chalotais: éducateur* (Paris, 1911), p. 108.
6   M. de Condorcet, *Sur l'Instruction publique* (second mémoire) (Paris, 1792), p. 275.
7   Polytechnique had been created under the name École Centrale des Travaux Publics in 1794. It was renamed in 1795. École Normale de Paris, created in 1794, survived only three months. It was reorganised and reopened as École Normale in 1810.
8   L. Liard, *L'Enseignement supérieur en France, 1789–1889* (Paris, 1888), vol. 2, p. 69.
9   A. Villemain, *Souvenirs* (Paris, 1856), quoted in R. Wilkinson (ed), *Governing Elites* (New York, 1969), p. 88.
10   A. François-Poncet's introduction to A. Peyrefitte, *Rue d'Ulm* (Paris, 1946).
11   École Centrale des Arts et Manufactures was privately founded in 1829.
12   On the concept of achievement orientation, see T. Parsons, *The Social System* (New York, 1951), pp. 48 ff.
13   G. Mosca, *Teoria dei governi e governo parlamentare* (Turin, 1925 edn), pp. 32–3.
14   Founded in 1821, the École des Chartes was refounded in 1829. See R. Pernoud, *Histoire de la bourgeoisie en France* (Paris 1962), vol. 2, p. 486.
15   E. N. Suleiman, op. cit., p. 53.
16   P. Ariès, 'Problèmes de l'éducation' in *La France et les Français* (Paris, 1972), quoted by Suleiman, op. cit., p. 42.
17   A. Leroy-Beaulieu's speech in memory of Émile Boutmy, quoted by R. Pernoud, op. cit., pp. 594–5.

18 See F. L. Ford, *Robe and Sword*, (Cambridge, Mass., 1953).

19 Cf. M. Vaughan, 'The *grandes écoles*' in R. Wilkinson, op. cit., pp. 94 ff.

20 F. K. Ringer (op. cit., pp. 172 ff.) notes 'the abrupt change in the social character of the École Polytechnique after 1880' (bourgeois representation declining from nearly 90 per cent to less than 60 per cent of enrolments) and relates it to the fact that the percentage of scholarship holders increased drastically at the time (from 31 per cent of matriculants between 1830 and 1880 to 57 per cent between 1880 and 1914).

21 F. Ringer, op. cit., p. 171.

22 T. Shinn, *The Dawning of an Elite*, p. 380, quoted in E. N. Suleiman, op. cit., p. 46.

23 See C. Chavanon, 'L'administration dans la société française, in A. Siegfried (ed.), *Aspects de la société française* (Paris, 1954).

24 See P. Sheriff, 'The state administration' in M. Vaughan, M. Kolinsky and P. Sheriff, *Social Change in France* (Oxford, 1980), pp. 66 ff.

25 See J. L. Bodiguel, 'Sociologie des élèves de l'École Nationale d'Administration', *International Review of Administrative Sciences*, XL (3), pp. 230 ff.

26 The extent to which *normaliens* were recruited from among more modest social mileux than *polytechniciens* has not been discussed, partly because this problem has already been tackled by R. J. Smith, 'L'atmosphère politique à l'École Normale Supérieure à la fin du 19ème siècle', *Revue d'Histoire moderne et contemporaine*, 20, pp. 248 ff., and partly because it is not directly relevant to the arguments put forward in this paper.

27 M. Vaughan and M. S. Archer, *Social Conflict and Educational Change in England and France, 1789-1848* (Cambridge, 1971), p. 185.

28 G. Mosca, *The Ruling Class* (New York, 1939 edn), p. 58.

7 'Plus ça change plus c'est la même chose': access to elite careers in French business

JANE MARCEAU
University of Liverpool

Introduction

This paper is *not* about the established business elite. It is *not* about the current leaders of France's biggest corporations as listed in the business journal, *L'Expansion*. It is *not* a description of the social origins and educational qualifications of the incumbents of such elite positions. Rather it is an attempt to explore the interactions of the social, economic and organisational processes which currently affect the chances of promising young managers of moving into the positions which later in their careers will give them the chance of running major companies.

The socio-economic characteristics of present incumbents of elite positions in French business are now fairly well known. Many studies have emphasised the narrow range of their educational qualifications and have indicated their high social origins.[1] Educational success and high family backgrounds have for long been effectively linked in company hiring, promotion and firing policies. They probably still are. They probably still constitute the framework of policies which will define the contours of the next generation of top managers. Thus simply stated, however, that linkage disguises a situation which is far more complex.

First, it should be remembered that within the business world things are not always as well ordered as overall statistics of this kind would suggest. Companies are not static and nor is their environment. Firms are subject to economic developments and technological changes beyond their control. Their directors respond to or attempt to control these factors — with organisational changes, with modified policies, including those of personnel. Company-perceived needs for specific skills vary over time, as is witnessed, for instance, by the '*oiseau rare*' analyses of the business journal *L'Expansion*. In different circumstances they offer different sets of opportunities and value different attributes. Finally, companies can only appoint to their controlling positions candidates who present themselves, directly or indirectly.

Secondly, there is never a perfect fit between numbers of qualified applicants and posts available. Not all graduates of even the best *grandes écoles* do equally well in their business careers, even when from similar family backgrounds. Conversely, many from high social origins do well even without a diploma. There is even a proportion that does well in business without either trump card.

The constitution of the pool of candidates effectively available is the result of large numbers of choices made as individuals seek the best way through a highly complex professional field. The characteristics of managers in the pool are the result of the interaction of pressures and preferences, of social and economic advantages or handicaps as well as individual skills, 'track record' and appreciation of opportunities. The choices made by employers are equally the result of such interactions, mediated by belief in the lessons of past experience and analysis of future advantage. Each side makes trade-offs between perceived opportunities and recognised costs. Finally, the factors affecting decisions are in unstable configurations, variable across industries and enterprises, changing over time and place; and careers leading to the top take place over many years — subject to the operations of other decision-makers, both in the private sector and in public policy, including education.

For these reasons, career paths are not the smooth progressions they frequently appear to be, when seen, for instance, from the 'top' looking down, from the board to junior management. Simple analysis of the characteristics of the incumbents of top business positions gives little real indication of how they got to hold their posts. Still less does it indicate the processes operating in the workplace to define the contours of the future recruitment stratum.

In other words, it is important when discussing elites in business in France, as elsewhere, to look more closely at the decisions taken over time by both sides: on the one hand, those of the existing controllers of businesses who offer the jobs which in succession constitute successful career ladders to the top; and on the other, those of individuals who decide to present themselves for any one of a number of possible opportunities.

This paper assesses data gathered in two studies, one of young French managers who held the degree Master of Business Administration (MBA) obtained in Europe's major business school, INSEAD (European Institute of Business Administration) and a second of similar people who obtained their MBA from Harvard.[2] Holders of MBAs in France usually come from high social and educational origins. In spite of their early ambitions, not all will however, make it to 'the top' in major companies. Some will; others will be eliminated from the race or eliminate themselves, while nevertheless choosing to remain in business. The paper uses a 'life cycle' approach to describe the principal factors affecting the decisions of individual managers. At each stage of his (and managers are still usually men) or her career, the elements of the decision are indicated. Starting with educational choices — in most cases the *sine qua non* of entry to the first steps in the business management ladder — and working through the variety of different business possibilities, the paper indicates both crucial influences and the cumulative interaction of handicaps and advantages. Influences on employer decisions are discussed as well as those affecting the motivations of individual potential members of the business elite. In this way it is possible to indicate the long-term processes by which some are chosen for positions of power, some are rejected and yet others eliminate themselves. The data are exploratory rather than exhaustive, and principally indicate the areas in need of further exploration for 'careers' in business remain largely unexamined in a systematic way.

Economic and organisational changes

Before looking more closely at influences on individual decisions it may be useful to point to certain more specific economic and organisational changes and their consequences which form the backdrop to the calculus of best advantage.

Some of these developments are familiar but need to be borne in mind in the subsequent analysis in the paper. The changes were especially pronounced in the 1960s and 1970s, the period most relevant here. The most important ones for the purposes of this paper may be summarised as follows: decline of family businesses in certain previously important sectors and an increase in salaried managerial employment; increase in size of firms and in particular a lengthening of managerial hierarchies, accompanied by an increase in the number of lower level supervisory positions; a change of focus from a principal managerial concern with production to one with marketing and also with the financial control of the enterprise; the consequent change in weight of certain functions within the enterprise; in some firms, a change to a divisionalised form of organisation rather than one based on functional specialisms.[3]

In parallel, the rise to dominance of certain companies and fields has meant the relative decline of others. At the same time, public policies, notably those related to the expansion of the education system, have changed the rewards available to the holders of specific credentials and have added new possibilities. These and similar changes constantly occur in any modern western industrial society, creating continually evolving configurations of opportunities and chances, favouring some groups, working to the disadvantage of others.

In the face of such developments, individuals in a society who wish to maintain or improve their socio-economic position (in relation to that of their parents) have to develop new strategies and make new investments in personal and educational resources. For example, as Bourdieu and his colleagues show, the changes occurring in France in the 1960s affected the chances of bourgeois sons of acquiring a social position equivalent in prestige and reward to that of their fathers and called forth specific responses. Bourdieu and his colleagues emphasise that to maintain their position, many sons of family businesses had to enter the public (i.e. more formal) managerial labour market and to enter it successfully felt it necessary to acquire extra increments of formally sanctioned cultural capital (diplomas). The best preliminary investments to make seemed increasingly to be in commercial and the newly introduced management education and reports in *L'Expansion* and elsewhere in the 1960s and early 1970s demonstrated the rise to prominence both of the 'new' functions (marketing in particular) and the success in them of the holders of diplomas from HEC, ESSEC and other leading commercial schools.[4] The analysis also specifically links this change further to the rise of a whole new set of managerial theories and practices, congruent with new forms of business organisation and ideology and notably a new emphasis on 'team work', on 'human relations', on 'dynamism' and even on the ability to speak English, the language both of the dominant economy and of the dominant theorists of management.

This emphasis is in stark contrast to the long established emphasis in French companies on production, with the privileging of engineering and an authoritarian and highly hierarchical organisational structure and ambiance. Such a change threw into doubt the desirability of many established educational paths and suggested the need for 'reconversion strategies'.[5]

Before 'reconversion strategies' come into play, however, other decisions have been made. The following sections indicate the major influences on educational choices and on decisions about early career paths. They show the roles of family, school system and organisational policies. They suggest the obstacles that need to be negotiated; the reasons for 'mistakes' and ways of correcting them; and finally the differences between theory and practice in many employers' decisions. First, however, how do some young people get on the path that leads to a business career?

The constitution of the pool of candidates

Entering the path to business: family and school

The business students investigated here came from extremely high social origins. They were even more consistently from the top social groups than the elite engineering and commercial schools. They were, moreover, very often from business backgrounds. Depending on exact definitions, 36 to 40 per cent of the students came from independent family businesses, with a further 11 per cent having fathers in senior and top management positions in other business enterprises. The upper echelons of the business sector as a whole, therefore, provided about half the total number of French students at INSEAD. The senior levels of the civil service and the liberal professions contributed another quarter. (See the tables in the Appendix to this chapter for information on students' backgrounds.)

The family backgrounds of the students concerned are significant because it is the parents who provide their children very early on with an image of their 'appropriate' socio-economic destination, an image very strongly internalised. The picture drawn includes elements of economic position – defined both in terms of revenue and in terms of leadership positions in economic organisations – and an associated social status and life-style. The inculcation of this image includes messages about the best means of achieving the desired objective. The families were unanimous in supporting a business career. Not one student chose the field in the face of parental opposition.

Within the business field there were a number of possibilities. Some students could enter their own family businesses. Many, however, did not and went to business school as a way of being successful outside their business of origin. In some cases, the companies were not doing well and families advised their youngsters not to enter them as a career. As one said:

'family businesses are meeting all kinds of difficulties, and anyway it is in a sector [wine] that does not interest me . . . The business has known a number of difficulties and there is not much of it left . . . Taking over a business that is not in a state of effervescence is difficult . . . My father did not advise me to enter it. He said that the market was good but the management [a grandfather and aunt] was bad.'

Moreover, family businesses, even those that are doing well, are complicated affairs. Two of the students indicated that although the businesses in which their father had a share were flourishing, they would not work in them, at least not at once, because relationships with members of their extended families – aunts, uncles, cousins – who were also in the business, made it difficult. They felt they must earn their spurs elsewhere and possibly enter the business later from a position of strength based on competence and experience of other companies.

They did not, however, envisage leaving the business world, the only one with which they felt they were thoroughly familiar. For the sons of businessmen or those of senior managers, a career in business most often seemed 'evident'. Frequently, no other was even considered. 'Let us say I was preconditioned', 'It was the best known occupation in my milieu'. As many said in their application forms to the business school, they had spent their childhood hearing about the business world and its problems and interests and reaching senior levels in it seemed to many the epitome of the *'belle carrière'*. Their family models presented few or no alternatives, even among cousins and uncles, as analysis of the wider families made in the study showed.[6] Strikingly, and an indicator of the strength of family influence, even where the students had thought of other careers they had abandoned them in the face of family disfavour or because they had 'discovered' that they were 'really best suited for business'.

For students without a business background as represented by the occupation of the father, the influence of the family in the choice of profession were much more intimately tied up with the verdicts of the school system and success within it. The father's profession sometimes tended to have rather a negative influence, as, for example, when the son saw the negative elements of certain potentially suitable careers – the army and navy no longer offered the same possibilities for high-ranking officers; life in the colonies, notably Africa (in whatever capacity) was perceived as a 'good-living trap', marvellous in the past but a life that changing circumstances meant one had to be wary of; pharmacy was perceived only as the life of the *'officine'* or as research; the civil service appeared as ultimately frustrating and as badly paid if one could not enter by the *voie royale* of the École Nationale d'Administration (for which several had tried). Thus, for most, the only avenue likely to offer the kind of position to which they aspired was business.

The interactions of family and schools

The tramlining effects of the education system combined with family pressures set many on the mathematical, and subsequently engineering or commercial school course, whose ultimate outcome is very likely to be a career in business. For the brilliant at mathematics, the choices at school, like the family ones, were almost 'automatic', and perceived as following the 'normal route'. Thus many, when asked to explain their choice, replied simply that they were '*très fort en maths*' or that they were 'not good enough at maths to enter the engineering schools, or at least not the best ones'. The preparatory streams, mimicking the prestige of the schools for which they prepare, are themselves hierarchically ordered, and the hierarchy is recognised by staff and pupils alike, with the generalist engineering schools' classes at the top and the commercial schools, whose students are disparagingly referred to as 'grocers', at the bottom. Knowledge of this hierarchy entered into the choices of the students:

> 'The stratification in my *lycée* was really precise; the best pupils went to *maths. sups.* [the maths preparation class], those who were less good went to preparation for commercial schools and those who were even less good went to the faculties. When you're seventeen, and even older, you feel you might as well consider yourself to be one of the best . . .' (Interview, 1974)

Pupils, then, were aware of the hierarchy established by the school system. They were also aware that on their success in that order depended to a considerable extent their subsequent chances on the labour market.

The latter awareness was much due to information and exhortations emanating from the family and notably the father. In some cases, the advice amounted to orders: 'My father imposed on me', 'I wanted or rather are wanted for me'. The parental views were particularly strongly expressed where the father himself was an alumnus of an especially prestigious *grande école*, and notably from the École Polytechnique: 'My father having been to *Polytechnique*, with the assistance of many kicks in the behind I *had* to enter the same school'. Even more directly, one student said:

> 'My father imposed my studies on me for many years because he wanted me to be in his image and afterwards I was obliged to operate a conversion strategy first through a doctorate in Economics and then through business school because at last I can do as I like. He [the father] forced me to prepare the *Arts-et-Métiers* as he had done himself.'

Perhaps the influence of the father, in interaction with the structures and values of the education system, may be summarised in the following quotation:

> 'That is to say, my father, one is always much influenced by one's parents, unless perhaps one has more strength of character than I have, anyway I know that maths, I did maths because one had to do maths. Maths in themselves had never much interested me but my father only

saw one thing, and that was the engineering *grandes écoles* because in his opinion they allowed a person to progress rapidly in industry . . . I consider that, in one way or another, I was a bit channelled, so that even if from time to time I felt attracted to other things, those feelings were smothered by this [father's] view of things . . . I got used to the idea of being an engineer . . . for the post that one can have . . . there was a bit of pride involved in it too.'

'I did not really want to be an engineer, in fact I was influenced by my family, my father being an engineer. It was the status that attracted me. At that time, it was natural to try to be the first, to overtake other people, the status of an engineer being preferable to that of a university man. In any event, I was attracted to business . . .'

The range of choice is, of course, very limited. Having discovered he was not good enough at sciences to become an engineer, he had to find a suitable alternative. Only two were effectively appropriate, HEC and *Sciences Po* – the top of the commercial school hierarchy, again a way of entering business.

The father, however, may not always be up-to-date. Even in terms of education, a son may have to reconsider his strategy.

'The market for engineers (*ingénieurs*) has weakened and there is less need for them . . . [while at the same time] . . . employers have realised that after all an engineer is not a poly-math and that it is not necessarily from engineers that one can systematically produce good managers (*cadres*) and moreover that it is not from an engineer that one can necessarily make a good management executive (*cadre du management*). That is what pushed me . . . into thinking of doing a business school.'

Entry to the business world: where to go and what to do?

Once qualifications good for entry to business have been obtained, a young person with ambitions to acquire early not only a high salary but also considerable independence and responsibility faces many new problems.

The heterogeneity of business is bewildering to the potential entrant. The business world is composed of major corporations, but also of small and medium companies. It is divided by product, by technology, by sector (manufacturing or service), by type of ownership and control, by time of creation or expansion. It is similarly diverse in its personnel policies and its managerial practices. A given position in one company does not in terms of power and responsibility correspond to that in another firm except perhaps at the very highest levels. Different types of firms offer different salaries, different career tracks and different responsibilities. Perhaps, more important here, they offer different 'entrepreneurial' and risk-taking opportunities to their most promising managers. Some promote on *ancienneté*, others on profits recorded. Big firms may enclose men in specialisms, thus limiting their power, while small ones, especially in fields such as consulting, offer access to power through outside influence. Ambitious young men have thus to pick their way through an enormously complex field of proferred opportunities. They have to judge which are real openings and which are *voies de garage*. They have to choose between sectors and functions, between staff and line positions, to weigh up the advantages of working at home or abroad, of choosing a large or a small firm, of being mobile or remaining in the same enterprise.

The choices they make involve preferences about trade-offs between salary and other attributes of a position such as independence and the decision-making power, both immediately and in the future, associated with it. Increasingly, they involve preferences for security over risk-taking, for career promotion over family life or vice-versa, for promotion within or mobility between companies with different configurations of all the characteristics outlined above. At every point in the *cursus*, in practice probably every two or three years, people developing business careers have to make important choices with a potentially long time-horizon, thereby involving their perceptions of future trends as well as their analysis of currently competing possibilities. The following section indicates the influences that play at different points on the career ladder.

Early mistakes: getting on the wrong track

Choosing size and type of firm, product and market, function or line positions is a highly complex matter. At this point, advice from people in senior positions is extremely important in minimising the risk of career 'error'. For those less 'in the know', making mistakes is easy and can be costly; entering fashionable areas can be a disadvantage. One interviewee, for instance, joined a large company on the computing side, thinking that to be an avenue to a management post.

> 'If that had worked, I would have stayed . . . but the company decided against using computers as a management tool and so I had to work as an engineer setting up an automated cell in a nuclear power station. This was boring and I left.'

Computing is perhaps a less 'noble' area and one which is too close to engineering for its practitioners to be considered good 'management' material.

Marketing, however, in the late 1960s was considered *the* function, *par excellence.* [7] However, even marketing is not guaranteed to lead to success. In recent years it has shown itself to be at least potentially a fragile function, unlike those which are the usual prerogative of the engineer, because it is highly dependent on the underlying or surrounding economic situation. Brought to prominence at a time of unprecedented economic boom, marketing may well suffer a setback at a time of economic recession. In such circumstances, finance, or even the despised production function may turn out to be better bets. Indeed, already by 1978, leading headhunters were reporting a return to a demand for engineers and for the more traditional qualities of command associated with possessors of a 'scientific' training (Interviews: Paris, London, Bruxelles, 1977–8). After the sales euphoria of the consumer dominated years, top managers with production units to run began to vaunt the virtues of the 'practical' manager, with his eyes on the production line, and to recruit from the *Gadzarts*, the graduates of the École des Arts et Métiers, whose salaries accordingly went up (cf. *L'Expansion*, 'Le Prix des Cadres', May 1978).

One of the 'new' functions may well do better, especially in the straitened financial circumstances of the 1980s and probably beyond.

One respondent in my study, who perhaps had had his nose a little nearer the wind, had carefully chosen finance as the surest way to 'the top'.

'In fact the only function, in fact *the* final function for a bloke, if he is pursuing a career . . . in business, is the financial function. Marketing, O.K., but it's very rare that a director of marketing becomes President and the only thing that's fun in a firm is to be President, at least I think so . . .'

From an upper-class family, in the business world, this man had entered banking as he believed it is 'nobler to sell money than socks'.

Judging the best sector to enter is not always easy. Even in the years of consumer boom, where expertise in marketing was much to the fore in the public mind and there proliferated in professional and business journals articles on the opportunities available in the commercial sector, business practices did not always keep up. Thus, while *L'Expansion* in the late 1960s and early 1970s advised entry to marketing and commercial functions and demonstrated the high salaries available to such *oiseaux rares*, young managers working in these sectors found such publicity a little *trompe l'oeil:*

'In France, there are lots of technical innovations but when it's a question of social relations, of marketing etc., that's not given much value. It's the same in the commercial sector. The French must have retained an old Catholic reflex which condemns moneymaking. Being a *directeur commercial*, that's not well looked upon.' (Interview, 1980)

It thus may not pay to put faith in business's own declarations about where its needs are, in part at least because these change extremely fast. Keeping not only abreast but front-running in the face of such changes demands a good deal of inside information, an abundance of 'flair' and much use of the *pifomètre*, an instrument rendered much more efficacious by appropriate networks of contracts.

The differences between 'ideology' and career realities mean often that ambitious young persons without sufficient inside knowledge of the business world will set out on the wrong track.

Business instability and the risk of growth, merger, and bankruptcy

Even when on the right track, however, the business world is sufficiently unstable for potential career disasters to strike unexpectedly. Opportunities in a given firm can change with great rapidity. In one case, for instance, a merger of two banks was:

'catastrophic where managers were concerned. There was an equal fusion at the top levels in the merger — in other words, the personnel were just added together at each level. Without this merger, I should at present occupy a higher post . . . Those who entered the bank two years earlier had had time to climb . . . I shan't be able to climb much further . . .' (Interview, 1980)

For this man, much depressed by the situation, not moving higher became dramatic: 'One can accept not getting promoted except that one is constantly pushed by family and friends . . .'

The experience of another young manager, working in an international company, illustrated the switchback nature of careers where companies are growing fast and where ambitious young men are entrepreneurial. A high salary is indeed frequently offered in return for considerable career risks. In this case, after the company he worked in collapsed, it took him ten years to earn again a similar sum. In the second job, having built up a successful company it was bought by an asset stripper. When interviewed, he was about to leave for the West Indies to start all over again.

Mobility for correcting errors

Mobility between firms and between sectors is a much remarked on characteristic of ambitious MBAs. Its value, however, as a means both of correcting errors of initial career orientation and of obtaining rapid promotion is not evident in French companies, at least in an unfavourable economic context.

> 'Should I change company [to overcome a perceived career blockage]? I don't know. Top management or the people just below them say they would move but in practice they don't because at that level it's hard to find a job elsewhere. Here salaries are very high. It is, of course, possible to accept a temporary drop in salary with the hope of rapid promotion *mais ce n'est plus l'heure, le malaise est partout*. There's a noticeable lack of will or willingness to take a risk and no longer be protected by length of service in the company. Here personnel rotation is low; few leave. For me to have promotion chances, the excess management personnel would have to leave . . . Inter-enterprise mobility is low. Only the best are able to leave because firms won't take on someone just average. *La crise favorise les personnes de niveau supérieur*, de qualification supérieure.' (Interview, 1980, my emphasis)

And another added:

> 'In my view it's a great mistake to stake one's professional cards on mobility, except where all one wants is to earn more money and to become extremely expensive. I think being a top manager is a vicious career – if you go for mobility, at the age of 60 years you have nothing, no roots, no enriching private life . . . Here we are not ambitious . . . When I ask questions of myself, it's not a question of whether I should change company to have more money or prestige but rather whether I shouldn't go to live in the country. I'm very fond of the country.' (Interview, 1980)

What to be: specialist or generalist?

Whether to aim at being a specialist or a generalist is the problem facing the young man ambitious to get ahead in business. The 'best' education favours the generalist. The École Polytechnique prides itself on educating the generalist and not the narrow specialist, to such an extent that the *polytechnicien* has to enter an *école d'application* before he is really considered employable. Prestigious business schools, too, play the generalist card and both their publicity and their curricula are geared to giving their students a 'global view of the problems of an enterprise'.

In practice, however, many firms wish to recruit specialists. They need people specialised in the latest financial techniques, such as inflation accounting, in the computing and information sciences, in modern marketing and sales tactics. They appreciate the skills of generalists in an abstract sense but almost always offer specialist employment. Even passage through a business school may not be enough to rid a candidate for a marketing job of his 'scientific' past, or to permit an engineer to enter the banking sector, the hunting ground *par excellence* in France of graduates from HEC and Sciences Po.

The utility of specialist qualifications varies by type of firm.

'That depends a lot on the kind of company and the kind of job. In the oil industry, for instance, it's clear that it's much better to be a specialist . . . But in other sectors, a more general training is better . . . , (Interview, 1980)

In contrast, there seems to be a unanimous view that it is the 'generalists' who make it to the top. At a certain point in almost every career, therefore, young managers who wish to advance have to devise ways of making the break from the specialist niche they occupy so that they can demonstrate their skills in other areas. It is at this point that the generalist background can be brought again into full evidence. The time to make the move is 'In the early forties . . . as a generalist, one has to make a choice at the moment at which one is most saleable'.

Becoming a generalist is hard, however, and perhaps becoming harder. Acquiring a generalist label means varied professional experience in a company, and now 'it's not very easy to change jobs in a firm; mobility has been reduced by the economic crisis and more and more people have similar qualifications.'

Even possession of 'management' qualifications may not be enough to effect the change. Indeed, many MBAs, in an attempt to escape the specialist image, to have a good knowledge of the market and to find a prestigious springboard for entry to high level posts, find it better to enter consulting companies, rather than large manufacturing firms.

Qualifications and performance

The crux of the question of career chances where access to top posts is concerned hinges around the relative importance accorded by employers to educational qualifications held and the professional track record established over the years of business life.

On the one hand, some young managers interviewed believed that:

'. . . after seven or eight years of professional experience, the diploma has no more importance. Rather, what counts are the results obtained, the success one has had in the posts occupied and, above all, the success obtained in the domain of human relations — rapid adaptation to new situations, capacity for working in a group, knowing how to be flexible while still maintaining a given objective. All that counts as much as the diploma itself.' (Interview, 1980)

In contrast to this, a number of respondents stated that in French companies the diploma held still constituted a *sine qua non* of movement into interesting positions. Indeed, it was suggested by some, both in 1974 and in 1980, that possession of a prestigious diploma and a certain *ancienneté* were able to disguise business incompetence.

'In France, length of service counts more than competence. If the two go together, it's perfect for one's career, if not . . . In this company, people from ENA or HEC have a label which authorises them to do just anything, to be in important posts even if they have no business sense. And even if they speak English badly! To do business, you have to be able to talk *coeur-à-coeur* with somebody. And the language of business is English. That's why the French are usually so bad at market prospection and why French companies are often obliged to employ foreigners.' (Interview, 1980)

In 1974, similar experiences were expressed.

'I had to move . . . I realised that people identify closely with their qualifications . . . in companies, qualifications count . . .' (Interview, 1974)

The same person went on to say:

'I could see that I need something extra . . . it is important to say that in France people are obsessed by the level of their qualifications . . . and it is quite painful, when it happens that one has failed to get into a so called *grande école*, to then find oneself not really inferior but left with the impression that one has not done as well as other people, and is somehow an idiot or stupid . . . [but] as soon as I was admitted to business school, at R.R. really I saw a red carpet unroll before me, I had conversations with people that before I had only seen for brief instants and there . . . I saw them for an hour, very friendly . . . They thought that perhaps in 4 to 5 years I should be their competitor . . . So, I have a medium-term objective . . . [to acquire] something that can only face all the HECs, the accountants, and even those who have doctorates in economics . . .'

Having particular diplomas is important for a number of reasons, as this respondent himself saw. Two are of particular salience.

(*a*) *Credentials of competence*   The holder of a given prestigious credential is expected to have not only the technical competence guaranteed by the level of teaching at the awarding institution, but also to be capable of rapid learning and general intellectual flexibility, able to turn his certified superior intelligence to any given task. This is the basis of the 'true generalist' and is the means in many large companies of selecting candidates for 'fast tracks', whether these are formalised into specific recruitment and promotion policies or whether they are implicit in the personnel decisions made in practice. Thus,

> 'It is certain, nevertheless, that the difficulty of the entrance examination does impose a degree of selection, and I would not pretend that I have the mathematical ability of a *polytechnicien*, but I also believe that what makes the difference afterwards is the different training (*formation*) of the schools themselves. There is no doubt that in the French *grandes écoles*, students are educated into a way of seeing things which enables them to behave differently in the environment they enter afterwards. From the moment you tell someone he will be a leader (*dirigeant*), that he is destined for responsibility, he behaves completely differently from someone to whom this has not been said, and that, I think, is important. *So, very often, someone who graduates from a French grande école is quickly associated with positions of power, and is promoted rapidly and develops quickly* . . . There is, in that, a phenomenon which places everyone else in an inferior position at least to some extent.' (Interview, 1974, my emphasis)

Here is the crux of the matter. This is how personal qualities interact early on with formal credentials to permit the rapid establishment of the successful track record in business which is ostensibly the objective criterion of selection for top positions. In effect, to him that hath, more shall be given.

(*b*) *The importance of relations*. Many analysts of the holders of controlling positions in French civil service and business have suggested the role played by informal networks of contacts based on common membership of alumni groups. Kosciusko-Morizet, in *La Mafia polytechnicienne*, for example, indicated the ways it works for the graduates of the École Polytechnique, the form . . . 'X'.[8] Clearly, the more powerful the positions

held by the alumni in question the greater are their possibilities of furthering the careers of their younger *camarades* and encouraging the continued
interaction described above. The distinctive '*tutoiement*' of these
camarades in the otherwise formal office atmosphere of French organisations distinguishes individuals and underlines special connections. Effective in the past, the power of such networks seems to exist among the
younger generation too — as was adversely experienced by several respondents.

'. . . in companies, qualifications themselves help a little but when it
comes to high-level positions, it is in general the 'old boy networks'
that count even if people don't admit it, and I saw in my firm that
graduates of ENA and *Polytechnique* were very well placed and those
from *Centrale* too. But those from HEC did much worse and people
like myself did very poorly.' (Interview, 1974)

It is indeed hard to distinguish the use of the 'diploma' itself from the
persona that possession of it implies and hence from membership of a
group with important contacts. Within the new system of needs the old
system of recognising potential managers, through the hierarchical level
of their schools, continued to predominate both at a time of shortage of
qualified 'managers' (the boom years) and more recently when organisations seem to think more in terms of internal promotion than external
recruitment for managerial *cadres*. The difficulties of the present economic
situation indeed may well encourage a return by employers to the most
traditional means of recognising management 'potential'.

Employers' views on management qualities: character or credentials?

'We do not recruit for a given post but for a whole professional life;
we don't look for scholastic achievements but for personality. To have
a candidate who has been a *moniteur* at Glenans [sailing school] or
president of the students' union, even to have been active in a political
party, that is what we like.' (Michel Thibierge, Directeur Adjoint à
la Direction du Personnel at Électricité de France (EDF), quoted in
L'Expansion, 1977)

The essential ambivalence of the attitudes contained within employers'
requirements for recruitment to *cadre* positions is directly mirrored in
this quotation. On the one hand, most large companies, officially or
officiously, use educational credentials as a selection mechanism at entry
to different posts and vary the salaries offered to successful candidates
accordingly. On the other, they insist that they seek qualities not implicit

in the formal educational qualifications of the candidates concerned and not inculated by school curricula. They underline that their selection systems (barrages of tests, interviews etc.) seek out these other qualities, while of course putting the selection on a 'scientific' basis presented as 'akin' to the scientific basis of formal examinations but more 'appropriate' to the demands of high-level business careers.

In the decades after 1945 the public conversion of French business to acceptance of the need for 'better' management was spectacular. Acceptance of this need meant in principle also acceptance of the desirability of candidates for senior management jobs being skilled in the 'new' management techniques, summarised in the curriculum of the MBA and consecrated with the label 'made in the USA' or the European institutional equivalent. As Story and Parrott (1977) put it:

> In no European country has American management been embraced so enthusiastically as in France . . . *le management, le marketing* and *le cash flow* became part of the French vocabulary and US corporations the model of business success . . . The whole love affair with American business started in the 1950s when streams of French businessmen poured across the Atlantic to sit at the feet of sales guru José Trujillo . . . The French enthusiasm for US management techniques was the more surprising in that French employers had until then (the 1960s) been among the most conservative in all Europe. In a completely hierarchical system in which promotion was decided more by education and family connections than by performance, the executives or *cadres* ruled their companies like feudal overlords.

Acceptance by French businessmen of American management methods seemed to represent a radical change in attitudes to a whole range of business practices, including senior personnel recruitment and managerial promotion. Story and Parrott go on to point to the increasingly competitive market which was a major stimulus to the change:

> 'In a protected market, these graduates from engineering schools were more concerned with turnover, production and technology rather than profitability, marketing, selling, budget control and long-term planning which are such important elements of the US business approach. Paternalistic and secretive, more concerned with status than with money, strong on theory but weak on practical experience, French managers were just no match for the aggressive products of the US system'. (Story and Parrott, op. cit.)

For many reasons, including a fear that an inefficient business sector would be unable to stand up to the assault of the Left after 1945 (as suggested by a writer in *International Management Development*, 1977) in the late 1950s and 1960s in France, a rash of book and articles appeared, emphasising that French business, and industry in particular, was suffering from the 'management gap'. This was the thesis behind the analysis of the 'American challenge', later made famous by Jean-Jacques Servan-Schreiber, whose diagnosis indicted French industry for spending too little on research and innovation and for peopling its controlling management positions with family members and retainers rather than trained and 'technocratic' managers.[9] With the implications that these would care only for the profitability of the company, rather than the position of its owners, this rhetoric indeed became a normative plea for 'managerial capitalism'.

Rather than interpreting this as a call for a fundamental change in structures, however, the business world chose to see the problem as principally one of education. Managers, both controlling and at more junior levels, must, it was thought, be trained in new techniques and a new outlook. In an age that believed in more and better education as the major force for change in both society and economy, *management* (as opposed to technical or commercial) education seemed an appropriate answer. By the 1960s, French top management seemed, by dint of hard persuasion from a small group of men in government, in public administration, and in private business, to have become convinced of the need to 'rationalise' management technique and seemed to believe whole-heartedly in the value of specialised education in business skills. In a world of rapid change, it seemed evident that managers needed to be taught how to 'adapt', how to 'think creatively', how to 'lead teams'. In an age of increasing incomes and consumer spending, marketing seemed an important 'science' to learn.[10]

When major companies made vast profits, absorbed others and conquered overseas markets, corporate planning and corporate finance came to occupy important places in company perceptions of their needs. Reorganisation needed 'reorganisation men'. All these activities demanded strategies and knowledge; all seemed to be capable of codification if not into 'disciplines' at least into discernible and teachable 'skills'. The advantages offered by business education to the managers of large companies thus seemed in principle convincing and to involve few costs. It might seem to follow from this that companies would overwhelmingly recruit their potential top managers from those holding the specific skills, certified by possession of the MBA.

In practice, however, the arguments have seemed less convincing. In many companies, management education has come to be a bonus given for good measure to those already selected for senior positions.[11] Discussion continues unabated about the relative importance of 'nature' and 'nurture' in the making of a 'true' manager and of the appropriate mix of 'personal' and 'professional' qualities, as well as about the best means for discovering 'potential'.

Assumptions about 'essential' managerial qualities are usually expressed in psychological and hence universal terms. Failing to recognise that organisational problems, the object of managerial concern, are a mix of 'technical' and 'ideological' factors, many observers try to describe what management is quintessentially about. Asked what they thought of on hearing the word 'manager', more than half of one survey's respondents put personal traits and leadership quality first.[12] Such factors as 'leadership, ability to communicate, social attitude, ability for teamwork, persuasiveness' went with 'sense of responsibilities, performance of duties, creative talent, superior technical knowledge and skills, decisiveness, personality, broad general knowledge, readiness to accept risks, vitality, ability to make things happen, intelligence'. It is clear therefore that:

> The director and manager must have a good general education, good breeding, ability to command, psychological talents . . .

and that

> A man in a leading position has a distinctive personality, good professional knowledge, strength, energy, common sense, leadership qualities, knowledge of human nature, organisational talents and rational thinking.

He must therefore have:

> Character, knowledge, corrected and improved by experience. The manager is determined by his character. Education and knowledge rank in second place . . . A manager must be vigorous, healthy, obliging and just.[13]

Such attitudes inevitably reduce the importance that leaders of industry and commerce attach to the role of business education and its possessors. The majority seem to believe that the most such education can achieve is the development or 'bringing out' of innate talents and abilities. As Xardel sums it up:

> Let's be clear; in a [business] school one acquires information (*connaissances*), one can develop aptitudes already existing in an embryonic state, but one can hardly create them.[14]

The high-level managers quoted in Xardel's study, paradoxically perhaps nearly all themselves products both of the French education system and American business schools, largely share the view expressed by Jean-Leon Donnadieu, Director General of Boussois-Souchon-Neuvesel, one of France's largest and most 'modern' companies, when he said that:

'What counts for a manager is that he must first and foremost be a business man, an *animateur*, that he must possess imagination, leadership and be opiniated. That can't be taught in schools!'

Another French *patron* has said, 'I believe no-one can say "I have trained a *patron*" '. Managers react with 'intuition', their 'sensitivity', their 'past experience'. The language used to describe the qualities necessary for decision-making at the level of these men, among France's most successful 'managers', verges on the mystical:

To conquer a market or lead a team of men towards victory, one must sometimes make use of the resources of emotion, of the irrational, of passion, or sometimes even of hate and the spirit of revenge.[15]

Where the language is not mystical it remains reliant on the military mode, much as it was in the nineteenth century.[16] The 'enemy' must be 'felled', 'forced to flee' or 'neutralised'. At the other extreme, the manager who succeeds is said to need qualities of 'openness', 'intuition', or 'sensitivity' with regard to other people, which he must possess in quantities greater than those of the common herd. The French Foundation for Management Education itself even went so far as to state:

Management is an art. It can therefore not be taught, even if one can develop it. It cannot be described rationally in its entirety and in its substance, even if one apprehends certain of its aspects. It is an affair of character and of personal qualities.[17]

Where then are these qualities developed? First, of course, in the home and school, favouring those with appropriate environments, but subsequently in another training area, as an officer in the armed forces:

'The best training for a manager is first military service, the responsibility for men, the fact of being an officer. Commanding a section of 60 to 80 men at the age of twenty is an extraordinary education! In relation to what one can learn as a student which is theoretical, [in military service] you are given power and learn practical matters . . . Commanding men young is fundamental.'[18]

To be a military officer one must almost always be from the *grandes écoles*, or at least have a degree from a university. Given the social and cultural mechanisms limiting access to the top educational institutions, *la boucle est ainsi bouclée*. By their reliance on personal characteristics, the controllers of French business are in practice relying on the most traditional values — albeit with a 'modernised' face — and hence on well-tried and traditional recruitment practices.

'Personal suitability' as measured by such criteria frequently disguises the demand for 'social suitability'. In other cases, or at higher levels, in more 'delicate' functions, social acceptibility may be more explicitly demanded. Once the first tests are passed and management potential established, conversations and discreet enquiry explore the more delicate question of life-style and network of *relations*. As a young Swede working in a French bank rapidly became aware:

'. . . The French are socially very bourgeois . . . if one doesn't have one's house in Cannes, one's chalet in the Alps or one's hunting stretch in the Sologne one is not *quelqu'un de bien*. Before taking you on, people check on how you correspond to these criteria.' (Interview, 1980)

Inheritance of access to such attributes (one does not need to own them as such) enables the young, while even on low salaries, to live in the appropriate way and, above all, to interact with the appropriate people. The importance of the 'external signs of life-style' is indeed twofold. First, possession of the signs is an indication of adherence to a system of values that is supportive of those of established business and society. Secondly, these attributes indicate possession of a network of relationships and, above all, of the material possibility of maintaining and increasing those relationships through their constant activation. Villas and chalets in suitable places permit invitations, both given and received, and hence interaction outside working hours with appropriate people. Membership of exclusive local clubs, notably in Paris, ensures a similar interaction in the local environment.[19]

Wives and other female kin have a primordial place in the upkeep of the effective networks implicit in the playing of a bourgeois social role, for the material symbols of the network are nothing without occupants.[20]

In the banks in particular, it would seem, the social persona, including the networks of relationships implied, is particularly important, both to recruitment and promotion:

'. . . the banking world has very archaic structures (like the insurance business) especially in France because banking is an old sector and there's no longer any competition (indeed there is often a need for holding back rather than fighting to get hold of a market). In this kind of situation it's more important to have contacts (*relations*) than competence . . . This is beginning to change. Where banks are having to establish themselves abroad they have to have more aggressive policies which mean a different promotion strategy, but at home . . .' (Interview, 1980)

Much clearly depends on the sector. Companies, as was underlined earlier in this paper, are organised on a great diversity of lines and specific studies are needed to assess the general importance of given practices and to weight each factor, or cluster of factors, one against the other. The elements described above do, however, seem sufficiently general to persuade many ambitious MBAs to leave the big company race.

Opting out and getting away

Many MBAs, aiming almost to a man at entry to business school for posts 'at the top', find out once again in the business world that they have to modify both ambitions and strategies for achieving them. Armed with their MBA credential and the 'whizz kid' image emphasised by business schools' own publicity, they frequently find that their reputation as 'go-getters', as 'super executives', may be a disadvantage. Their 'itchy feet'[21] allow them to seek out and take advantage of a wide range of opportunities, to acquire a wide range of expertise, but firms frequently hold different perspectives. Mindful of the interests of the company as a whole, employers:

'are anxious to assemble a wide variety of competences and to give priority to no particular school. My recruitment criteria are suitability for a post but also the future of the group, the balance of the future hierarchical pyramid.' (Louis Rosset, head of the executive service of Pechiney-Ugine-Kuhlmann, one of France's major multinationals)[22]

Although in practice such firms do increasingly use 'Le Prix des Cadres' (*L'Expansion*, June 1980) diplomas and even business diplomas as qualifications necessary for access to top posts, such credentials still are not sufficient and the way to the top is often deeply mired in bureaucratic regulations about *ancienneté* and the approved range of salaries. MBAs frequently find a lack of fit between their perceptions of their capacities and the use companies are willing to make of them, as was suggested by almost half the alumni contacted in my 1973–5 survey.

These analyses vary in the degree of blame for this lack of fit they attach to the management in place. For some MBAs, French firms 'know little about the talents of an MBA'; they are 'impermeable to Anglo-Saxon terminology and ideas'. For others, the fault lies clearly with the outlook of present managers, running enterprises perceived as 'covered with dust', as 'based on gerontocracy', with their leaders 'fearing change' and imposing organisational structures which are too constricting. The existing managers 'trained on the job' do not accept the 'young who are in a hurry' and the latter, in an 'over-structured firm' do not find 'a climate that would allow them to mature rapidly'. These factors mean above all that MBAs feel underused and hence unappreciated, both in terms of the functions they are offered and the possibilities open rapidly to them. They feel that companies 'do not ask for a high enough level of competence'; that the managers in place 'do not want to give up their prerogatives and refuse to decentralise'. In essence, perhaps, as one respondent said, 'Companies see MBAs as staff: MBAs see MBAs as line.'

So many drop out of big company competition. More than half, either immediately on graduation or later find that they can enter smaller companies at a higher level.

> MBAs have a good reputation but many business structures make it hard for them to get positions of responsibility for fundamental problems . . . [the best companies] are medium-sized, distributing technical products in an expanding sector, oriented towards export or towards rapid diversification. There it is possible to be in general management and to exploit to the full one's knowledge of industrial milieux (Survey respondent, 1974)

The ideal career was indeed summed up by one respondent:

> One must make one's mistakes in a big company, prove one's efficiency in a medium-sized one and finish by earning a lot of money in one's own business (Survey respondent, 1974)

and one added, echoing a general sentiment,

> No to secure middle levels of management, yes to top management judged by results.

The search for a post in top management, where one is judged by results, would seem to be the key to MBAs mobility. Time is short. Major decisions need to be taken between 35 and 45 years. Disappointments are many, the roads to the top not clearly known and not clearly marked in a changing economic and organisational environment. Many, therefore, make trade-offs that remove them from the race to the traditionally defined 'elite' positions in business. Those who remain in the big firms were shown in the survey to be also frequently from *patronat* families and often to possess prestigious engineering diplomas. And yet these, too, had opted out of the race to membership of the purely French business elite. Those who were high-flying were largely to be found in multi-national or American enterprises and not in the purely French business milieu.

Conclusion

This paper has attempted to look behind the statistical description of the socio-economic and educational characteristics of the incumbents of elite positions in French business, to explore in more detail the mechanisms leading to the results. While detailed studies of the current recruitment stratum for these positions are not available, analyses of the social and educational characteristics of present incumbents of more junior positions suggests that fundamental economic changes, organisational responses to those changes and a considerable expansion of the education system have merely meant that *plus ça change, plus c'est la même chose*. This is not, however, the whole story.

The data presented above were chosen to illustrate certain specific social and economic processes and individual reactions to these that influence the outcome of any given person's career choices within the business world and hence the effect of individual choices on the aggregate picture. They suggest that in spite of many changes, and indeed because of some that indicate to employers an increased need for avoiding 'mistakes' in recruitment and hence a need for greater reliance on well-tried mechanisms of selection, the top managers of major French companies are likely in the year 2000 and beyond to be chosen from milieux very similar to those of business's present leaders. The structures of business are such and the influences on early career choices so systematic that major changes in recruitment patterns to business positions as careers are unlikely. Once on the track, the hazards encountered act on the one hand to necessitate the use of many 'external' business connections or assets and, on the other, to discourage a multitude of candidates from presenting themselves. Those who come from 'inappropriate' backgrounds are discouraged early; many from 'suitable' social but novel educational backgrounds have professional expectations which make it difficult for them to accept the constraints of a bureaucratic career in a large organisation for the period required. The 'unsuitable' are thus eliminated; many of the 'potentially suitable' eliminate themselves. In this sense there should be a question mark in the title of the paper.

The true criteria of recruitment to top level positions in important French businesses remain still largely obscure. The extent to which particular new qualifications or incumbency of particular positions (such as personal assistant to a senior director) provide long-term 'best bets' for an ambitious individual is not wholly clear. Analysis over twenty years of important change, however, suggests the longevity of the value of the most traditionally prestigious diplomas and the most traditionally important methods of career advancement − the mentor, the *camaraderie*, the network of *relations* − personal, familial and professional − and the inheritance of access to the attributes of the most bourgeois life-style, albeit 'modernised' to include skiing as well as shooting. Acquisition of a 'new' credential, a new piece of cultural capital, is not usually sufficient to change career chances fundamentally; as a crown on the head of the already culturally, socially and economically well-endowed it does, however, serve a legitimating function, guaranteeing the 'appropriateness' of the 'expertise' officially rewarded.

It is difficult in the analysis of business careers in France, or elsewhere, to separate the man from the post. Looking at the components and determinants of careers almost by definition involves examining the characteristics, the personal qualities, the educational and professional past of the man as well as the organisational situation of any given position. It is on the basis of this that men make career choices and that men are chosen for careers. It is here that the social constraints, expectations and aspirations built up over a long period of time, including time dominated by the family of origin and each stage of the educational experience, come into play and determine in large part what are conceived of as desirable career choices. Those who 'opt out' of the race for top positions in major corporations do not define themselves as suitable 'bureaucratic' material for the climb up from step to step in what they themselves seem to perceive as a fixed hierarchy of levels. By defining the steps in terms of the company rather than of their own ability to influence the outcome − an influence in practice in 'successful' careers which seems fairly large − they are led early in the game to reject the trade-offs which must be made in careers potentially leading to greater ultimate social and economic power and to prefer instead the advantages of high salary, 'modern' life style and a more evidently entrepreneurial existence to those of devotion to a company, to the need to 'prove' (by a 'challenge-success' career or by the more widespread 'position-promotion' one) one's capabilities to a long series of people in established positions. MBAs are encouraged in this by the 'generalist' ethos of business schools and the emphasis placed there on access to policy-making while young, allied to the belief that formally certified 'competence' should be given its due.

On their side, businesses are highly reluctant to formalise their promotion criteria, especially where the most senior levels of the company are concerned. While in France, businesses specifically use the decisions of the formal education system as a basis for recruitment to a career path, and indeed link salary to them beyond that stage, a number of other factors also come into play and the choices of men to promote are probably legitimated in other terms. Possession of a diploma from a *grande école* disguises the social and character considerations that companies use in recruitment at entry and provide justification for differential initial treatment of recruits. These differences then become self-perpetuating. As long as the educational selection depends so much on extra-scholastic characteristics as it seems to at present, that long will the relative chances of following successful business careers in French businesses remain largely unchanged. Thus, while changes in business organisation could in principle mean new opportunities for young managers and a change in the characteristics of the recruitment stratum, in France even in the '80s they do not seem to. Specific paths to the top may alter and thereby affect individual candidates' attitudes to their decisions. While in overall statistical terms the social composition of potential elite candidates in major businesses in France may seem likely to resemble closely that of the existing elite, in terms of individual career chances there are many uncertainties. While overall the education system may work to reproduce quite closely the chances of bourgeois sons in France of achieving controlling positions in major business, these chances are by no means sufficient for success. Equally many, and perhaps increasing numbers, prefer to be advisers to men in high places rather than to occupy those places. In that way they obtain many of the rewards while taking few of the risks. Equally, not all who are called can ultimately be chosen. Those that are so chosen in the year 2000 will probably have more in common than not with their predecessors of the 1960s and 1980s, or even of the 1950s, even in the 'newer' sectors of the economy. Once again in France, where elite recruitment is concerned, it seems largely to be true that *plus ça change, plus c'est la même chose*. Where other business policies are concerned, however, and hence the chances of more fundamental change, the significance of this remains to be assessed.

Notes

1 N. Delefortrie-Soubeyroux, *Les Dirigeants de l'industrie française* (Paris, 1961); A. Girard, *La Réussite sociale en France* (Paris, 1961); D. Hall and H.-C. de Bettignies, 'The French business elite', *European Business*, no. 19 (1968), pp. 1–10; D. Monjardet, 'Carrière des dirigeants et contrôle de l'entreprise', *Sociologie du Travail*, vol. 13, no. 2 (1972), pp. 131–44; P. Bourdieu, L. Boltanski and M. de Saint-Martin, 'Les stratégies de reconversion: les classes sociales et le système d'enseignement', *Information sur les sciences sociales*, vol. 12, no. 5 (1973), pp. 61–113.

2 The data on which this analysis is based were collected in one study of several hundred French students and alumni of INSEAD over the period 1973–5 and in a second study of Europeans holding MBAs from INSEAD and Harvard carried out between 1977 and 1980. The first was financed by the British Social Science Research Council and the second by the French CORDES. Information was gathered by analysis of academic records, interviews and question-naires.

3 For a more detailed discussion of these changes see, e.g., G. Dyas and H. Thanheiser, *The Emerging European Enterprise* (London, 1976) and Lawrence Franko, *The European Multinationals* (London, 1976).

4 Bourdieu, Boltanski and de Saint-Martin, op. cit.

5 Ibid., passim.

6 Jane Marceau, *The Social Origins, Educational Experience and Career Paths of a Young Business Elite* (Fontainebleau, INSEAD Monograph, 1976).

7 Bourdieu et al., op. cit.; Dyas and Thanheiser, op. cit., p. 36.

8 J. Kosciusko-Morizet, *La Mafia polytechnicienne* (Paris, 1973).

9 Jean-Jacques Servan-Schreiber, *The American Challenge* (Harmondsworth, Middx., 1969), orig. pub. as *Le défi américain* (Paris, 1967).

10 See P. Bourdieu et al., *L'Encyclopédie de la technocratie* (Paris, 1976) for an account of the development of this discourse.

11 See a series of articles in *L'Expansion* in the 1960s and 1970s.

12 F. Harmon, 'European top managers struggle for survival', *European Business*, no. 28 (1971), pp. 4–19.

13 Ibid., p. 14.

14 Dominique Xardel, *Les Managers* (Paris, 1978).

15 Ibid., p. 27.

16 A. Melucci, *Idéologies et pratiques patronales pendant l'industrialisation capitaliste: Le cas de la France* (Paris, 1974).

17 Quoted in Xardel, op. cit., p. 61.

18 Jouve, PDG at twenty-nine of the *Groupe Expansion*, quoted in ibid., p. 58.

19 P. Bourdieu and M. de Saint-Martin, 'Le patronat', *Actes de la recherche en sciences sociales*, nos. 20–1 (1978), pp. 3–82.

20 J. Marceau, 'Le rôle des femmes dans les familles du monde des affaires', in A. Michel (ed.) *Les Femmes dans la société marchande* (Paris, 1978), pp. 113–24.

21 J.-C. Willig, ' "Send the bosses back to school!" complain young MBAs', *European Business*, no. 28 (1971), pp. 20–6.

22 Quoted in J. Fontaine, 'Les grandes entreprises jugent les grandes écoles', *L'Expansion*, no. 109 (1977), pp. 64–71.

Appendix

Table 7.1   The social origins of INSEAD students

Socio-professional category	Number			% known origins		
Patrons of industry and commerce	135			36.5		
Liberal professions	49		} 270	13		} 72.5
Cadres supérieurs* − public sector	45 } 86			12 } 23		
Cadres supérieurs − private sector	41			11		
Cadres moyens (middle executives)	50			13.5		
Artisans/small shopkeepers	20			5		
White-collar workers	8			2		
Manual workers	8			2		
Farmers	14			4		
Other/unknown	45			11% sample		
Total	415					

Cadres supérieurs are 'managers' or 'executives' in the widest sense and here include high level teachers and career officers, as in the INSEE classification, to whom we have added senior civil servants (very few). The second category, *cadres supérieurs* in the private sector includes only the managers in private business.

Source: J. Marceau, *The Social Origins, Educational Experience and Career Paths of a Young Business Elite* (Fontainebleau, 1976), p. 20.

Table 7.2 Social origins — students grandes écoles (%)

Socio-professional category	INSEAD	Poly-technique	Mines (Paris)	Centrale	ENA	HEC	ULM Lettres	ULM Sciences	ESCP	ESSEC
Patrons and cadres supérieurs	59.5	24	28	30	19	38	25	16	13*, 28† {41}	6*, 25.5† {31}
Liberal professions	13 {72.5}	10 {37}	8 {37}	5 {36.5}	17 {45.5}	8 {53}	10 {38}	14 {35}	12 {53}	12
Senior civil servants		3	1	1.5	9	7	3	5		
Ingénieurs	13.5	20	13.5	13	6	11	5.5	14.5	12	16
Teachers		15 {46}	8 {41.5}	11 {39}	11 {30}	5 {29}	25 {42.5}	21 {46.5}	5 {27}	4 {39}
Middle executives		11	20	15	13	13	12	11	10	19
Artisans/shopkeepers	5	5	6	8	8	13	4	6	8	9
White-collar workers	2	5	4	6	7	2	8	6	6	4
Manual workers	2	4	5	4	4	1	5	2.5	2	2
Farmers and farm workers	4	2	6	5	6	2	3	3	2	3
Other	–	1	1	–	–	–	–	–	–	–

* Industriels
† Cadres supérieurs

Sources: Study by *Centre de Sociologie Européene*, 1967.
ESCP and ESSEC data – Ministère de l'Education Nationale.
Service de Statistique, 1971.

School Names:

ENA	École Nationale d'Administration
HEC	École des Hautes Études Commerciales
ULM	École Normal Supérieure
ESCP	École Supérieure de Commerce de Paris
ESSEC	École Supérieure des Sciences Economique et Commerciales

Table 7.3 Socio-professional categories of a national sample of fathers and sons — 1970 (%)

Fathers \ Sons	2	3	4	5	6	0	1	7	8
2 Owners, industry and commerce	28	11	13	9	33	2	1	2	2
3 Higher managers and liberal profs.	7	42	24	7	14	2	0	2	3
4 Middle managers	5	21	32	11	25	0.5	0	2	4
5 White-collar workers	8	10	18	15	42	1	1	2	3
6 Manual workers	6	3	11	9	64	1	1	2	3
0 Farmers	7	2	4	5	35	39	6	1	2
1 Farm workers	8	1	4	6	56	7	16	1	2
7 Service personnel	8	4	18	12	50	1	2	3	3
8 Other	11	11	20	10	33	1	2	2	11

The numbers refer to the INSEE category numbers

Source: Adapted from C. Thélot, 'Les tableaux de l'enquête "Formation et qualification professionnelles" sont disponibles', *Économique et statistique*, vol. 41 (1973), pp. 62–3.

8 The contribution of the École Nationale d'Administration to French political life

ANNE STEVENS
University of Sussex

This chapter attempts to evaluate the contribution of the École Nationale d'Administration (ENA) to post war French political life in terms, firstly, of the institution itself, its initial inspiration, its persisting ethos and its activities. Secondly, it examines some of the activities and attitudes of former students of the School. It argues that the main importance of the ENA lies not in any particular political stance which it may have inculcated (although its claim to be quite a-political must be discounted) but in the style and approach it has engendered and the status and opportunities it provides for its former students.

The place of the School in the education of a number of the most prominent political leaders in France today is well known, but it may be appropriate to recall some of the background facts. The School was founded in 1945 to select and train candidates who would in due course come to occupy some of the most senior posts in the administration. It replaced the separate selection processes of the various *grands corps* — the *Conseil d'État*, the *Inspection des Finances*, the *Cour des Comptes*, the diplomatic and prefectoral corps — and also the individual competitions for *rédacteurs* — general administrators — run by most of the various ministries. For successful candidates the School provides a two-and-a-half-year training. The details of the course have varied considerably over the past thirty-five years, but many of the initial principles remain intact. Both the selection process and the institution and nature of a common training had been the subject of much discussion and some experiment over the previous century and a half, and the School owes much to this background.

During its thirty-five years the School has contributed to the education of one president and one prime minister. Some twenty-four other former students of the School have held office as ministers or junior ministers, and amongst the posts involved have been the most senior ministerial offices — Finance (Ortoli, Fourcade), Justice (Peyrefitte), Foreign Affairs

(François-Poncet). 2.9 per cent of the candidates at the 1978 election were former students of the ENA and thirty-three of them were elected. Of the major political groupings only the Communist Party does not have former students of the ENA in prominent positions. Former students of the ENA are also active, although markedly less so, at local level. Recent figures are hard to find. In 1972 forty-six former students had served as mayors, ten as members of a *conseil général* and fourteen had held the two posts simultaneously. Some had, of course, combined such a post with a position as a *député* or minister (Alain Peyrefitte, Mayor of Provins, for example).[1] Outside parliamentary politics former students of the ENA are active within what has come to be called the *Nouvelle Droite*.[2] Clearly a significant proportion of those at the top of French political life have passed through the School. While they represent only a very small proportion of the three thousand or so former students of the School, they are a particularly visible and important group. It is there-fore not inappropriate to ask about the aims of the School and its ethos.

From its inception the aims of the School went beyond mere admini-strative efficiency. Certainly such efficiency was, and has remained, an important consideration. Michel Debré, in his initial report on the motives for the foundation of the School, condemned bureaucratic *paperasserie*, and later amplified his criticisms:

> si, par absence de politique démographique et par absence de politique d'hygiène la population française diminue en quantité et en qualité depuis de longues années; si, par absence de programme et de plan l'économie française, agriculture et industrie ont pris un retard bien antérieur aux ruines de cette guerre; si depuis vingt ans, nos grandes villes se sont aggrandies dans le désordre, la saleté et la laideur, c'est pour une bonne part la faute de l'administration. . . .'[3]

However, as the passage quoted indicates, Debré's criticism went beyond the castigation of inefficiency and torpor. The administration, he clearly felt, should be active in formulating the new policies which the new regime demanded. The sentiment that any regime needed to train its servants in ways of thought and action that would be consonant with the maintenance of that regime was not new. Thus Napoleon wished the young *auditeurs* of his Conseil d'État to be men 'qui lui soient sincèrement dévoués . . . qui se formeront, pour ainsi dire, à son école et qu'il pourra employer partout où le besoin de son service les rendront utiles'.[4]

In 1848 Hippolyte Carnot's short-lived École d'Administration was based, he said, on democratic ideals, on the idea of equality which befitted a Republican regime. It was intended to train republican officials to replace the royalists. In 1936 Jean Zay, Minister of Education in the Popular Front Government, was prompted by similar sentiments. The preamble to his abortive bill to establish an École Nationale d'Administration pointed out that the State was obliged under the existing recruitment and training system to employ servants from amongst those classes whose interests and ideals might not coincide with those of the nation as a whole.[5]

Similar motives lay behind the foundation of the present ENA. The old administrative elite had become discredited during the war years. A new spirit was needed. Debré described it.

> En notre temps plus peut-être qu'à toute autre époque, il appartient à l'administration de préparer avec soin et dans tous les domaines, les éléments d'une grande politique, d'établir les plans à longue échéance et de veiller à leur exécution conformément a l'intérêt supérieur de la nation. Cette obligation ne suppose pas seulement . . . les caractéristiques traditionnelles des agents de nos services, mais bien davantage: la force de caractère, l'unité des vues, le souci de la réalisation rapide, la volonté de réussir.[6]

If one of the aims of the School was to imbue its students with a spirit which would go beyond mere administrative efficiency, another was to provide a training which, while sufficiently specific to be useful, was also sufficiently wide and general to prepare its students, who would not know until the end of the course what posts they were to occupy, for a very wide range of possible future responsibilities. It has not always been easy to find a balance. The founders of the School were convinced of the necessity of providing a common training to overcome the problems of division within the administration, but the earliest form of organisation in the School involved four specialised sections and a final year of vocational training following the students' choice of the posts they were to fill. The criticisms to which this gave rise resulted, from 1958, in an era of *polyvalence*. After 1971 the School reverted to two distinct sections, but there is a common core of subjects undertaken by all students. Ezra Suleiman has stressed the importance of recognising that the aim of the ENA and of the École Polytechnique is to provide a training that will fit their former students for any senior post. Of the *stage* — the first year of practical placements that has been an almost unchanging feature of the ENA since the beginning — he says: 'The *stage*, then, is ideally suited to a group of leaders that does not wish to circumscribe the area over which it exercises decisive influence.'[7] He later comments: 'generalised skills enable the elite to occupy posts that have little connection with its prior training. The members of the elite become politicians, bankers, industrialists, international civil servants; and even when they remain in the public service they occupy posts for which their training has not prepared them.'[8] As he points out, 'the schools have always had to tread a narrow path between maintaining that they were preparing the elite of a particular sector and maintaining that they were preparing the elite of the nation as a whole. The latter view is now the more accepted one. . . .'[9] It is clear that in these aims – and it should be noted that these are only two amongst the several aims with which the School was founded – the School goes beyond any intention simply to produce specific skills, and provides a soil that may well prove fertile for the nurturing of political ambitions and leadership.

The School has, over the years, developed a particular ethos. The approach of its staff members, the tone of official publications describing it, the reminiscences of former students, all reflect this. What are the guiding ideas behind this ethos, and how far do they reflect a particular political stance? The three main ideas which have persisted with considerable tenacity since the foundation of the School seem to be the importance of the role of the State and the high moral status of service to it, the primacy of 'the general interest', and the desire for efficiency.

Jacques Chevallier, who has analysed the ideology of the top administration, has pointed out that any official will speak very frequently of the State which he regards as

> une entité qui le dépasse et à laquelle il rapporte l'intégralité de la puissance . . . L'Etat apparaît aux fonctionnaires comme le centre d'intégration et d'unification d'une société qui serait, sans son intermédiaire, vouée au désordre, à l'éclatement, à la dissolution . . .[10]

Former students of the ENA are conscious of the extent to which the role of the State was stressed during their training.

> au moins pendant les premières années l'enseignement de L'E.N.A. était très centralisateur, très dirigiste, très 'colbertiste'. La haute administration était presentée comme 'l'aile marchante' de la société française, tenue pour ignorante, mineure et irresponsable.[11]

The second guiding idea behind the ENA is the notion of the administration as the guardian of the general interest.

> Pour les fonctionnaires il existe bien un intérêt général, autour duquel la société peut être unifiée, intégrée, solidarisée. Mais cette intérêt général n'est pas réductible à la somme des intérêts particuliers . . .

intérêt général et intérêts particuliers sont en relation d'opposition dialectique: l'intérêt collectif de la société entre inévitablement en conflit avec les intérêts individuels des membres contre lesquels il doit être défendu et imposé.[12]

As early as 1956 Alain Gourdon, a former student of the ENA, writing for Mendès-France's *Cahiers de la République* spoke of the School as having an almost jesuitical belief in the possibility of inculcating virtue. This virtue consisted of the rejection of any rigidity of intellectual position and a belief in the possibility of arbitration between conflicting demands. The Bloch-Lainé Committee which reported on the ENA in 1969 recognised this aspect of the School's ethos and defended it.

Peut-être le réproche de hauteur ou de distance que l'on adresse aux anciens de l'ENA ne correspond-il au fond qu'à cette volonté de maintenir entre les intérêts particuliers, la neutralité et l'impartialité requise par le service de la collectivité?[13]

However, as Bernard Gournay pointed out in 1964, the top civil servants were obliged to give the notion of the general interest some content. This content he analysed as involving efforts to produce technical and economic progress, to encourage modernisation, expansion and rationalisation through 'good administration' which would bring the various social and economic groups to perceive where their own best interest lay.[14]

Gournay thus links the idea of the general interest with the third guiding idea behind the ENA, that of efficiency. This current of thought can be found, for instance, in the tendency of both teachers and students of the School to think in terms of the 'right answer' to any given problem. The structure of the School encourages this — the final assessment is made largely on the basis of examinations with questions the answers to which must be capable of being marked.

One common factor behind all these guiding ideas is that all involve some stress upon the notion of the 'de-politicisation' of problems of administration and even of policy. This aspect of the top administration has been noted by many observers. In the 1960s Bauchard noted the admiration which many of the then students of the School felt for Bloch-Lainé, based in part upon his indifference to politics. Both Gournay and Ridley described this emphasis upon 'depoliticisation',[15] and more recently Jacques Chevallier noted that 'Les fonctionnaires se prévalent de leur "apolitisme" . . . [ils] sont dégagés de tout lien d'allégeance, totalement désintéressés et détachés des "contingences circonstancielles" . . .'.[16] The American, Riemer, observed the pressure on the ENA students to conform to the doctrine of an impartial State and civil service, making judgements on a purely 'objective' basis. As one of the students remarked of his colleagues 'Ils sont habitués à faire comme s'il n'y avait pas de politique'.[17]

To accept this emphasis upon the absence of 'politics' at its face value, however, is to ignore a by now considerable stream of comment and criticism which assesses the contribution of the École Nationale d'Administration to French political life in terms of its role as a *séminaire du régime*, producing politicised officials who actively support the governing coalition which governed from 1958 to 1981, some of whom moved over into the world of active politics.[18] It is not difficult to find evidence to support such conclusions. Firstly, the nature of the regime is determined by a constitution which was very largely the responsibility of the ENA's founder, Michel Debré, and a small team several of whose members were former students of the School. The installation of a new regime, with its intention of restoring authority to the executive, coincided with the arrival in more important and visible posts of a number of former students of the School who had been making their way up through the administration over the previous decade. This could be seen as more than a co-incidence.

Secondly, former students of the School have provided for the Fifth Republic a number of ministers and junior ministers. Every general election since 1958 has seen an increase in the number of Members of the National Assembly who are former students, and they have mostly been members of the parties which made up the Gaullist/Giscardian coalition.

Thirdly, public discussion has tended to emphasise the role of ENA graduates. Both journalists and academics have studied their role – Pierre Birnbaum's book *Les Sommets de l'État* is a particularly striking example of such a study. Former students of the School have undertaken increasingly visible posts, as they have reached the highest posts of an administrative career, and also as the proliferation of powerful bodies (the regional planning body DATAR is an obvious example) with 'political' aims but with civil servants, often ENA graduates, at their head, has opened new opportunities. If *Giscardiens* replaced *Gaullists* in such posts it was still amongst the former students of the ENA that Giscard found supporters suitable for such appointments. Of the fifty-two *Giscardiens* outside the field of education cited by Yves Agnès in a recent *Le Monde Dimanche* article twenty-six were former students of the ENA.[19]

Against any over-simple conclusions that might be drawn from such evidence, however, three considerations may be set. Firstly, the political orientation of former students of the ENA is very varied and by no means always favourable to the Government. The ENA students of the late 1960s and early 1970s had a reputation for turbulence, and in 1970 the School was threatened with closure when a number of the students supported a statement denouncing the Government's law and order policies. Two surveys of the political opinions of former students of the ENA in the early 1970s showed over one third of them supporting the parties of the Left. (Certain key appointments in the Mauroy Government have involved former ENA students. *Ed*.)

Secondly, there is no evidence to show that it is necessarily the ENA which determines the political orientation of its former students. The ethos of the School exists, but is only one of many influences which act upon the students. That many of the most radical criticisms of the School have come from its own former students suggests this. It seems probable that the ENA has more influence upon the former student's style, than upon the content of his ideas. Style is a vital part of success in the French educational process and the ENA is in this respect no exception. The examining boards, both for the entry and the final examinations, emphasise this, stating that only exceptionally should a candidate depart from the accepted form of answer. But a common outward style does not also presuppose a common intellectual or political viewpoint. The biographies of those former students who have succeeded in political life suggest that other influences often brought them into such activities. Bernard Stasi, for instance, was active in the MRP from the age of seventeen, and Françoise Gaspard, elected as the Socialist mayor of Dreux whilst still a student at the ENA in 1977, had been a member of the Socialist Party since 1971. President Giscard replaced his grandfather in his parliamentary seat, while for Gaullist leader Chirac the determining factors seem to have been his service in Algeria and his close association with Pompidou.

Thirdly, the debate about the extent and nature of the politicisation of the top administration as a whole remains open. The subject is considered in more detail by Dr Ella Searls in Chapter 10, and the persistence in office of the same governing coalition for over twenty years (1958–81) makes conclusions particularly difficult to draw.

The first section of this chapter has described the operation of the ENA in terms of its aims and its ethos, arguing that while it eschews any overt political orientation, and while criticisms of it as a *séminaire du régime* are usually exaggerated, it nevertheless is concerned, as it has always been intended that it should be, with more than the mere execution of policy. Its students are inevitably involved in considerations of policy and politics. The second part of the chapter goes on to consider more specifically the contribution which the École Nationale d'Administration may make to the political careers of those of its students who turn to this field of activity. Some factors which may help to explain the success of its former students may emerge from these considerations. Three aspects will be considered: the question of the nature of the training, the question of access and opportunities provided through the School, and the complicated question of the status and legitimacy enjoyed by those who are former students of the School.

The training provided by the ENA since 1971 has been based upon the assumption that the students need to acquire three techniques, which are defined as the techniques of decision-making, of negotiation, and of administrative research. In addition, the School aims to provide the students with a number of ancillary tools, chiefly of a quantitative nature, and to improve their foreign languages. The technique of decision-making is dealt with through two courses, one on administrative texts and documents, and one on budgetary and fiscal problems. The ENA courses are based upon files of documents upon which the students draft their answers to problems. The problems set develop an ability to deal with a mass of information competently and quickly, and to weigh up the facts of a situation and the legal position concerning them. The teaching is much concerned with inculcating the correct style and form for administrative documents but is also likely to encourage students to take a wide overview of problems.

The techniques of negotiation are, it is felt, fostered by courses on international relations, involving especially a study of the processes through which a particular treaty or accord was reached, and by a consideration of industrial relations linked to the period of practical placement spent in an industrial or commercial concern. Administrative research and enquiry are undertaken in the seminar groups, which are assigned a topic to study and required to produce a report including practical policy suggestions. In their final months at the School the students undertake further in-depth study of two other topics.

This type of training seems to convey two advantages to the future politician. Firstly, it gives him practice in skills which may be very useful to a politician. Jean Saint-Geours, himself a former pupil, summed up this advantage:

Qu'apprend-on à l'ENA? Peu de choses sur le plan des connaisances proprement dites. Beaucoup dans le domaine des réflexes et de l'angle de vision . . .
   A l'ENA [l'élève] . . . apprend bien les disciplines de l'analyse subtile et rigoureuse, et l'art de la synthèse élégante et puissament

simplificatrice. Car l'utilisable l'emporte sur le vrai. S'il est nécessaire de comprendre, il est encore plus nécessaire de transformer pour l'action et la conviction. Des exercices répétés forgent un mode d'expression pur et clair comme un idéal d'intelligence: outil remarquable pour le diagnostique et arme redoutable . . . dans les combats de la vie politique et administrative.

L'ENA dote surtout ses élèves d'une structure de comportement et d'une dynamique de l'esprit qui combine indissolublement le sens de l'État, la conscience missionaire et le goût du pouvoir.[20]

Saint-Geours rightly stresses the usefulness of the ENA training as a tool; he also remarks upon the linkages between administrative and political life, and speaks of the development of a 'missionary conscience' which is an attribute that might be considered more suitable in politician than administrator.

The second advantage which the training provided by the ENA may confer is the development of a way of looking at problems which takes into account a political dimension. Inevitably the political orientation assumed has been that of the Government of the day. Riemer remarked upon this aspect of the training when he pointed out that the problems set in the major courses tend to involve policy considerations, and the student is required to be 'realistic' in his answers — implying that he assumes the continuation of the policy of the Government in office. The final examinations for one *promotion* (Guernica, 1976), for instance, required the students to produce notes for a ministerial speech to the Economic and Social Council for the examination in Budgetary and Fiscal Problems and, for the examination in international relations, to draft a statement for a high level OECD meeting setting out the French position on primary products. Amongst the supporting documents with which they were provided were copies of speeches by the Foreign Ministers of France, Britain, West Germany and the USA. In both cases the students were told that the examining board would look at the 'realism' of the solution given. It has, indeed, been a criticism of the ENA training that it produces people who have been asked to take a broad overview of problems, to pretend that they are ministers, or at least members of ministerial *cabinets*, and who are consequently ill-fitted for the less exalted posts that many of them will fill at least in their early years. Such training is however, un-doubtedly an asset for those who aspire precisely to the highest levels.

The training of the ENA thus conveys certain specific advantages to the aspiring politician. However, the mere fact of recruitment to and passage through the ENA can offer other advantages which may in fact be much more important. These further advantages may be described as advantages of access, and of legitimacy.

Entrance to the ENA is the first step on a road which may potentially lead to two positions within French society either or both of which provide a particularly favourable launching point for a political career. These are membership of a *grand corps* or a post within a ministerial *cabinet*.

Entry to the *grands corps* – the *Conseil d'État,* the *Inspection des Finances*, and the *Cour des Comptes* – depends upon the rank achieved in the final assessment examinations of the ENA. Those at the top of the ranking have first choice of the posts on offer, and throughout the ENA's history have almost invariably chosen posts in these *corps*. It is a striking fact that members of the *grands corps* are heavily over-represented amongst those who have successfully undertaken political activities. For example, despite the very small size of the *corps*, they provide 2 per cent of the *Conseillers Généraux*.[21] Although less than 10 per cent of all ENA graduates are members of one of the *grands corps* over half of all the former students of the School who have served as ministers or members of the National Assembly are members of the *grands corps*. It is interesting to speculate as to the reasons for this. They are probably all interlinked, but three possible factors which may contribute to an explanation can be advanced.

Firstly, membership of a *grand corps* provides a good deal of intellectual, professional and personal freedom. Although in the early years the tasks demanded of *corps* members may be demanding – the inspection tours of a young *inspecteur des Finances*, for example – the new *corps* member quite quickly becomes able to determine his own pattern and load of work and to organise the division of his time and effort. The atmosphere of freedom which this produces is certainly conducive to the development of the personal interests of *grands corps* members, including the pursuit of political activities. Ezra Suleiman, in an article in *Le Monde* in 1978, pointed out the consequences:

Il est patent et public qu'un certain nombre de fonctionnaires occupent des postes de responsabilité à la tête de groupements politiques nationaux tout en exerçant leurs fonctions dans une administration centrale ou dans un corps de contrôle. De deux chose l'une: ou bien ils n'exercent pas réellement leur fonction, et dans ce cas c'est une subvention indirecte que le gouvernement accorde à de groupes politiques. Ou bien ils tentent de continuer à exercer leur fonction, et dans ce cas la régle fondamentale de la neutralité et de la réserve en pâtit necessairement . . .

After quoting several examples of the political activity of top officials Suleiman continued.

> Il est de notoriété publique qu'en fait seul un nombre restreint des grands corps sont capables de bénéficier de ce système pour des raisons qui tiennent aux privilèges de fait et de droit dont jouissent les membres de ces corps.[22]

If the 'space' available to members of the *grands corps* is one reason for a greater tendency to engage in political activities than other former students of the ENA, so too is the ease of communication and contact between *corps* members. It is clear that the 'club' atmosphere within which the members of some *corps* work can in some cases account for the recruitment of members of political activity. Thierry Pfister, in his study *Les Socialistes*, instances particularly the *Conseil d'État*, where the influence of some of the older members was, he says, important in attracting some of the younger members of the *corps* to political activity.[23]

It is also probable that success in political activity is but one aspect of greater success which *grands corps* members enjoy compared to other former students of the ENA in many fields of administrative life. Jean-Luc Bodiguel's study of the former pupils of the ENA demonstrated the extent to which they could be divided into two tiers.[24] He showed that in terms of career patterns, access to senior and responsible posts, remuneration and movement into the private sector, members of the *grands corps* did significantly better than other former students. Many interlinking factors account for this — long-standing prestige, the corps' attractiveness to able entrants, the existence of the corps' 'networks', their strategies for maintaining and enhancing their standing — but they have until now combined to ensure high social status for the corps. The usefulness of such status within the political parties was explained by Jacques Lautman when he observed

> Le fait est qu'en France, à l'exception du Parti Communiste, les partis politiques tendent à avoir parmi les membres de leur appareil une structuration des positions assez largement analogue à l'hiérarchisation du préstige des professions et métiers dans la société. Autrement dit, les partis politiques ne constituent pas, ou peu, des voies d'accès aux positions de commandement différentes de celles des examens et concours de la République.[25]

Passage through the ENA may lead to one of the *grands corps*. It may also, both for members of the *grands corps* and for others, lead to a post within a ministerial *cabinet*. The important role of former students of the

ENA within the *cabinets* is undisputed. The first ENA graduates to enter ministerial cabinets did so in 1950, and by June 1972, as Jean-Luc Bodiguel has shown, some 28 per cent of all former students had done so.[26]

The growth of the proportion of senior officials, and thereby of former students of the ENA, within ministerial *cabinets* has been documented by Mme Siwek-Pouydesseau, and some of the pressures which have led to this position are described by Ezra Suleiman.[27] The major problem attached to this phenomenon is the interpretation to be attached to it. Is a ministerial *cabinet* so essentially political an institution that mere service within it is to be regarded as evidence of attachment to the political line of the minister? This is the viewpoint that journalists — Yves Agnès in his *Le Monde Dimanche* article, for instance — often explicitly or implicitly adopt, and it is shared by some more serious observers of the French administration. Others — Ella Searls, for example, and Bernard Gournay[28] — have seen service in a *cabinet* simply as a normal stage in a career involving no more political commitment than a discreet readiness to apply the Government's policies. The outcome of the debate between these two interpretations is important in discussions of the politicisation of the top administration as a whole, which have been pursued elsewhere.[29] In this context the important point is that the politically ambitious ENA student, particularly if he or she is a member of one of the *grands corps*, or has achieved a fairly high ranking in the final assessment examination, is likely to be able to achieve a post in a ministerial *cabinet*; and while, for many, this will simply lead on to further administrative posts, for those who so choose, this can be an advantageous starting point for a political career. As Lautman remarks, 'bien entendu le passage par le cabinet aide à trouver, ou plutôt à se voir accorder, une bonne circonscription'.[30] The career of Jacques Chirac is particularly exemplary in this respect. It is no doubt a matter of insights, of knowledge, of experience, and above all, of contacts.

Passage through the ENA gives its former students a useful training, and may give them access to some of the key positions which can assist a political career. But more important than either of these advantages is the status which it conveys. On the whole former students of the ENA are not expected to have to prove their worth by any protracted process, either to the political parties or their constituents. It is accepted that they may legitimately aspire to positions of influence. They are likely, so to speak, to enjoy the benefit of the doubt. Jacques Lautman, in the passage quoted above, observed the extent to which the structure of the political parties reflected that of society as a whole. Clearly the whole question of the emergence and survival of acceptable elites is a very complex one. There are, however, three factors which seem to be particularly relevant to the case of the ENA, which may also help to illuminate the question in a wider context. They are: the position of the ENA as the culmination of the educational process; the extent to which this elite has succeeded in ensuring that its values are accepted by society; and the cumulative effect of success.

The educational process in France can be seen as a series of hurdles. At each stage those who successfully clear one hurdle are propelled inexorably towards the next. In interviews with former students of the ENA it emerged that a number of them were not aware of having made a conscious decision to enter the School. Each step had simply led 'logically' to the next. Families who are ambitious for their children launch them upon this course at an early stage. As Michel Sidhom remarked, 'La véritable sélection commence . . . en partie au moment de l'inscription en classes préparatoires . . . mais aussi, et surtout, dès l'entrée en classe maternelle.' The ENA owes its position as one of the culminating points of this process to its status as one of the *grandes écoles*. Although it differs from some of the other schools in recruiting at postgraduate level, it resembles them in providing skills which are seen as being vocational and access to the service of the state. It occupies a position between the Institut d'Études Politiques (and can draw on the prestige created by the success of the predecessor of the Paris Institut, the École Libre des Sciences Politiques) and the *grands corps*, from whose prestige it also benefits. The result is that the School attracts a sufficiently large number of candidates to be able to select rigorously. As Suleiman observes 'The specialised Schools do not hide the fact that their task is essentially that of training leaders who are rigorously selected precisely because they are distinguished by their superior qualities. . . . Life for those who have experienced the rigour and pace of work within these institutions has consisted of a long series of hurdles. To arrive at their present position they have always had to be the most successful of their generation.'[32] President Giscard was probably not the only politician whose image has benefited from the aura surrounding the 'high-flier'.

Daniel Gaxie has suggested that the fact that the proportion of former students of the ENA is higher amongst members of the National Assembly than amongst electoral candidates indicates the existence of a *'prime à l'ENA'* – either such candidates tend to be offered safer seats, or the electors prefer them.[33] All this suggests that the political parties and the electorate tend to accept the claims of the ENA students to superior qualities. Their values have been accepted and diffused within society. This process has been particularly closely examined by Ezra Suleiman. He has shown the extent to which the generalised skills, the efficiency and the competence of top officials have made them attractive to industrial and commercial concerns. The phenomenon of *pantouflage* is important. While only some 10 per cent of the former students of the ENA are active outside the administration, they hold some of the most senior and key positions, especially in the banking and financial sectors (Jean Saint-Geours, Claude Pierre-Brossolette). Birnbaum points out that 12 per cent of the 'patrons' of the one hundred top companies – public and private) in France are members of the *Inspection des Finances*.[34] Jacques Chevallier speaks of a process of osmosis:

> L'appel aux hauts fonctionnaires permet aux entreprises de tirer parti de leur compétence technique, de bénéficier par transfert de leur légitimité, ainsi que de s'assurer les contacts nécessaires avec les milieux politiques et administratifs.[35]

Suleiman has argued that this process of osmosis in effect works both ways: on the one hand the officials' notions of the general interest have undergone a change which has favoured modernisation, industrialisation and growth, but on the other hand 'the elite [in this context the *grands corps*] having a near-monopoly on the key positions of society, comes to set standards by which it judges potential aspirants for such posts. It ultimately succeeds, to a greater or lesser extent, in having its own criteria accepted by society'.[36]

The extent to which an analogous situation obtains in political life is perhaps best illustrated by considering how many of those former students of the ENA who have been elected to the National Assembly have also held ministerial positions. Before the 1978 election twenty out of the twenty-five former students who had been elected as members of the governing coalition had done so at some time.

Finally, the legitimacy of the former students of the ENA rests also upon the success of their predecessors. There is undoubtedly an expectation that a former student of the School who turns to politics may expect to be rewarded with office and a distinguished career, and this must to some extent be based upon the fact that their elders have already achieved this. 'Les succès faciles d'un Attali ou d'un Dijoud font rêver certains.'[37]

Against this image of a widely accepted legitimacy a number of other facts must, however, be set. Firstly the situation is not necessarily the same at local level as at national level. The major achievements of the former students have been in the central organisations of the parties, and in groups such as the Giscardien 'Clubs Perspectives et Réalités', or the left-wing Socialist ginger group 'Centre d'Études, de Recherche et d'Education Socialiste' (CERES) — which was, of course, the creation of a group largely composed of former students of the ENA. While this is of course largely the automatic consequence of the concentration of top officials in Paris, it is also possible that it reflects a certain distrust at local level of the Parisian and the technocratic.

Distrust of the former students of the ENA at local level is perhaps best exemplified by the attacks of Gerard Nicoud, whose association CID-UNATI reflects right-wing opinion amongst the self-employed and the small businessman. Inveighing against 'La dictature des technocrates de l'ENA', in 1978 he invited his adherents not to vote for any former student of the School, whatever their party.

Distrust of the products of the School also exists at national level. There have been attacks from both Right and Left — such as that of Jacques Chirac at the School's thirtieth anniversary, denouncing his former fellow students' tendency 'à travailler dans l'intérét du public sans lui et au besoin malgré lui'. In 1978 the Socialist Claude Estier attacked the political orientation of the School, accusing it of rigging its results in favour of those associated with the governing coalition. Such attacks have not hindered the successful political careers of those who have reached influential positions in the parties, but they may have had some effect on public opinion. Gaxie noted the tendency for those candidates who had attended the ENA to stress their youth, dynamism and ambition rather than their provenance when presenting themselves to the electorate.

The contribution of the ENA to French political life is complex and not easy to summarise. In conclusion, it may be worth noting that the School, founded with fairly wide-ranging aims and by a team much of whose inspiration was essentially Gaullist, existed largely uncriticised under the Fourth Republic, providing its former students with access to a number of politically sensitive posts, for example, in the *cabinets*. Following the advent of the Fifth Republic the greater coincidence between the ethos of the School and the aims of the regime may have been responsible for tempting more former students into political life, as may the success of some of the first to attempt active politics. Guy Drouot maintains that it requires the prospect of early office to tempt a former student of the School into politics.[38] It is possible to account for the attraction of both Giscardianism and the re-launched Socialist Party in the 1970s in these terms. In fact many of the most notable ex-ENA Socialists were politically active before the Party's revival, and on the side of the governing coalition, as Francis de Baecque has shown, the tendency of top officials who have been both Parliamentarians and ministers to stay in politics if they lose their ministerial posts suggests motives other than pure opportunism.[39]

The French administration has no tradition of political neutrality at the top. The regulations since 1945 have expressly stated that any Government needs as its closest collaborators officials upon whom it may rely, and allows political opinions to be taken into account at that level in the making of appointments. The passage between the administration and political life has never been difficult. It is in this context that the ENA has set out to select and train very able young people. As in other fields, it has tended to be those who have made it into the *grands corps* who have been best placed to seize the opportunities. In these circumstances it may perhaps be argued that had the French political system failed to attract at least a number of the School's products, then it would indeed have to be regarded as impoverished.

Notes

1 Daniel Gazie, paper for 'L'Énarchie, mythe ou réalité? discussion organised by the Association Française de Science Politique, 27 April 1979, and J. L. Bodiguel, *Les Anciens elèves de L'ENA* (Paris, 1978), pp. 191 and 262.
2 The Club de l'Horloge, presided over by Yvan Blot, a former student of the School, was named after the large clock in the room in the School's former premises, rue des Saints-Pères, where the club first met.
3 Quoted by J. F. Kesler, 'La création de l'ENA', *Revue Administrative*, no. 178 (July-August, 1977), p. 357.
4 Quoted in Louis Fougère (ed.), *Le Conseil d'État 1799-1974* (Paris, 1974), p. 66.
5 See Guy Thuillier, 'Les Projets d'École d'Administration de 1936 à 1939', *Revue Administrative*, no. 177 (May–June, 1977), pp. 237-8.
6 Présidence du Gouvernement, *La Réforme de la fonction publique* (Paris, 1945), p. 16.
7 Ezra Suleiman, *Elites in French Society* (Princeton, N.J., 1978), p. 165.
8 Ibid., p. 166.
9 Ibid., p. 173.
10 Jacques Chevallier, 'L'Idéologie des fonctionnaires: permanence et/ou changement', paper presented to the colloquium 'L'Administration et la politique en France sous la Ve République', 30 November–1 December 1979, p. 19.
11 Bernard Gournay, personal communication, October 1977.
12 Jacques Chevallier, op. cit., p. 29.
13 Commission d'étude des problèmes de l'École Nationale d'Administration, (Commission Bloch-Lainé) *Rapport* (Paris, 1969), pp. 25-6.
14 Bernard Gournay, 'Une groupe dirigeant de la société française, les grandes fonctionnaires', *Revue Française de Science Politique*, vol. XLV, no. 2 (April, 1964), p. 231.
15 P. Bauchard, *La Mystique du plan* (Paris, 1963), see p. 73. F. Ridley, 'French technocracy and comparative government', *Political Studies*, vol. XIV, no. 1 (February, 1966), pp. 34 ff.
16 Jacques Chevallier, op. cit., p. 26.
17 Reynold Riemer, *The National School of Administration: Selection and Preparation of an Elite in Post-War France.* Unpublished doctoral thesis presented to Johns Hopkins University, Maryland, 1976, pp. 310-11.

150   *Anne Stevens*

18 In her contribution to the discussion 'L'Énarchie, mythe ou réalité?' 27 April 1979, Marie-Christine Kessler examined the criticisms levelled at the School.

19 Yves Agnès, 'L'État Giscard', *Le Monde Dimanche*.

20 Jean Saint-Geours, *Pouvoir et finance* (Paris, 1979), pp. 23-33.

21 Daniel Gaxie, loc. cit. For a further analysis of the activity of senior officials – not exclusively former students of the ENA – in local and national politics see Francis de Baecque, 'L'interpénétration des personnels politique et administrative', paper presented to the colloqium on 'L'Administration et la politique en France sous le Ve République', 30 November-1 December 1979.

22 Ezra Suleiman, 'Fonction publique et politique', *Le Monde*, 20 July 1978.

23 Thierry Pfister, *Les Socialistes* (Paris, 1977), pp. 80 and 131.

24 Jean-Luc Bodiguel, op. cit., p. 128.

25 Jacques Lautman, 'La Liberté d'engagement n'est pas la même pour tous', *Le Monde*, 4 August 1978.

26 Jean-Luc Bodiguel, 'Les anciens élèves de L'ENA et les cabinets ministériels', *Annuaire internationale de la fonction publique (1973-4)*, p. 361.

27 Cf. Jeanne Siwek-Pouydesseau, *Le Personnel de direction des ministères* (Paris, 1969), passim; and Ezra Suleiman, *Politics, Power and Bureaucracy in France* (Princeton, N.J., 1974), pp. 233 ff.

28 Cf. Ella Searls, *Political-Administrative Relations in the Fifth French Republic.* Unpublished doctoral thesis, London School of Economics, 1976, p. 385; and Bernard Gournay, 'La Politisation de l'administration en France', *Res Publica* (1971-2), p. 189.

29 Anne Stevens, 'Politicisation and cohesion in the French administration', *West European Politics,* Volume I, no. 3 (1978), pp. 68-80.

30 Jacques Lautman, loc. cit.

31 Michel Sidhom, 'Les avantages des classes aisées', *Le Monde*, 28 June 1978.

32 Ezra Suleiman, 'Self-image, legitimacy and the stability of elites: The case of France', *British Journal of Political Science*, vol. 7, no. 2 (April, 1977), pp. 199-200.
    Jacques Chevallier remarks (op. cit., p. 36) that officials lay claims to two types of legitimacy – one based on technical expertise, the other on democratic considerations. In connection with their technical expertise he says, 'La création de l'ENA a contribué a développer chez les fonctionnaires le sentiment de leur absolue supériorité; leur réussite à un concours difficile et prestigieux suffirait à démontrer leurs capacités intellectuelles, leurs connaissances techniques et leur assurer le monopole du savoir et de la compétence.'

33 Daniel Gaxie, loc. cit. Admittedly, in 1967 sixteen former students of the School stood for the first time unsuccessfully, and only six former students of the School were elected for the first time.

34 P. Birnbaum, *Les Sommets de l'État* (Paris, 1977), p. 141.

35 Jacques Chevallier, op. cit., p. 45.

36 E. Suleiman, *Elites and French Society* (Princeton, N.J., 1980), p. 140.

37 Odon Vallet, *L'ENA toute nue* (Paris, 1977), p. 128.

38 Guy Drouot, *'Les Fonctionnaires députés sous la Ve République.* Doctoral Thesis, University of Aix-Marseille, 1975, cited in Francis de Baecque, op. cit., pp. 36-7.

39 Francis de Baecque, op. cit., p. 37.

Appendix I: *Former students of the ENA who have served as Members of Parliament or Ministers to March 1978*

(*a*) *ENA graduates elected as Members of Parliament*

Date of first election	Governing Coalition (Fifth Republic)	Opposition
1956	Giscard d'Estaing,* Arrighi	
1958	Peyrefitte*	Chandernagor
1962	Guéna,* Charbonnel,* Bailly,* Prioux, Duhamel*	
1967	Poniatowski,* Dijoud,* Granet,* Limouzy,* Chirac,* Bernard	
1968	Soisson,* Stasi,* Lecat,* Malaud,* Lelong,* Billecocq,* Ortoli*	
1969 (by-election)		Rocard
1973	Guermeur, Mesmin, Ligot*	Joxe, Chevènement
1975 (by-election)	Rufenacht*	

*Has held post as Minister or Junior Minister

(*b*) *ENA graduates who have served as ministers or equivalent without election*

	Governing Coalition (Fifth Republic)	Opposition
	Deniau Fourcade (elected to Senate 1977)	Cheysson (Commissioner of the European Communities)
	Jobert Lenoir	

Appendix II: *Graduates of the École Nationale d'Administration returned in the French general election, March 1978*

Previous Members of the Chamber of Deputies					Elected for the first time 1978			
Name	Constituency	Date of First Election	Grand Corps?	Graduated	Name	Constituency	Grand Corps?	Graduated
Rassemblement pour la République (R.P.R.)								
J. Chirac	Corrèze (3) (Ussel)	1967	C.C.	1960	M. Aurillac	Indre (1) (Châteauroux)	C.E.	1953
Y. Guena	Dordogne (1) (Perigueux)	1962	C.E.	1947	J. Boyon	Ain (1) (Bourg)	C.C.	1959
G. Guermuer	Finistère (7) (Douarnenez)	1973	–	1967	J.-C. Pasty	Creuse (1) (Guéret)	–	1963
J. Limouzy	Tarn (2) (Castres)	1967	–	1958	P. Séguin	Vosges (1) (Epinal)	C.C.	1970
A. Peyrefitte	Seine-et-Marne (Provins)	1958	–	1947	J.-E. Mancel	Oise (5) (Beauvais-sud-ouest)	–	1977
A. Rufenacht	Seine-Maritime (6) (Le Havre)	1975	–	1968				
Union pour la Démocratie Française (U.D.F.)								
P. Dijoud (P.R.)	Hautes Alpes (2) (Briançon)	1967	–	1966	F. de Branche (P.R.)	Mayenne (3) (Mayenne)	–	1967
P. Granet	Aube (3) (Troyes)	1967	–	1960	F. d'Aubert	Mayenne (1) (Laval)	C.C.	1971
G. Ligot (C.N.I.P.)	Maine-et-Loire (5) (Cholet)	1973	–	1956	J.-F. Deniau	Cher (1) (Bourges)	I F	1952

Name	Constituency				Name	Constituency		
G. Mesmin (C.D.S.)	(Paris 20) (Muette, Auteuil)	1973	I.F.	1954	C. Fèvre (P.R.)	Haute-Marne (1) (Chaumont)	–	1964
J.-P. Soisson (P.R.)	Yonne (1) (Auxerre)	1968	C.C.	1961	F. Léotard (P.R.)	Var (2) (Hyères)	–	1973
B. Stasi (C.D.S.)	Marne (4) (Epernay)	1968	–	1960	G. Longuet (P.R.)	Meuse (1) (Bar-le-Duc)	–	1973
					J. Douffiagues (P.R.)	Loiret (1) (Orléans-sud)	C.C.	1966

Parti Socialist (P.S.)

Name	Constituency				Name	Constituency		
A. Chandernagor	Creuse (2) (Aubusson)	1958	C.E.	1951	L. Fabius	Seine-Maritime (2) (Grand Couronne)	C.E.	1973
J.-P. Chevènement	Territoire de Belfort (1) (Belfort)	1973	–	1965	C. Pierret	Vosges (2) (Saint-Dié)	–	1972
P. Joxe	Saône-et-Loire (5) (Chalon Nord-Louhans)	1973	C.C.	1958	A. Richard	Val-d'Oise (1) (Pontoise-L'Isle Adam)	C.E.	1971
M. Rocard	Yvelines (3)	1969	I.F.	1958				

Majorité – not attached to any Parliamentary group

Name	Constituency			
J.-P. Lecat	Côte-d'Or (3) (Beaune)	1968	C.E.	1963
P. Malaud (C.N.I.P.)	Saône-et-Loire (1) (Mâcon)	1968	–	1956

Abbreviations:

C.C.	Cour des Comptes	C.N.I.P.	Centre national des Indépendants et Paysans
C.D.S.	Centre des Democrates Sociaux	I.F.	Inspection des Finances
C.E.	Conseil d'Etat	P.R.	Parti Républicain

9 Political control and persuasion in contemporary French

DENNIS AGER
University of Aston

Language is a social activity; as such it is subject to constant development and no language is static while it is still in use as a means of communication. Hence many problems for the linguist; one of these is to determine the means by which change takes place and to examine the processes by which such change comes to be accepted, as well as the actual nature of the changes involved. Most linguists would, I feel sure, consider that attempts at direct control of the process of language change are more or less doomed to failure, whether such attempts involve the imposition of change or resistance to change; yet on the face of it there is no reason to suppose that an elite will have less success in imposing its will on language than on any other aspect of social life.

Most research in the area of language planning and language control has been devoted to the problem of developing countries, particularly those attempting to devise a language policy which will enable them to confront problems such as decolonialisation, the demands of linguistic minorities for political and social rights, the needs of international trade and the desire for international status. In the developed countries research tends to focus on the problems of linguistic minorities or on the 'misuses of language as an instrument of symbolic persuasion or oppression'.[1] In either we are examining cases of the exercise of power, usually political power, and as such the effect of and influence of the elite must be present.

French offers a good example of a language and society in which direct control of language is attempted, and has been attempted for more than three centuries. The motivations for control have included overt attempts to establish or maintain national unity, and the pressures to achieve this were particularly strong at the time of the Revolution. But prior to this the value of centralised control of language in ensuring the homogeneity of an elite such as the Versailles court was well seen by Richelieu, and motives based on such social priorities need to be considered along with the political ones. Expertise in language manipulation, whether it be evidenced by the ability to translate Latin verse, turn a couplet or persuade a council, rarely comes naturally; education plays a considerable role at least in developing the ability, and motivations for control based on educational priorities are not absent from nine-teenth-century debates on the widening of educational opportunity. In more recent times pressure for control of language has had a base in economics; unfair competition or consumer protection have been advanced as direct reasons for controlling the use of particular terms. And even more recently the drive to communicate effectively, efficiently, can be identified in the wish to control and clarify specialised scientific and technical vocabularies.

This chapter examines one aspect of such attempts to control language on behalf of an elite. Means and processes of linguistic control in France in the use of language by a political elite to control or guide *la base* will be examined and exemplified. The paper will not be concerned with the question of efficiency in communication, a problem principally for the scientific elite; also the working assumption will be made that 'elite' can be regarded as equivalent to 'ruling group', and that this elite is fairly homogeneous.

The language of political control

In the Western democracies the political elite must consist both of members of the ruling group and of members of the 'opposition', however formed or represented. Insofar as France is concerned, therefore, and for the purposes of the present paper, ex-President Giscard and members of his coalition form one part of the political elite; members of the Socialist Party, the Communist Party, other left-wing and right-wing groups, and members of non-official opposition groups are included also, insofar as they form and change political opinion. It is no easy task to determine how political opinion is formed and changes, of course, but again for the purpose of this chapter it will be assumed that political leaders are also leaders of opinion; that, by participating in the political debate, they form the opinions of others. From a linguist's point of view it might therefore be thought that we are dealing with the speech of individuals, and that group characteristics, or the notion that there can be a common language of 'control', is defeated before we start. Particularly if we study the language of outstandingly successful politicians – de Gaulle, for example – the view that their achievement is unique may be reinforced; nonetheless there appears to be sufficient commonality of expressive procedures among many politicians to make a group analysis possible, and the work of researchers analysing political expression by different means, both in France and elsewhere, seems to be sufficiently promising for us to accept that there are characteristics common to processes of political control and that relevant linguistic processes can be identified and described.

Most research in the language of politics has concentrated on 'the covert and insidious use of language as a means of institutional labelling and symbolic control'.[2] St Clair instances *Mein Kampf*, the language of white racism in America, the derision of American Indians, and shows how labelling opponents has enabled the creation of attitudes of superiority on the part of ruling groups, provided these are in a clear position of political supremacy. Qualities such as intelligence, humanity or adulthood (maturity) are perceived as good and as contributing to the maintenance of the in-group, whereas the opposite characteristics are ascribed to the opponent; similarly attempts are made to label non-members of the group as deviant — 'if you're not with us, you're against us'.

A political elite therefore controls opinion; and controls it in speeches, debate and discussion and documents by various definable linguistic processes. As politics is the spoken culture, opposed to the written culture of government, speeches in particular have an important role to play, and the spoken language of control represents the instrument by which the elite 'manipulates' the mass.

The process of control which takes place in a political speech can be seen as developing over five stages or phases: getting people to listen; describing the situation; analysing the situation and interpreting it; proposing an attitude or an action based on that interpretation; and getting that attitude or action adopted by others. The last of these requires powers of persuasion if it is to be successful, and the present discussion is limited to that aspect of the control process.

In analysing the success of a persuasion process — and indeed of any communication — we need to bear in mind a schema of the communication situation.[3] In essence this is made up of the speaker, the hearer and the immediate and wider situation in which they find themselves: the text itself; and the interaction between speaker and hearer as the text is actualised. The speaker too needs to be aware of the nonlinguistic aspects of his message — the size of the audience, the nature of the room in which he is speaking, the purpose of the meeting, relevant recent events and so on. In particular he needs to be aware of the interaction between himself and his audience and of the nature of the feedback he is receiving. But social psychologists and many sociolinguists can make too much of the undoubted importance of these factors; in the final analysis it is the power of the language which persuades, and the linguistic content of the text is a most important factor in political success. Nonetheless the linguistic content relates in various ways to aspects of the message, to certain speaker characteristics, and to characteristics of the interaction:

Message

Intellectual content derived from beliefs and values of the speaker; Logic and coherence of the message.	The linguistic content is likely to show qualities of cohesion, clarity and an appropriate level of complexity.

Speaker characteristics

Sincerity Competence Likeability Leadership qualities	The linguistic content is likely to show the effectiveness of the projection of the self; the idiolect of the speaker himself will characterise it.

Interaction characteristics

Rapport with audience Feedback	The linguistic content is likely to show how the speaker directs support for his own views and opposition to the views of the 'enemy'; how he causes enthusiasm and encourages action.

We may illustrate the last section of this analysis from a speech by Marchais delivered on 11 September 1977 and reprinted in *L'Humanité* (see the Appendix to this chapter), and from work by Roche on election addresses by Valéry Giscard d'Estaing (VGE) and François Mitterrand (FM).[4]

Roche has carried out a large number of analyses of the style used by candidates for the Presidency in various elections since 1965. Clearly candidates appealing for support from the electorate, particularly in the texts of television or radio broadcasts, use persuasive techniques designed for the mass of the population, and their speeches are likely to be marked by generalities insofar as the content is concerned. Nonetheless there are clear contrasts of style as between the candidates, and although it would be rash to assume that the successful candidate is also the one most successful in his oratory, the stylistic contrasts highlighted by Roche may go some way to comment on the defeat of the unsuccessful. Roche's method consists of taking frequency counts of certain aspects of language use such as the proportion of nouns or verbs, sentence length and so forth; the method, although simplistic, nonetheless reveals stylistic characteristics of considerable interest. Thus in comparing VGE's 1974 second ballot address with that of the first round, one notices an increased dynamism (more verbs and adverbs), more force (verbless sentences decrease) and greater clarity (an increase in inverted word order, high-lighting important points). An increase in negation and in interrogation, however, may well indicate a greater degree of humility.

In comparing VGE with FM, one or two other characteristics stand out. VGE uses only one third as many negative forms as FM; his sentences are longer and more carefully structured; FM uses half as many 'insistence' forms as VGE. The difference of individual styles becomes particularly clear in a comparison of the use of the personal pronouns *je, nous,* and *vous,* shown in the following table together with de Gaulle's usage, and shown also in the two *tours* of the election:

Candidate		Je	Nous	Vous
1974				
VGE	– 1st ballot	53	13	34
	– 2nd ballot	52	16	32
1974				
FM	– 1st ballot	39	43	18
	– 2nd ballot	59	22	20
1965				
dG	– 1st ballot	25	50	25
	– 2nd ballot	55	30	15

(Figures shown are percentages.)

The regularity of usage of *je* in VGE is noticeable, as is the dramatic increase in the usage in the case of both FM and dG, both of whom may well have felt on the defensive in the *second tour*, needing to present themselves more strongly than before. *Vous* is rarer in both FM and dG, both of whom seem to have used abstractions (*la France, la société, l'Europe*) more frequently than VGE – thus avoiding addressing the elector directly. *Nous* is consistently high in dG; FM drops between the two dates, and VGE increases slightly.

The procedures and devices available in French to correspond to the overall communicative function of persuasion are not, however, linked to lexical items alone, and a count of the relative frequency of occurrence of items, valuable though it is as an analytical device, does not necessarily reveal the full complexity of the linguistic tissue. The peroration pronounced by Marchais in September 1977 in his speech on the occasion of the *fête de l'Humanité* of that year may indicate the complexity of the descriptive task involved.

Marchais says, within the 500 words or so of this section of his speech, that there will be a political battle with the bourgeoisie; that the Parti Communiste Français is the natural political party to conduct the battle and he lists the aims and desires of the Party, including what it does not want. He appeals to workers to join the Party, because they need it; to read its organ, *L'Humanité*, and to advance together to victory. The previous parts of the speech had been devoted to attacks on Giscard and the majority, but also to putting a final nail in the coffin of the *programme commun*.

One or two 'standard' rhetorical devices are used here and there in the peroration — inversion (*rarement . . .*) and the rhetorical question (*Que voulons-nous . . .*); but the main rhetorical movement is dependent on repetition — of the clauses dependent on *que* after *nous voulons*, of phrases such as *vous avez besoin, il faut que* or even words such as *quand* or *pour*. This rhetorical movement — the building up to the climax point, marked by *Voilà ce que nous voulons* (and even this phrase is repeated) — is introduced by a mention of the name of the Party and ended by a similar mention; but at first it is accompanied by *leur*, implying a certain distance, while at the end of the speech we hear of *ce parti qui est le vôtre*.

Such a switch of adjective is paralleled by the switch from *nous* to *vous* just after the climax of the peroration; in speaking Marchais is careful to reserve the distancing third person for the bourgeoisie (*elle*) or for the *grands capitalistes* (*ils*), and to associate himself directly with his audience. It is interesting also to note that alliteration is reserved for 'the enemy' — *ses profits, sa puissance, ses privilèges* and *le pouvoir et le patronat* and *face aux formidables moyens*; that the word '*grand*' is reserved for them also; and that their place in this peroration is not large, the main stress being placed on notions of togetherness — with the use of *nous* and *vous* — on desires and wishes — with the use of *vouloir* — and on need — with the use of *vous avez besoin*.

The peroration holds few surprises on the level of language; clichés such as *le combat sera rude* or *la liberté pour tous* are expected and offered, giving a sense of security to the audience. The same is true of the use of set phrases such as *Chers amis et camarades*, and presumably no one will object (whatever their political allegiances) to the list of desires and wishes. One slight surprise perhaps in the mention of a *France libre, indépendante et riche*; but the language chosen in this exercise in political persuasion indicates, on whatever level one analyses it — lexis, sentence structure, paragraph development or the use of specific rhetorical devices — that whether such choices are conscious or unconscious they respond directly to the communicative function and hence to the setting in which the speech is delivered; their effectiveness in controlling and directing the enthusiasm of the audience, in establishing and reinforcing the control over the mass by the elite, is measured both by the actual terms used and also by the relationship between these terms and the communication situation involved. Lexis selection alone, sentence structure alone, rhetorical devices alone cannot be isolated as the sole or even the main actualising device used; the total use of presented language is involved, and the analyst's task is not merely to identify the terms but also to examine their role in the spoken discourse; any indication of the content alone of a peroration such as this is quite inadequate to explain the observed effect, the arousing of enthusiasm and the move to action.

Notes

1   R. St Clair, 'The Politics of Language', *Word*, vol. 29, no. 1 (April, 1978), p. 42.
2   Ibid., p. 53.
3   D. E. Ager, 'Language learning and sociolinguistics', *IRAL*, vol. XIV, no. 3 (1976), pp. 285–97.
4   J. Roche, 'Deux candidats, deux styles: Valéry Giscard d'Estaing et François Mitterrand', *Travaux de Linguistique et de Littérature* (Strasbourg), vol. 17, no. 1 (1979), pp. 273–89.

Appendix: Speech by G. Marchais on 11 September 1977, on the occasion of *La Fête de l'Humanité*. Reprinted in *L'Humanité*, 12.9.77, p. 3 (extract).

Chers amis et camarades,

Nous entrons dans une période de grande bataille politique. Rarement dans notre histoire l'enjeu en a été aussi important.

Pour la grande bourgeoisie, ce qui est en jeu, ce sont ses profits, sa puissance, ses privilèges. Elle ne va pas y renoncer de bon cœur. Elle va tout tenter pour éviter la défaite et pour empêcher le changement.

Le combat sera rude. Mais les travailleurs, pour l'emporter, peuvent compter sur leur parti, le Parti communiste français.

Que voulons-nous, nous les communistes?

Nous voulons que la vie soit plus douce pour tous ceux qui souffrent aujourd'hui. Nous voulons que dans les familles populaires on puisse acheter et de la viande et des fleurs. Qu'on puisse se soigner quand on est malade et s'habiller chaudement quand il fait froid. Nous voulons qu'on aide les enfants à suivre à l'école, que les jeunes aient du travail, que les vieux aient à manger et à se chauffer. Nous voulons la dignité. Que les usines ne soient plus des bagnes. Que l'usure, l'épuisement, l'accident ne soient plus le lot des travailleurs. Nous voulons la liberté. La liberté pour tous. Que les travailleurs puissent exercer leurs droits. Qu'on écoute les gens quand ils parlent. Voilà ce que nous voulons: un monde débarrassé de la crainte du lendemain, un monde où l'homme se sente un peu plus chez lui.

Vivre au pays

Et pour cela, il faut, entre autres, qu'il soit possible à chacun de pouvoir — comme on dit — vivre et travailler au pays. Regardez notre fête: elle se tient sur le thème des régions. Oui, nous voulons des régions vivantes, fières de leur identité, dans une France libre, indépendante et riche. Nous ne voulons plus voir fermer les usines, casser les machines au gré des intérêts égoïstes des grands capitalistes. Nous ne voulons plus les voir spéculer sur la monnaie nationale, exporter les usines et les capitaux, sacrifier des régions et des branches entières de notre économie.

Ils ont fait assez de mal comme cela. Maintenant, il faut qu'ils cèdent la place. Il faut que notre peuple soit enfin maître chez lui.

Voilà ce que nous voulons.

Si vous êtes d'accord avec cette politique, alors rejoignez sans attendre ce parti qui est le vôtre: le Parti communiste français.

Face aux formidables moyens dont diposent la réaction, le pouvoir et le patronat, vous avez besoin d'un Parti communiste influent et actif pour vous défendre. Vous en avez besoin pour créer les conditions d'un succès qui réponde vraiment à vos espérances.

Et vous avez besoin aussi du journal qui défend chaque jour vos intérêts et qui vous dit la vérité. Lisez *l'Humanité*.

En avant, amis et camarades, tous ensemble, pour assurer la victoire et le changement!

PART III POWER

10 Ministerial *cabinets* and elite theory

ELLA SEARLS
University of Newcastle upon Tyne

Introduction

The Fifth Republic, which was governed by the right from its inception in 1958 until this year, has continually been the target for accusations about the elitist nature of the regime. It is argued that not only the Government, but also the whole state machinery has been infiltrated by anti-democratic, unrepresentative, bureaucratic forces. Alternatively, it has been claimed that the administration, and certain sectors of the industrial world have been politicised. The breeding ground for these claims is indeed fertile. Firstly, the fact that there was no real change of government for over twenty years led to a strong possibility of patronage and collusion amongst decision-makers. Secondly, the nature of the politico-administrative system, where there is a close overlap of both function and personnel, gives rise to the possibility of a ruling elite.

This chapter analyses these contentions in the light of a study of ministerial *cabinets*, which function at the interface between politics and administration. *Cabinets* provide a useful focal point for a consideration of elite theories as they are themselves key elements in the decision-making process and also provide a route between the political and administrative worlds. Hence *cabinets* not only provide a forum for observing the activities of an elite, but also give the opportunity for assessing theories about the formation, mobility, and interests of elites. This chapter contends that although there is much fuel to fire elite theories, many of the theories are oversimplified or difficult to substantiate on a closer analysis of the politico-administrative structure.

Theories about the regime

After the initial concern with constitutionalism and the powers of the presidency much of the comment on, and analysis of, the Fifth Republic has been concerned with 'who actually governs France?'. Many of the theories, polemical attacks and analyses are poorly substantiated or circular in argument, and taken as a whole are wide-ranging enough to be contradictory or mutually exclusive. The Fifth Republic has been seen as being governed by the *énarques*,[1] presidential advisers,[2] ministerial *cabinets*, a technocracy,[3] administrators from the *grands corps*, an overriding presidency,[4] a ruling class[5] or ruling *élite* — the list is endless. Common to most of these approaches is an agreement that the powers of the President have increased and the powers of Parliament and the individual *député* have declined. This imbalance in the 'normal' checks and balances of the political system leads to disquiet about the distribution of power.

These approaches can usefully be grouped as follows:

(a) The *ruling class* approach which sees the state being dominated by a ruling group from a particular socio-economic class, who constitute the administrative-industrial elite. It is contended that the significance of the Fifth Republic is in the particularly high degree of penetration of the system by the capitalist class. Pierre Birnbaum in *Les Sommets de l'État*[6] gives a lucid, well argued example of this type of approach when he contends that the Fifth Republic has witnessed the consolidation of the leaders of the industrial world and the leaders of the politico-administrative world. Once in a position of mutually strengthened power this ruling group has extended its domination not only into economic spheres of activity, but to that of the whole state:

C'est-à-dire vers des lieux où s'exerce le plus efficacement un contrôle sur la société civile où la vie socio-culturel en général.[7]

He sees this process taking place at the expense of the professional politicians:

La haute fonction publique a bien envahi les sommets de l'appareil d'Etat et tient définitivement a l'écart le personnel politique professionalisé.[8]

Within this process the Giscardians have an even more favoured background, and closer links with the higher administration and industry than the Gaullists. Key mechanisms by which the ruling class (or is it the servants of the ruling class?) consolidate their power are the *cabinets* and the promotion of personnel from *cabinets* into the industrial sector. Hence the *cabinets* under the Fifth Republic are one of the mechanisms which contribute to the decline of the autonomy of the state from the economic sector. This approach will not be discussed further in the context of this chapter.

(b) Those who fear the penetration of the administration by political forces leading to a *politicisation of the administration.*

(c) The *technocratic state* school which stresses the de-politicisation of the state — that is to say those who see all the key institutions within the state being taken over by civil servants.

(d) Finally, there is now an increasing number of studies which lay more emphasis either on the decision-making process and policy outputs or on attitude formation and stances taken up by the various decision-makers.[9] Each of these two approaches in themselves has obvious limitations but taken together they help to build up a picture of the power structure of the state.

We now turn to a more detailed discussion of approaches (b), (c) and (d).

(b) The politicisation of the administration

Two interrelated developments — the 'stability' of the Fifth Republic, the advent of majority government, and, consequently, the seeming facility for the executive to meddle with the administration, and reward trusty servants with key posts in the administration, on the one hand, and the fact that an increasing number of civil servants are serving in political posts, such as ministerial *cabinets*, and then in some cases returning to the administration, on the other — have led to many fears that the administration was no longer neutral and had become identified with the Gaullist and, even more closely, the Giscardian regime. This state of affairs is contrasted with the Fourth Republic where politicians came and went and civil servants exercised power with little political control.

There is considerable information to back this up. Although there was no purge of the administration in 1958, there was a gradual replacement, or moving sideways of those who were antagonistic to the regime. There has also been during the course of the regime a placing of civil servants who have been particularly loyal to the government in key posts (especially through the route of ministerial *cabinets*), although there has not been a great number of non-civil service party men who have been given administrative posts. The numbers involved are difficult to estimate, for as one Socialist civil servant interviewed commented: 'It's difficult to say how far the administration has been infiltrated as so many of the higher civil servants are by sympathy Gaullist or Giscardian anyway.' One third of all *directeurs* in the central administration are ex-*cabinet* members who owe their positions to grateful ministers — although this is usually largely because of their administrative expertise rather than

political loyalty — and a large number of heads of government corporations, naturally enough, are pro-Government men.[10] However, this
general picture may be misleading, and one can pick out both logical
and empirical flaws in the arguments about the politicisation of the
administration:

(i) On a closer analysis, the general threads in the argument about the
administration being more political under the Fifth as compared to the
Fourth Republic are woven together in a rather fragile way.

(ii) Although some sectors of the administration can be seen to be strongly
supportive of the Gaullist regime, others clearly opposed it (e.g., some
sectors of the *Conseil d'État* and/or of the Ministry of Finance).

(iii) It may be rather simplistic to argue that civil servants moved or
appointed as the result of political pressure are necessarily still whole-
heartedly committed to the Government. Although they will be in general
sympathy to the regime, they may have very divergent views on specific
policy issues, particularly once they have lost ties with the politicians
with whom they formerly worked. The degree of loyalty of ex-*cabinet*
members to the Government will of course vary considerably depending
on the strength and reasons for their political commitment.[11]

(c) The technocratic state/the triumph of the administrative elite

Many commentators are more concerned about the implications of the
infiltration of civil servants into the political world; as Suleiman comments,

> The predominance of civil servants in key institutions — the State
> bureaucracy, nationalised industries, the private sector and political
> posts proper — has given rise to an alarming fear: the rule of the State
> by a group (or class) of specialists sharing a common background,
> a common education and a common ideology.[12]

It is the large number of detached civil servants or ex-civil servants —
working in *cabinets* and the public sector, or serving in the Government
— *coupled with* the apparent weakening of Parliament and party political
forces which has given rise to concern. Again, there is much fuel for this
particular fire. It is true that civil servants, in particular those who have
been trained at the *grandes écoles* and especially those from the École
Nationale d'Administration (ENA) provide much of the personnel not
only for *cabinets* (about 90 per cent of members are now civil servants)
and for semi-governmental organisations, but also for the political sector.
Furthermore, ministers now no longer have to be members of Parliament
in order to hold their governmental posts,[13] although most in fact do

stand for Parliament as soon as possible,[14] and more pertinently, a number have worked in the civil service prior to becoming ministers. Of the 1980 Government eleven out of the twenty ministers had reasonably strong links with the administration. Of the 67 Republican Party Deputies who obtained seats in the 1978 legislative elections, 15 had been civil servants within the previous five years; and 6 per cent of the total membership of the 1978–81 National Assembly attended the ENA.[15]

Once again, however, some provisos should be added to these arguments:

(1) The civil service, which is a highly thought-of profession in France, has always had a fairly close association with the political world. Civil servants are allowed to stand for political office (as long as this does not conflict or overlap with their administrative duties, which it sometimes does) and the neat, if unreal, separation between 'politics' and administration which exists in Britain, for example, has never been held strongly in France.

(ii) It may well be the case that civil servants working in a political capacity are able to separate the two functions (this will be further discussed below in the case of ministerial *cabinets*).

(iii) There is a danger of exaggeration, generalisations, and jumping to conclusions in analyses of this type. For example, if a minister started off his career in the *Conseil d'État*, but has been detached from it either in an industrial or political capacity for twenty years, how far will his administrative origins continue to influence his behaviour?

(iv) Finally, many of the theories too quickly make the assumption that there is one cohesive administrative elite governing France. Either this is done by concentrating too heavily on socio-economic background[16] and administrative training, or by lumping different *corps* and groups of civil servants together and treating them as a coherent whole. Whilst it is obviously the case that all civil servants have something in common, this does not necessarily mean that they all share a common interest. Several recent studies[17] have shown that not only do groups of civil servants hold different ideologies and policy preferences but that it is often the post which they hold, rather than the background which they have, which determines their priorities and loyalties.

Hence both of these interpretations have their limitations, and taken together are contradictory. **The approaches (d)** which analyse the priorities of actors within the policy making process, and consider policy output and the groups influencing it, have more to offer. There are of course limitations in this type of analysis. Firstly, the approach, as any other, has a certain bias and rests on a set of assumptions (which are not always made explicit) about the nature of power. Secondly, an approach which emphasises policy output or interaction of actors as a measure of power (the classic example being Dahl's *Who Governs?*) of necessity assesses the visible face of power.[18] However despite the limitations of this approach it is the one which has been adopted in my analysis of ministerial *cabinets*.

Following on from this general review of elite theories the following points are of relevance:

(1) Any conceptual framework is necessarily constrained by the fact that for so long there was no radical change of Government in the Fifth Republic. Consequently, it is difficult to test two alternative basic hypotheses of elite theory — that is to say the existence of a ruling elite *impervious to influence and change*, or the existence of an elite which shapes the direction of change and adapts to it. Although there was a change of Government from the Gaullists to the Giscardians, for various reasons this represents a rather small shift in the political spectrum. The Mitterrand/Mauroy administration is too new for testing.

(2) It is necessary to know not only the socio-economic background of the proposed elite (in this case the administration) but also *how* this background affects their mode of action, and their interests.

(3) In particular, the dynamics and constraints of the decision-making process (i.e., the framework in which they act) and the pressures on the so-called elite must be considered.

(4) Finally, in making conclusions about the existence of a ruling administrative elite, there is a danger of omitting the realities of politics.

The remainder of this paper will consider these issues, beginning with a brief discussion of the constraints of political realities.

The political system under Giscard

Presidentialism

Giscard d'Estaing won the presidential election of 1974 with a slim margin of votes. Although he had the undeniable advantage of being a 'favoured son of Pompidou',[19] in Parliament, the National Federation of Independent Republicans (renamed the Republican Party in 1977) was still the minority within the majority — a minority which had never been forgotten by some *pur et dur* Gaullists, such as Michel Debré, for what was seen as their half-hearted support for the Gaullist regime in the late 1960s. Although Giscard's political position improved with the 1978 legislative elections, party political factors continued to shape his presidency and arguably increased his need for support within the administration.

Following on in the tradition of de Gaulle and Pompidou, VGE took a strong grip on the presidency. In many ways his supremacy over the Government increased during his seven years in office. He held many more *conseils restreints* (a classic way of circumventing any possibility of decision by the Government as a whole) and issued more presidential directives than his predecessors — most of which were directly to individual ministers, rather than through the Prime Minister.[20] Indeed, generally speaking, the office of the Prime Minister — whose strength in the Fifth Republic may have been underestimated by commentators — was weakened under VGE. Initially Giscard chose Jacques Chirac, the leader of the Gaullists, as PM in an attempt to appease the Gaullists and assure them of his credibility. The fact that Chirac was excluded from the decision-making process by the President and was often unsupported in inter-ministerial disputes, resulted in his 'leaving' office in 1976 to pursue his political ambitions in another manner. He was replaced by the economist, non-parliamentarian Raymond Barre, who in Giscard's words 'was appointed as Prime Minister in order to sort out the economy'. Barre was extremely useful to Giscard both as a policy adviser and as a buffer for Giscard's unpopular policies. The two, and their staff, worked in harmony, as a tandem, and their combined force was felt by other ministers and their *cabinets*. *Cabinet* members who had served under both Pompidou's and Giscard's presidencies claimed that scrutiny from the President was stronger under the latter, along with a weakening of the direct control of the Prime Minister. This reflects a harmony of policy between the two.

The nature of presidentialism has very much shaped the functioning of *cabinets* during the regime. If *cabinets* are to be seen as the pinnacle of the administrative elite, then the *cabinets* of the Prime Minister and the President are certainly the elite of the elite. They have considerable control over the activities of *cabinets* and the relations between them are often much more characterised by conflict and bargaining than by consensus. The nature of these relationships is, however, very much determined by political factors. If the *cabinet* of the President is extremely powerful this is normally because the President invests it with that power.[21] This is not, incidentally, always the case with the ministers and their *cabinets*.

The political position of Giscard – l'État UDF?

It is rather difficult to write with conviction of the passing of the Gaullist State – l'État UDR – and the coming of the Giscardian – l'État UDF – as many journalists have done. It is certainly true that the style of the regime changed. The medallioned Gaullist *barons*, linked together through the Resistance ('a secret network', according to Giscard) gave way to the athletic, discreet, clean-living Giscardian troops. It is also true that Giscard was the leading theorist of both the PR and the UDF (Union pour la Démocratie Française – a confederation of the PR and other centre-right parties, founded in February 1978) – a party and a federation which have different ideological roots to the RPR (the Gaullist party). However, there are several points to note:

(1) The policies of the two parties – PR and RPR – are not substantially very different. They certainly have the same 'world view' of politics and the differences[22] over social, foreign and economic policy[23] are in essence not very great. The conflicts between them over policy issues are a manifestation of a much greater conflict over territory and posts.[24]

(2) During his presidency Giscard was in an essentially unsettled position. It remained unclear in the long term what the composition of a presidential majority would be. This uncertainty, coupled with his need for Gaullist support with the National Assembly led to his retaining considerable numbers of second rank Gaullist ministers in the Government. It appears that, apart from the usual professional and personality clashes, the Giscardian and Gaullist ministers worked well together. Certainly, at the level of ministerial staffs there was usually complete co-operation. There were exceptions to this rule. For example, a fervent PR activist working as a *chef de cabinet* interviewed, claimed that he preferred getting information and help from a Republican minister rather than a Gaullist; he stated that if necessary he would use contacts in the staff of a Republican junior minister to circumvent the Minister himself (Table 10.1).

(3) The shape, strength and future of both the Parti Républicain and the Union pour la Démocratie Française remained uncertain during Giscard's presidency. The PR, which originally incorporated the political dreams of Giscard, in many ways did not live up to his expectations. It has remained in some respects a party of local *notables*, a party incapable of winning new electoral ground and, according to Michel Pinton (*délégué général* of the UDF), a party incapable of responding to the exigencies of being a 'presidential party'. Partly as a cause and partly as a result of its political weakness, its structure and personnel were continually changing, largely in accordance with the needs of the President. Consequently, it had little impact *as a party* on the politico-administrative system. The more recently formed UDF, which was an 'umbrella organisation' incorporating the parties supporting Giscard as President,[25] is in the ambiguous position of being half party, half federation. It too cannot be said to have *colonised* the administration as a party to any great extent.

This is not to say that there were no links between Giscard's advisers

Table 10.1 *Political affiliations of ministers under VGE*

Governments[3]	UDR or attached	Gauche Démocrate	MSL[4]	Radicals	RI (PR)	Pres.[5] Maj.	Mouvement Réformateur (Radicals plus some ex-MRP)	Union Centriste (other ex-MRP)	Non Affiliated	Non Parliamentarians[6]
May 1974–Aug 76	[1]M – 5 [2]JM – 7			Still affiliated to Mouvement Réformateur	M – 3 JM – 5	–	M – 3 JM – 3	– JM – 3		M – 4 JM – 4
Aug 1976–Mar 77	M – 5 JM – 4			M – 3	M – 3 JM – 5	JM – 2	Absorbed into Radicals or UC (CDS)	CDS M – 1 JM – 2		M – 6 (5 – Pres. Maj. 1 – RI) JM – 5 (3 – Pres. Maj. 1 – RI 1 – Rad)
Mar 1977–Apr 78	R.P.R. M – 3 JM – 7		JM – 1	M – 1	M – 2 JM – 8	JM – 2	–	M – 2 JM – 3		M – 7 (5 – Pres. Maj 2 – RI) JM – 4 (3 – Pres. Maj 1 – RI)
Apr 1978–Jul 79	M – 6 JM – 4	JM – 1			U.D.F. M – 9 JM – 10				M – 1	–
Jul 1979–May 1981	M – 5 JM – 5	JM – 1			M – 11 JM – 12				M – 1 JM – 1	–

Notes:

1. M – Ministers
2. JM – Junior Ministers
3. Only the principal Government changes and reshuffles are given here.
4. *Mouvement Socialiste et Libérale.*
5. The term 'Presidential Majority' was used by VGE after the end of May 1974 to characterise the direction of the Government. It was used officially as a party label post-January 1976 till 1978, although Giscard himself stopped using the term after the end of 1976.
6. Between 1974 and 1978 there were a large number of non-parliamentarians as ministers. By and large they were Giscardians without parliamentary coats on. In the 1978 legislative elections most were elected under the UDF label.

or former advisers — and the parties supporting him — and the administration. Indeed the opposite was the case; but the point to remember is that it is the President who invests individuals with power. For example, in the well disguised setting up of the UDF during 1977 — when the Radicals and the Centre des Démocrates Sociaux were drawn, rather hesitantly, into alliance with the PR — many *cabinet* members played a key part. The skilful negotiations, persuasions, and bargaining were largely conducted by Jean-Pierre Soisson (the PR Secretary-General) and Pinton, but they obviously had considerable contact with the President; indeed, two of his staff, Riolacci and Aucouturier were involved in a supervisory or advisory capacity in most of the negotiations. Other key actors who had had recent experience of *cabinets* or were currently *cabinet* members were Jacques Douffiagues (PR), Jean Paolini and Bernard Prades, Jean-Louis Langlais (CDS) and Daniel Doustin (from Barre's *cabinet*).[26]

Furthermore, Giscard was by no means adverse to placing former collaborators in key positions within the state. Apart from members of his *cabinet* whom he has rewarded with posts in the administration (e.g. Philippe Sauzay as Prefect), many of his ex-advisers are to be found in the financial world — for example Claude Pierre-Brossolette is now director of Crédit Lyonnais and Jacques Calvet is director of the Banque Nationale de Paris. Obviously, it is difficult for people placed in such positions to ignore the President's wishes, and in many cases their views could have been expected to correspond to his: however, the constraints and priorities of any current post may well override allegiances of the past.[27] Finally, although the parties and electoral coalitions which originally formed around Giscard are in a state of flux, it is true that many of the long-standing activists have strong contacts within the administration. For example, of the ten current, permanent, non (ex-) ministerial members of the Political Bureau of the Republican Party, eight are ex-*cabinet* members. Others such as Philippe Pontet, *conseiller référendaire* at the Court of Accounts, have a varied and sound grasp of the administration.

To conclude, whilst the links between the Giscardians and the administration were strong, they should not be seen as an indicator that the Giscardians had 'taken over the state' nor that the administration was dominating the Government. It is easy to exaggerate the links and hard to estimate the impact which they have had. These issues will be examined a little more closely in a consideration of the role of ministerial *cabinets*.

Ministerial cabinets

Background/composition

Ministerial *cabinets* are the personal staff who are attached to each minister. They work directly for the Minister, are responsible to him and their legal existence is tied to him. Although not unique to the Fifth Republic[28] they have undoubtedly increased overtly in power and strength since the early 1960s. The contributory factors to this growth have been the advent of 'majority government', the increased stability of governments (though not *necessarily* of ministers), the growth of the executive power and the consequent changes in the decision-making process.

The number of members of ministerial *cabinets* has been regulated by law since 1911. The current legislative position which has operated since 1954 stipulates that each *cabinet* may include, among others, one *directeur*, one *chef*, two *chefs adjoints*, a secretary and two *chargés de mission* or *conseillers techniques*. In all, the number must not exceed ten, except that *cabinets* in the Ministries of Foreign Affairs, Finance and Interior are allowed to have one extra member whilst *cabinets* of junior ministers must not exceed seven. Most *cabinets* also, in fact, have a number of both unofficial and/or secret members. The inflation in the size of *cabinets* was a matter for concern and criticism during the Giscardian regime and there were several attempts at reducing the numbers and rationalising the activity of *cabinets*. Raymond Barre issued several directives to ministers encouraging them to limit their staff to seven or eight members (as one *cabinet* member complained 'yet another one of his little schemes to economise!'), and Giscard also asked ministers to try to clarify and rationalise the role of their *cabinets*. In particular, he requested that the dividing line between the work of the top civil servants in the ministry and the *cabinet* be more defined.

Giscard, as the 'good leader' setting an example, made an attempt to control the numbers in his cabinet, in response to criticisms that the President's staff were taking over from the Government.[29] In 1974 Giscard's personal staff (excluding the military personnel) numbered only seventeen compared to twenty-six in the last *secrétariat général*[30] of Pompidou. However, during the course of Giscard's presidency the number crept up to twenty-three (February 1980). Consequently, he has been criticised for allowing this increase and thereby potentially enabling his *cabinet* to exert greater control over the Government and the administration. However, it is argued that the increase was accounted for by members who dealt with general political matters, image building, public opinion and communication. This type of argument about numbers and functions is not always very helpful since the size of a *cabinet* is not necessarily an accurate measure of its strength. Many of Giscard's ministers (for example, Christian Bonnet, Minister of the Interior and Jacques Barrot, Minister of Health) responded to requests for cutbacks in size, but it should be noted that often these types of cutbacks increase the use of unofficial collaborators.

Civil servants now account for about 90 per cent of the members of ministerial *cabinets*. Most are detached from their *corps* or administrative post for a period of years to serve with a minister. The *grands corps* are obviously the favourite choice for ministers (about 40 per cent) as their knowledge of the administration, contacts, and expertise make them excellent advisers. However, other specialist civil servants — for example, engineers, inspectors and financial administrators — also play a key role, usually serving in the *cabinet* of their 'home' ministry. This large number of civil servants who serve in what are essentially political bodies obviously gives rise to concern for those who see the domination of the whole state apparatus by an administrative elite or the dilution of political authority by the bureaucracy. This interpretation ignores the possible change of allegiance of *cabinet* members originating from the civil service, or an alternative explanation that it may contribute to an *increased* control of the civil service by their politically loyal colleagues.

Obviously, the number of ex-*énarques* (students of the ENA) serving in *cabinets* is now high,[31] as the school has become the training ground for most higher civil servants. In 1980 about half of all *cabinet* members had attended the ENA compared with 12 per cent in 1960. Some *cabinets*, such as those of Giscard, Michel d'Ornano and Jean François-Poncet had considerably over half their members from the ENA whereas others, such as that of Yvon Bourges, Minister of Defence, had only two or three members. A point to be made is that even ministers who feel that they 'dislike the breed from ENA' often see the strategic advantages of having at least one ex-*énarque* in their *cabinet*. At the very least, the 'old boy network' of the ENA facilitates contact between former members and may, for example, help the passage of an interministerial dossier or the resolution of a delicate problem. At the very most it can be seen as a mechanism for the interchange of elites.

The socio-economic background of members of ministerial *cabinets* is similar to that of the higher reaches of the French administration — that is to say predominantly Parisian and bourgeois (if not aristocratic), often with industrial or civil service roots. Most members have degrees in law and were educated at the Paris *facultés* and the *grandes écoles*.[32] They are also often linked together through family, cultural and social ties. For those who view sociological factors as not only a necessary but also a sufficient condition of a ruling elite these facts are not without importance. In the case of ministerial *cabinets*, I found that this type of link and shared background was of great importance in *facilitating contacts,* particularly of an informal nature, but that professional background, administrative allegiances as well as political affiliations (especially of the minister) were also of importance.

Sample studies of the political allegiances of members of the ministerial *cabinets* during both the Gaullist and Giscardian presidencies showed that although most were in sympathy with the regimes many were not 'politically active' before their entry into a *cabinet*. It should be noted that in most cases the political sympathies of potential *cabinet* members are gleaned in one way or another by the *directeur de cabinet*. Civil servants who are known to be lukewarm about the Government are normally excluded from entry. The number of party activists working within *cabinets* is small although of course some politically active ministers use their *cabinet* as a finishing school for some young activists. The distinction between Giscardian and Gaullist *cabinets* is not as clear and definite as many would maintain. Under de Gaulle many Independent Republicans were to be found in *cabinets*, as are Gaullists in the *cabinets* of Republican Party ministers in the present system. Similarly, a large number of *cabinet* members easily served ministers of differing political complexions.

Cabinet members spend varying lengths of time in the compelling world of advising ministers. Some may only stay two or three years and then return to the former posts, or acquire new, more lucrative or interesting ones. Others may follow a minister, or flit between *cabinets*, for fifteen years or more. In general, it is difficult to estimate the impact which the passage through a *cabinet* has on promotions. Firstly, often 'high flyers' are invited to serve as *cabinet* members before they go elsewhere – that is to say, they may have been already heading for a promotion before their entry into a *cabinet* (this is often the case, for example, in the Ministry of Finance). Secondly, in some cases, promotions are difficult to assess from the outside. For example, it may be a diplomat's *preference* to obtain a post in Venice rather than in Washington – or a Prefect's preference to serve in Indre-et-Loire rather than in Meurthe-et-Moselle (some areas such as the South of France are always popular) – and this may not always be apparent to the outside observer.

Bearing this point in mind,[33] the following observations can be made. Firstly, about 9 per cent of *cabinet* members moved into the political world on leaving a *cabinet*: the majority of these were civil servants who had become *cabinet* members as a prelude to a political career; some

however, became 'politicised' whilst serving in a *cabinet*. About 5 per
cent of *cabinet* members took up posts in private industry or, more
likely in the public sector – e.g. as Director of *Gaz de France* – on leaving
a minister's team. Of the remainder, 42.9 per cent had no noticeable
change in their career pattern within two or three years of leaving a
cabinet whilst 43.5 per cent obtained some sort of promotion – for
example, they moved from the post of *sous-directeur* to that of *directeur*,
or from a *sous-préfet* to *préfet*. Most of these promotions, although
'helped along', do proceed through the normal channels. However, it is
not unknown for a minister to try to push an illegal promotion for one
of his ex-collaborators.

Two questions about the subsequent careers of *cabinet* members arise
which are of relevance for this chapter. Firstly, to what extent are promotions one of the mechanisms by which the Government infiltrates the
state – that is to say how far are they part and parcel of the politicisation
of the regime? Or secondly, conversely, how far do they demonstrate the
existence of an elite working within the key decision-making centres of
the state machinery? Answers to these questions involve not only pointing
out the numbers of promotions which take place, but also, more importantly, weighing up the respective pressures on, and freedom of action of,
the person who has been appointed by a thankful minister to a position
of responsibility in the administration or in a public corporation, or who
has used professional ties to secure a post in the private sector. For even
though an individual may want to use his new post to carry out policies
of his former minister he may be constrained in doing so by clients, boards
of directors or shareholders. Most ex-*cabinet* members interviewed
explained that once in the private sector or in a public corporation they
found themselves subjected to new market or financial pressures which
tended to determine their priorities. It was often the case that *cabinet*
members contacted ex-*cabinet* members or pro-Government men working
in the administration or outside, to ask for advice or to help to ensure
the execution of policy. In many cases, however, these contacts were
working within new constraints and *sometimes* found it difficult or un-
desirable to help members of their old *cabinet*.

Furthermore, no evidence was found that ministers systematically
tried to infiltrate the industrial/administrative structure with their supporters. If there is a greater patronage in this respect during the Fifth
Republic, it is associated with majority government. Many ministers
interviewed often found the rewarding of ex-collaborators an 'obligation
to be fulfilled'(!) – rather than a way of infiltrating the state machinery –
and were relieved when ex-collaborators accepted posts which they

suggested or found for them. This is not to say that they did not try to use and exploit useful contacts once they had been placed. Although many 'Giscardians' are to be found in key posts within the state, many prominent Gaullists still hold important positions. For example, Jérôme Monod is Vice-President of Lyonnaise des Eaux and Jacques Friedman is President of the Compagnie Générale de la Maritime.

The functions and role of ministerial cabinets

It is a view widely held by commentators, civil servants, and indeed by some *cabinet* members themselves, that *cabinets* can broadly be divided into two categories — that is to say the *cabinet technique* and the *cabinet politique*. However, this distinction is somewhat misleading, as are the general contentions about civil servants working in *cabinets*. For all *cabinet* members are political animals in the sense that they are functioning at that interface where administrative issues become political or political decisions need some interpretation. Even the so-called *techniques* in the team are tuned in to the political aspects of any one policy; their job is to see administrative issues in a political light *and to act accordingly*. Many civil servants working in *cabinets* alluded to the fact that, not only did they see more of the political repercussions in administrative dossiers, but that they never turned a blind eye to them, or ignored them, as they may have done formerly in the *services*. Having said this, it is true that some members are principally concerned with the political aspects of the minister's work — i.e. press, constituency, Parliament, interventions etc. — whilst others tend to work more closely (often in a supervisory capacity) with one or two *directions* in the ministry, or concern themselves with administrative problems or difficult dossiers which cut acro s many divisions within the ministry.

The actual functioning and power of the *cabinets* vary enormously depending on the aptitude of the minister, the nature of the ministry, the personnel of the *cabinets* and the political situation. Essentially, the *cabinet* is there to advise the minister, to protect him, and to facilitate his work load. At the very least, this will mean receiving Deputies, arranging visits, 'ensuring' a smooth passage for ministerial legislation,[34] and helping the minister to 'run' the ministry. At the very most, it can mean the *cabinet* acting as the key decision-maker by supplanting both the ministry and the administration, controlling and often usurping the functions of the *services* and acting as a forceful interministerial negotiating body. On the whole, most *cabinets* fluctuate between these two poles, certainly protecting the minister and saving him political embarrassment and acting as one of the decision-makers in a complex process of bargaining. Certain elements of elite theories do have some applicability and validity when applied to *cabinets*. However, the author found that no one theory gave a framework in which *cabinet* activity could be successfully explained, and in this sense the *cabinets* highlighted the inadequacy of much of the literature at a micro level.

On the one hand, *cabinets* themselves function at a vital position in the decision-making process and are hence instruments and sources of power. The background of *cabinet* members reflected their elitist origin and status, and under the Gaullist and Giscardian regimes in no senses did the 'institution' serve to 'open up' or 'democratise' the power structure — that is to say the background of *cabinet* members was similar to that of other leaders in society. In this sense *cabinets* bolster up the sources of access of the existing elite. Furthermore, the administrative and professional backgrounds of *cabinet* members not only gives them a certain expertise in particular areas, but also facilitates contacts with their colleagues in other areas of the administration. Hence *cabinets* provide a mechanism for elite interchange.

On the other hand, it was found that although a certain type of administrative background gave the *cabinet* member a frame of reference, it did not necessarily determine the way in which he acted. For in nearly all cases studied, the loyalty to the minister and a desire to ensure the execution of his policy, overrode all previous loyalties and commitments. The evidence on the power position of *cabinets* showed that although most *cabinet* members clearly sought to influence their minister, there was not much evidence of attempts to dominate him, to the extent of weakening the political force. Cases of a high degree of control by the *cabinets* normally occurred where there was a weak ineffectual minister. Without a *cabinet* system this control would have been exercised by the civil service. Indeed in the majority of cases it was found that the existence and role of *cabinets* improved ministerial control of the bureaucracy. Most policy formation and the execution of major reforms came from a close contact between three or four decision-makers irrespective of the posts which they held. That is to say, it was difficult at this level to point to the domination of any *corps* or body such as the *cabinet* or a *service*.

It was found that *cabinets* did provide a route for a degree of politicisation of the administration, which was closely linked to presidentialism. All *cabinets* had links with *députés* and pressure groups, and many had links with the party. Under Giscard a tentative conclusion was that the UDF, by its very nature, had more influence on *cabinets* than did the PR (or RPR?). However, this perhaps should be viewed as being part and parcel of the domination of presidentialism. Although this influence was there, the domination and infiltration of 'the UDF' was still weak at the time of Giscard's defeat. However, it should be noted that this politicisation of the administration is in itself not necessarily anti-democratic as it may provide a mechanism for effecting the policy of a democratically elected government. On the other hand it may signify the infiltration of a ruling elite into different decision-making bodies and a weakening of one of the possible alternatives (and hence checks) to governmental power.

Conclusion

This chapter has looked at some general theories about elites in the context of the French politico-administrative structure. It is hard to conclude as to the existence of *an* administrative elite, for although civil servants function in key positions with the state, they do not appear to *rule* nor to have a group identity which cuts across the posts which they hold. Similarly, although there has been some infiltration of the state apparatus by supporters of both the Gaullist and the Giscardian Governments, there is little data on the long term implications of this infiltration.

However, it is important to view the case of France in a broader context. Typically, Western political structures lead to the concentration of power in the hands of a few. What one is concerned about is the protection of society from this concentration of power. It is normally assumed that this can be achieved by the representative nature (in terms of responding to pressures) of the ruling group, the separation of the structures of government, and the changing of the rulers by election. In order for governments to implement programmes on which they were elected they need to build effective bridges of communication between the political and administrative worlds. There are several ways in which these bridges can be built: in Fifth Republic France the building blocks are alternatively civil servants and politicians. This close intermixing must give cause for concern, since it may lead to the decline of checks and balances and the emergence (or triumph) of a ruling group which functions, without opposition, in key positions in the state.

In the final analysis, the question of relevance in the general context of elite theory is whether these links which are built up between the political world, the administration and the industrial sector are maintained and sustained *over time*, and, in particular, *over a change in government*. If the personnel and interests change, then the close overlap which occurred under the Gaullist and, increasingly, the Giscardian regimes can be viewed as part of the 'style of governing'; if they do not,[35] then the grounds for arguing the existence of a ruling elite are obviously much

Danger of ruling group

stronger. Thus, the answer to the questions posed in this chapter awaits an examination of the implications of the very recent changes in the presidency and in the majority governing the country.

Notes

1 J. Mandrin, *L'Énarchie ou les mandarins de la société bourgeois* (Paris, 1968).
2 For a recent journalistic analysis of this type (which incidentally to a certain extent tries not to paint too black and white a picture) see 'Les 30 hommes du Président', *L'Express*, June 1980. See also, B. Badie and P. Birnbaum, 'L'autonomie des institutions politico-administratives: le rôle des cabinets des Présidents de la République et des Premiers Ministres sous la Ve Républic', *Revue Française de Science Politique* (April, 1976).
3 See for example, P. Bauchard, *Les Technocrates et le pouvoir* (Paris, 1966).
4 The fiercest criticism of supreme presidentialism comes of course from thwarted ex-ministers, see for example, J. Chaban-Delmas, *L'Ardeur* (Paris, 1975).
5 See for example, P. Birnbaum, *Les Sommets de l'État* (Paris, 1977) (with 1980 addition), and P. Birnbaum, 'La classe dirigeante', *Pouvoirs*, no. 8 (1978).
6 See also Serge Mallet, *Le Gaullisme et la gauche* (Paris, 1965), and Henri Claude, *Gaullisme et grand capital* (Paris, 1966).
7 P. Birnbaum, *Les Sommets de l'État*, op. cit.
8 Ibid.
9 See for example: Ezra N. Suleiman, *Politics, Power and Bureaucracy in France* (Princeton, N.J., 1976), and *Elites in French Society* (Princeton, N.J., 1978); V. Wright, 'Politics and administration in the Fifth Republic', *Political Studies* (March, 1974); Anne Stevens, 'Politicisation and cohesion in the French administration', *West European Politics* (October, 1978); Diana Green, *Economic and Financial Decision-Making in the Fifth French Republic*, unpublished Ph.D. thesis, London School of Economics, 1976; and Ella Searls, *Politico-Administrative Relations in the Fifth French Republic: A Study of Ministerial Cabinets 1959–1974*, unpublished Ph.D. thesis, London School of Economics, 1976.
10 See D. Derivry, 'The managers of public enterprises in France', in M. Dogan (ed.), *The Mandarins of Western Europe* (London, 1975), and P. Birnbaum, *Les Sommets de l'État*, for an impressive amount of information on this point.
11 For a succinct unravelling of these arguments see E. N. Suleiman, 'The French bureaucracy and its students: towards the desanctification of the state', *World Politics*, vol. 23, no. 1 (1970).
12 E. N. Suleiman, *Politcs, Power and Bureaucracy in France,* op. cit.
13 Indeed by the 'incompatibility rule' they have to give up their seats to their *suppléants* (substitutes) if elected.
14 Incidentally, the lack of interest of ministers in Parliament is one of the myths perpetrated by the administrative elite school.
15 Five ministers – Peyrefitte, François-Poncet, Deniau, Soisson and Lecat – were former students of the ENA. Matteoli had a long Foreign Office career, Papon was a Prefect, Saunier-Seïté a university administrator of long standing and Beullac, Méhaignerie and Giraud all had long administrative careers in one of the specialist *corps*.
16 For a general criticism of this type of approach see L. Edinger and D. Searing, 'Social background in elite analysis', *American Political Science Review* (1967), pp. 428–45.
17 See for example, V. Wright, 'Politics and administration in the Fifth Republic', op. cit.

18 For a criticism of Dahl's pluralist modes of power and a discussion of the importance of trying to evaluate the hidden force of power see P. Bachrach and M. S. Baratz, 'Two faces of power', *American Political Science Review*, vol. 56, no. 4 (December, 1962).

19 Although like de Gaulle, Pompidou did not name his 'successor' it seems apparent that VGE was foremost amongst those whom he felt capable of succeeding him.

20 On this point, see P. Avril, 'Ce qui a changé dans la Ve République', *Pouvoirs*, no. 9 (1979).

21 The exception to this is the case of Pompidou's *cabinet* who tended to take the reins of power in the last two years of his presidency during his terrible illness.

22 On the differences in doctrine see P. Dabezies, 'Gaullisme et giscardisme', *Pouvoirs*, no. 9 (1979).

23 On the differences in economic policy see for example Diana Green, 'The economic policies of the Barre Government', paper presented at the annual conference of the Political Studies Association, University of Exeter, April 1980.

24 For an elaboration of this point see my paper 'The consolidation of presidential power in France', for Reading Seminar Series 'Political Expression in Western Europe in the 1970s' (unpublished).

25 Notably the PR, the Radical Party and the Centre des Démocrates Sociaux (ex-MRP – Christian Democrats).

26 See D. Seguin, *Les Nouveaux giscardiens* (Paris, 1979) for a detailed and apparently accurate account of the devising of the new federation. The only weakness is an underestimation of the role which Jean Lecanuet, President of the CDS and a former presidential candidate in 1965, played in the negotiations.

27 This is obviously much less the case with former collaborators of the President than those of ex-ministers.

28 Ministerial *cabinets* in the form in which they exist today can be traced back to the beginning of the nineteenth century; for a discussion of the development of *cabinets* see my doctoral thesis, *Politico-Administrative Relations in the Fifth French Republic: A Study of Ministerial* Cabinets *1959–1974*, op. cit., chapter 1.

29 This was a criticism that was particularly made of Pompidou's staff.

30 At the beginning of the Fifth Republic, the President's *cabinet* and *sécretariat général* were separate; however, they are now merged into one body, although some of the President's staff carry out the more formal, administrative functions of the *sécretariat général*. For a fuller, though rather outdated discussion of this, see P. Verrier, *Les Services de la Présidence de la République* (Paris, 1973).

31 This will be a natural increase as the School was only founded in 1945.

32 For a discussion of the impact of the educational system in perpetuating inequalities in France see, Jane Marceau, *Class and Status in France* (Oxford, 1977).

33 It should be noted that the following figures are worked out for a sample of 250 *cabinet* members whose careers were assessed two or three years after they had left *cabinets* during the Gaullist regime. It is difficult, due to the time period involved, to give definitive figures for the Giscardian period; however, a survey of the careers of half the *cabinet* members who had served in *cabinets* during 1974–6, revealed much the same pattern.

34 Although Parliament's role may have been weakened under the Fifth Republic, most ministers still put enormous effort into ensuring that they have the right amount of support in Parliament (particularly in committees) for their legislation. The amount of negotiations which take place increases dramatically in politically difficult situations – for example, late 1979 and early 1980.

35 For a discussion of the probable adaptability of the administrative elite, see E. N. Suleiman, *Elites in French Society*, op. cit.

11 The French Deputy as a member of the elite

A. J. PETRIE
University of Exeter

I hope it will not be thought inappropriate to begin this chapter on a personal note. I recall a few years ago having a long and fascinating conversation with an elderly Deputy who had first been elected to the then Chamber of Deputies in 1936. He reminisced nostalgically about the period of his youth when he first decided to go into politics, recalling how in those days — the 1920s — a Deputy 'was really somebody' and how he and many other politically aware young men of his generation saw election to the Chamber as the crowning summit of a successful political career. His own experience of success was short-lived, however. No sooner had he gained election to the coveted seat in the Chamber than it all seemed to turn sour: for twenty years and more, crisis followed hard upon crisis — the slump, the internal disturbances of France in the late 1930s, the war and the Occupation. A brief moment of revival and optimism and then the chaos and turbulence of the Fourth Republic, the Algerian War, the return of de Gaulle and the virtual eclipse of parliamentary government. By the late 1950s the Deputy's role and position in French life has sunk to its lowest ebb, a state of affairs given constitutional and political recognition by the drastic reduction in power accorded to Parliament — and the National Assembly in particular — by the 1958 constitution, and by the haughty disdain of President de Gaulle for the claims and pretensions of a group of men whom he considered most responsible for France's plight.

For ten years, my interlocutor continued, he and his fellow Deputies had to endure the punishment thus meted out to them. It was only after the crisis of 1968 and the passing of de Gaulle the following year that things slowly began to improve. The younger generation — the legislative intake of 1967 and 1973 — were in his view fortunate to be entering the Assembly at a time when it was beginning to win back some of its former standing and political function. His explanation for this upturn — a crisis of executive self-confidence brought about by 1968 and the departure of the father figure the following year — seems simplistic and inadequate.

But he did nevertheless discern the fact of a renewed role for the Assembly and an enhanced opportunity for Deputies to participate in public policy-making which few others have discerned, and it is this, I think, which poses for us the interesting question of just how far can the French Deputy now be regarded as a member of the governing elite of France.

That this question can be posed at all might come as a surprise to some. While it is indisputable that the Assembly retains a symbolic importance, conferring the stamp of republican and democratic legitimacy upon the Fifth Republic, the prevailing view nevertheless remains that as far as the hardware of politics is concerned the Assembly plays no more than a peripheral role at best, and often virtually no role at all. This attitude is reflected by the published literature on the subject in two rather striking ways. In the first place, there is the astonishing fact that the only scholarly study of the post-1958 Parliament that has yet appeared remains Williams's work[1] — an admirable but relatively slender piece published, significantly, in 1968, and now inevitably dated. To this day, no French political scientist has considered the National Assembly of his own country under the present constitution a worthy object of study. This remarkable lacuna is perhaps partly explained by the other rather singular feature of the literature: what may be termed the 'Suleiman syndrome',[2] which suggests that France, especially under the Fifth Republic, may be regarded as a technocratic-administrative state controlled by a tightly-knit like-minded, socially cohesive, extremely capable and highly-trained cadre of administrators — not all of whom necessarily occupy strictly administrative positions — who form, virtually alone, the entire governing elite of France.

Given that this group is supposed to control not only the executive departments but also the major economic interest groups (including of course those of the very substantial public sector) and even the main non-Marxist political parties, it can be seen that this view leaves little or no scope for other institutions, whose role is thereby relegated to peripheral and unimportant spheres of activity. It is further noteworthy that this view is shared by both Marxists and Gaullists (although with vastly different value-loadings) — the two dominant intellectual strands in France during the past twenty years. It is also a view which, if not pressed too far, does carry a certain plausibility, particularly if one confines one's attention to the period before about 1970-3 when the technocratic strand in French government seemed to be in the ascendant. It is significant in this regard that there are almost no major studies of the French political system that draw on any substantial empirical material dating from after 1973. Yet it is precisely this recent period which has witnessed the upturn in Deputies' roles and functions after the nadir of the 1950s and 1960s.

Even the two important behavioural studies of Deputies, by Woshinsky[3] and by the CEVIPOF team in Paris[4] were both published in 1973, and draw on interview data collected in 1969/70 — a time when the new trends were as yet scarcely detectable and also a time when the Assembly was as untypical of itself as it has ever been, with the opposition parties traumatised and decimated by the law-and-order backlash vote of 1968. The result is that these two studies, which between them provide the only systematic data on Deputies' socialisation and motivational character- istics reveal patterns which must now be treated with reserve as descriptions of contemporary realities. It would seem, then, that almost wherever one turns in surveying the literature on modern French politics, the picture that emerges is one that is drawn essentially from the 1960s, with the post-Pompidou era included if at all merely as an afterthought to an established pattern set by the first ten to fifteen years of the Fifth Republic. Yet now, with the passage of time, it is possible, I think, to suggest that this particular period of French political history is a period of major transition and readjustment, both of attitudes and institutions. As such it is scarcely the most appropriate period to take as a bench- mark against which to assess and interpret subsequent events.

We shall return to this theme in greater detail later, but at this point it would seem advisable to offer some clarification of the concept of 'elite' as the term is to be used here. Elites are of course notoriously elusive phenomena, both conceptually and empirically. There is no wide- spread acceptance among scholars of any informative and non-trivial definition of what elites are, what they do and think *qua* elites, or how they can best be discerned in the real world. This is not, however, the occasion to enter into a discussion of elite theory.[5] It will suffice here to propose a simple schema for elite analysis which would appear not to conflict seriously with any of the major modes of elite theory but which also will aid us in our task of description and analysis.

The schema consists of a simple 2 × 2 matrix, employing functional and attitudinal variables as the two dichotomised dimensions. The functional variable can be dichotomised into *power* and *status*. By this is meant an elite which can be characterised as either a power elite in the sense of holding a quasi-monopoly of political (i.e. authoritative public) power in a society; or a status elite which enjoys the diffuse social influence stemming from a society's stratification system. Now obviously these two variants are far from mutually exclusive; on the contrary there is bound to be a considerable area of overlap between them — members of a power elite enjoy high (though not always the highest) status, while members of a status elite find that their social influence includes, importantly, privileged access to power. The basis of the distinction, therefore, lies less in its content than in its origins: a power elite owes its elite position primarily to its possession of power, while a status elite owes its perhaps almost identical elite position primarily to its possession of rank.

Cutting across the functional dimension we can postulate an attitudinal dimension which may in turn be dichotomised into two categories: on the one hand a social group whose claim to inclusion in its societal elite is *accepted* by other social groups who are already incontestably members of that elite; while on the other hand a social group may not be accepted by established elite groups even though its elite status is *ascribed* by the society at large. Such groups clearly possess some claim to be included in the elite, for the very fact that a society at large believes them to be included confers on these groups a social influence they would otherwise lack, even though such a claim may be disputed or rejected by other, perhaps rival, elite groups. Accepted elite groups on the other hand find themselves part of a wider interlocking elite network irrespective of their ascriptive elite status at mass level, which may be high or low. Again, these categories of ascribed and accepted elite status are far from mutually exclusive: as in the power/status dichotomy referred to above there is a large measure of overlap between them, and indeed it may be thought the mark of a successful elite group that it enjoys both qualities simultaneously. Nevertheless the distinction remains, I believe, a valid and useful one, especially for the purpose of description and analysis of groups whose elite status is ambiguous, tentative or partial — such as the group we are concerned with in this paper.

Functional dimension

	Power	Status
Accepted		
Ascribed		

Attitudinal dimension

Figure 11.1

Figure 11.1 represents the schema just outlined in diagrammatic form. It is a matrix in which we can place elite groups according to the nature of their claims to be members of an elite. It is most certainly not intended to be a contribution to elite theory — as such it would be absurdly simplistic and naive. It is simply intended as a straightforward framework for the purpose of analysing a specific elite group whose claims to elite status are, it is suggested, ambiguous in ways which the schema's analytical categories bring into focus.

Let us now, therefore, turn to the subject of this paper, the French Deputy. It would seem useful to examine the Deputy's claim to elite status in the light of our schema at three separate and contrasted historical moments. We shall examine briefly and in summary fashion the Deputy's elite status first in the early 1920s, which could, arguably, be regarded as the high point of French parliamentary democracy; then again during the period, approximately from 1956 to 1962, which could be regarded as the complete reverse — the lowest ebb of parliamentarism in France. We shall then be in a position to look in somewhat more detail at the position of the Deputy in the present period — the late 1970s.

The Early 1920s

By the early '20s the Third Republic was half a century old and already held the longevity record for post-Revolution regimes. The principle of republicanism, hotly contested at the outset of the regime, was now firmly in the ascendant as one by one the pockets of anti-republican resistance had been eliminated — by colonisation (as with many of the administrative corps, though not all), or by concordat (as with the Church) or simply by absorption, as with the bulk of the conservative (or 'moderate') political forces of the time. But not only was republicanism as such triumphant: it was increasingly translated in people's minds as government by parliament consisting of freely and universally elected Deputies whose will would override that of the indirectly elected Senate. Those democratic ideas had crystallised round the Radical party and later the Socialist and Communist parties who were at this time making substantial electoral gains. The regime was further fortified by having emerged unscathed from the First World War — surely the severest possible test of any regime, let alone a French one. Parliamentary democracy was not just a slogan — it actually worked.

At the centre of this, the point at which the values, myths and institutions of the regime converged, was the Deputy. He expressed in his elective office the new-look democratic republicanism espoused by an increasing popular majority; he expressed in his *cumul des mandats* the relentless drive towards national integration that modern communication permitted and the modern party system ensured; he expressed in his legislative functions the principle of parliamentarism that seemed to be the secret of effective and legitimate government for France; and as *ministrable* and minister he expressed the subservience of the political executive to the will of the sovereign people. He was male, middle-aged, middle-class and middle-brow − a comfortable and reassuring symbol of the age of the small man.[6] The old Deputy quoted at the beginning of this chapter was not mistaken − the Deputy of that era 'was really somebody'.

Yet his elite status was not unambiguous or undisputed. In terms of our schema, the Deputy was clearly a member of the power elite. He really did make binding decisions on matters of public policy − if the bureaucracy or the government proposed, the Deputy it was who disposed. True, the regime was showing the first signs of what in 1924 broke out as the first crisis of *immobilisme*: the need to break legislative deadlock by conferring special powers on an authority figure. But this still lay in the future and in any case its problematic nature was not fully perceived: if doing nothing was the way to give least offence all round, then perhaps it was the best solution − after all, there was always tomorrow.

The Deputy, then, was a leading member of the power elite and, clearly, was there by virtue of his ascriptive quality as the embodiment of legitimate government. But to this ascriptive status was *not*, in general, added an accepted status by other power elite groups such as the Church, the armed forces, and, pre-eminently, certain important sections of the bureaucracy. At this stage the majority of the traditional administrative *grands corps* − in particular the Diplomatic Corps, the Finance Inspectorate and the Conseillers d'État − were still for the most part self-recruiting and staffed by members of the upper bourgeoisie and aristocracy for whom the political values of republicanism were still something close to anathema.[7] They were saved, however, from outright self-destructive hostility to the will of elected governments by their strongly entrenched traditional ideal of public service. Nevertheless it remains true that the political and bureaucratic wings of the decision-making elite did not fuse into an interlocking whole, but continued to regard each other with wary suspicion, prepared at all times to scotch any perceived attempt to encroach upon the powers and prerogatives of the other. Furthermore, if the political wing, in the form of the Deputies, were tempted to assert their undoubted political power too strongly over the resistance of the bureaucracy, they remained uncomfortably aware that the bureaucracy in its turn was composed of representatives of the traditional status elite of France, which still enjoyed very considerable social influence. It was as if French society as a whole was prepared to ascribe power to the Deputies on condition that this power would not be used to overturn or threaten the social order represented by the status system. It was, in effect, a tacitly agreed stalemate: the Deputy was thrust into the lime-light as a leading element of the power elite in return for certain under-stood restraints on the exercise of this power. In terms of our schema then the Deputy was kept firmly in the bottom left-hand cell.

The period c. 1956–62

This point in French history represents, in parliamentary terms, an almost total contrast to the earlier period discussed above. What had occurred during the intervening years was, of course, the progressive accumulation of increasingly conclusive evidence that the parliamentary mode of govern-ment, at any rate in its French guise, was simply not capable of facing up to the succession of challenges, both internal and external, that had con-fronted France almost without respite for over twenty years. The historical facts are too well known to bear repetition here, as indeed is the dismal catalogue of the political system's largely unavailing efforts, whether in the form of the Third or of the more radically parliamentary Fourth Republic, to come to terms with them. It will suffice here simply to observe that the final crisis of the Fourth Republic, from 1956 to May 1958, was also, in retrospect, the death-throe of the traditional mode of French republican democracy. It was this mode which, as we have seen, reached its apogee in the early 1920s, which placed the National Assembly, trustee of the sovereignty of the people and expression of the people's will, at the nexus of the political system. Now, by the late 1950s, after a generation of almost unrelieved failure, Assembly government was finally discredited, and with it the Deputies who personified it — 'ces princes qui nous gouvernent' as the fundamentalist Gaullist Debré had sarcastically dubbed them.[8]

The Deputy thus found his position undermined on all fronts. Although constitutionally he was designated as the leading element in policy making, armed with a wide range of controls over the Government and, through the Government, over the bureaucracy, in practice he found himself unable to exercise this power. The only practical power left to him was the power to further weaken the authority of governments over the institutions which had traditionally rivalled the Deputies' elite claims and which now were acting almost autonomously from outside control: the armed forces and the bureaucracy.

But not only were the Deputies deprived of the power that was technically theirs; they also saw their ascriptive claim to membership of the power elite dwindle to almost nothing. The evidence is overwhelming of not only a loss of public confidence in the ability of Deputies to do the job they were entrusted with but of an increasing determination to give the job to someone else — an executive president, or a rival elite of *novi homines*. The growth of anti-system parties at the expense of the 'third force' parties — and the ultimate triumph of one of them in 1958; the spate of sneering and contemptuous publications directed at the Deputies and their 'house without windows'; the increasing opinion poll evidence of the low level of public esteem enjoyed by Deputies, and their low ranking in the public's preference order of people capable of solving national, local and even personal problems: all this points to a crisis of legitimacy which the Deputies experienced alongside the erosion of their power.

Small wonder, then, that the triumphant Gaullists of 1958 swept aside the despised model of assembly government in favour of an executive-dominated regime, and in doing so deliberately and willingly humbled the Deputies by removing them from the centre of policy-making. Not only did they get away with this symbolic destruction of the traditional pillar of republicanism — they were applauded for it all the way to the polling booth. So began, for the Deputies, a decade of penitence for their past misdeeds and extravagances, real and imagined. The low point was reached, perhaps, in 1962, when the French people endorsed de Gaulle's studied slight of Parliament on the question of the direct election of the President, and gave him a docile and obsequious parliamentary majority when the Deputies had the temerity to object. But this episode has another side to it: it showed that the Deputies were not necessarily a spent force. They could still bring governments to heel — and the fact that it was now a much rarer and more laboriously-achieved event lent it added significance. In the high-tide of de Gaulle's personal ascendancy this fact was somewhat masked — but it was there, as a pointer to the future for those who had eyes to see.

The situation today

Having sketched out, inevitably cursorily, the circumstances of the Deputies' fall from their traditional grace, we may now turn to the circumstances of the late 1970s, and the new role that the Deputies are in the process of defining for themselves as a new phase of French republican democracy takes root after the charismatic interval of de Gaulle. This new-style republicanism may be characterised as a governing formula that shares the trusteeship of popular sovereignty between the Assembly and the directly-elected President assisted by a hand-picked Government whose primary, but not sole, responsibility lies upward to the President. It may be suggested that the relationship between the Assembly and the President has moved from one of total legislative subservience during de Gaulle's reign, by halting and uncertain stages to a relationship today that comes fairly close to *potential* (though not yet actual) equality. This change is well symbolised by the contrast between de Gaulle's action following the Assembly's defeat of the Government in 1962, and Giscard's action in 1979 following the defeat of his budget.

This relationship between the Assembly and the executive, while certainly a far cry from the model of Assembly supremacy that character- ised earlier regimes, does nevertheless represent a very significant advance in the Assembly's influence compared with the early years of the Fifth Republic. But more significant, perhaps, is the fact that the Deputies themselves seem increasingly prepared to accept the role of junior partner in decision-making. For them of course it represents a vast improvement upon the systematic exclusion and humiliation they suffered at the hands of de Gaulle. But it is not just that they are grateful for small mercies: there is an awareness that it is no more than realistic in the modern world to accept that legislatures can on the whole do little more than provide a fine tuning and a legitimising stamp of approval for policy made else- where by experts and interested groups. And with this awareness has come a degree of restraint toward the executive that one would hardly have thought possible even ten years ago — and in return, the executive has shown more flexibility and willingness to treat the Assembly as a partner than would have seemed possible in the recent past.

Let us look at some of the evidence. In the first place, Deputies are less likely than they used to be to seek open confrontations with the Govern- ment — confrontations which they are almost certain to lose. Take, for example, the use of the motion of censure. In the ten years from 1959 to 1968, there were tabled seventeen motions of censure, while in the succeeding decade to 1978 there were only eight, of which three were 'routine' in that they were tabled simply to force a debate on the Govern- ment's general policy.[9] Conversely the number of parliamentary questions asked by Deputies has risen dramatically: if we conflate the different types of question (written, oral with and without debate, and *'questions au Gouvernement'*) we find the following as set out in Table 11.1.

This nearly threefold increase in the number of parliamentary questions asked, coupled with the halving of the frequency of motions of censure,

Table 11.1 *Number of parliamentary questions asked by Deputies in selected years*[10]

1959	3899
1964	5747
1969	6264
1974	8921
1977	9149

does seem suggestive of a changing attitude on the part of Deputies vis-à-vis the executive. If this is so, it is certainly paralleled on the executive side by an increasingly tolerant attitude toward the Assembly. One indication of this is the dramatic drop in the use of the notorious *vote bloqué:*[11] in the ten years up to 1968 it was used no less than 115 times, while in the subsequent ten years it was used only 25 times.[12] A similar dramatic drop (though the numbers involved are perhaps too small to be significant) can be seen in the use of the almost equally notorious Article 49-3 of the constitution, which provides that a bill is adopted without debate should the Government decide to pledge its responsibility on it.

Of course, these statistics by themselves, though highly suggestive, tell us nothing specific about the attitude of Deputies. But this statistical evidence is reinforced by evidence gathered by the author from interviews with Deputies. These interviews were conducted on various occasions between 1970 and 1979, and although they were not conducted with the present purpose in mind they nevertheless do give some admittedly unsystematic but nevertheless revealing indications.[13]

In the first place there is no doubt that the general level of morale of Deputies is now considerably higher than it was ten years ago. They feel that, in general, their work is more important and more appreciated than it was, both by the Government and by the public at large. This seems to be especially true of younger Deputies and (as one would expect) members of the Gaullist and Giscardian ex-*majorité*, but the differences between different age groups and parties do not seem all that great.

In 1970 one detected a strong element, especially among opposition Deputies, of resentment at the fact that their services, expertise and democratic credentials had for so long been scorned and ignored by the executive, and in particular by the younger, technocratic element within the bureaucracy that was by then beginning to make its mark. It was almost as if one were witnessing a dying political class being thrust aside by a new and up-and-coming elite. Yet ten years later one was scarcely able to detect any sign of such feelings. Indeed, far from feeling a sense of hostility toward a group of usurpers, there was instead a sense of guarded like-mindedness (if one may put it this way), a sense that both sides had come to realise that each depended on the other's goodwill if both were to peform their functions optimally.

Many Deputies, it seems, attribute this change of attitude – which they themselves recognise – to the election of Giscard to the presidency. Whatever Deputies may think of his ideas about the need for concerted decision-making and government by the centre, they do acknowledge that his commitment to these notions has produced a major change of attitude and behaviour on the part of the administration toward the Assembly. Officials, they say, are now more accessible, more willing to part with information and more willing to listen to Deputies' views on policy questions. Even Elysée staff now attend committee hearings – something that was unheard of in the days of de Gaulle and Pompidou.

The most significant aspect of this change, however, lies in the apparent realisation by Deputies – of all parties, including the Communists – that it offers them an opportunity and demands from them a response. The opportunity is for political rehabilitation and a role once again – even if relatively modest – in policy-making; but the realisation of this is conditional upon Deputies responding to the administration's greater openness and flexibility with restraint and a willingness to forgo the temptation to seek public credit for forcing policy changes upon a reluctant Government. As one Deputy put it to this writer: 'We can get things done, but only if we don't brag about it. They don't like being shown up publicly as having lost a battle.' Another Deputy – a Socialist of the CERES persuasion – explained how important it was to disguise anything that a bourgeois government might construe as ideologically motivated and to present it instead as a 'constructive' suggestion based on 'technical' merit. Even then, he conceded, the chances of it being accepted were slim – but at least that was better than no chance at all.

It is of course all too easy to overdraw a picture that is based on such scattered, fragmentary and impressionistic evidence as has been presented here. Certainly it is not our intention to suggest that the Deputies have been restored to their former importance, nor that all the old divisions, between parties and between legislature and executive, are now firmly interred beneath a topsoil of harmony and sweet reason. Yet clearly *something* has changed in the last decade. The changed political atmosphere and the difficult economic circumstances of the 1970s have eroded the self-confidence and technocratic supremacist pretensions of the bureaucracy. At the same time an increasing number of top administrators have gained not only ministerial experience but also, by further extension, legislative experience too; and this has had the effect of papering over the traditional social and political divide between Deputy and civil servant. On the legislative side, the continuing passage of time and the steady generational replacement of Deputies has dimmed the nostalgia for the 'good old days' which, in any case, are now accepted by many beyond the Gaullist ranks as being bad old days rather than good. Then again there was the nuancing during the late 1970s of the earlier trend towards bipolarisation of the party system, with its strict and relentless logic of *majorité* and opposition, ins and outs. These lines of division became softer and more blurred as a range of intervening possibilities for alternative majorities presented themselves as a result of the tensions within the ex-*majorité*, the ups and downs of the left alliance, and the continued refusal of centrism to die the death predicted for it. It is too early to judge the impact of the Socialist victories of 1981, but it must be remembered that the PS is itself a coalition with a strong parliamentarist base.

The combined effect of these forces has, I suggest, been to create the new role for the Deputy. He is once again a participant — albeit a modest one — in decision-making. He is a constitutive element in an elite sub-system composed of Government, bureaucracy, strategic group leaders and Deputies. These elements interact according to well-defined behavioural rules designed to minimise conflict, confine what conflict remains to non-public arenas, and to create a forum for expertise, information and — the Deputy's commodity *par excellence* — democratic legitimacy. The achievement of these objectives requires of the Deputy that the price of his limited participation is self-restraint, courtesy and understanding toward the sensibilities and commitments of other actors, and a willingness to operate in non-public forums.

Insofar, then, as this picture may be accepted as an accurate portrayal of the Deputy's contemporary role, then it is clear that he has re-entered the power elite from which he had been for a period all but excluded. Interestingly, however, it would appear that whereas in the heyday of parliamentary government the Deputy's elite position was ascriptive (by virtue of the spread of the republican ideal) but was not accepted — or at best was only grudgingly accepted — by rival elites, particularly the bureaucracy, today the position is the exact converse. The Deputies are now accepted — at least conditionally — by the one rival elite that matters, but their ascriptive status remains low. There is still little sign at mass level that the Deputies have recovered significantly from the low standing to which they had sunk by the early 1960s. But this may indeed be the price the Deputy of tomorrow will have to pay for his continued membership of the power elite: for if his influence is dependent upon its restrained and discreet use away from the public gaze, then the public will have no reason to alter its view that the Deputy, while embodying French republican legitimacy, and while sustaining or opposing the government of the day, is nevertheless of little practical use when it comes to getting things done.

A final point, virtually a postscript. Up to now we have been considering the Deputy as a member (or not, as the case may be) of the *national* elite; that is, the Deputy in his capacity as a legislator, a member of the National Assembly. But of course there exists in France, perhaps more than in many developed countries, a well-defined system of *local* elites, whose structure, in contrast with the national elite structure, has remained markedly stable over a long period of time.

While this does not form a central focus of our present study, it would clearly be wrong to omit altogether what is an important elite function of the Deputy, and what is an even more important element in the local elite structure. For, except in the most highly urbanised areas of France, the Deputy continues today as he did a century ago to be the local notable *par excellence*. Not only does he typically hold significant local elective offices – *maire* of what may often be the *chef-lieu* of his Assembly constituency, and often *conseiller-général* of his *département* as well[14] – but, arising from his elective status (and in some areas of conservative coloration, from his social status as well), he enjoys a diffuse prestige and influence over the locality in which he is known and with which he is identified. All this is well-known and scarcely requires spelling out.[15] What is of relevance to the present topic is the fact that the Deputy's elite situation at local level would appear to be such as to place him rather more in the category of the status elite than of the power elite. Although it is true that he is seen at grassroots level as a representative of political power who may be approached for the satisfaction of political and administrative demands, his function is seen more as an intermediary, or intercessor, than as a dispenser of power himself. This does of course carry its own social and political standing, and one, moreover, which spills over into other aspects of local life; but it scarcely places the Deputy squarely inside the power elite. Even as *maire* of a considerable town and chairman of a *conseil général* his powers are severely circumscribed, and are seen to be by the public at large. He can influence but not dictate; bring pressure but not make the decision. He may proudly flaunt his sash of office, share a drink at the corner bistro with a handful of deferential constitutents;

but before he can actually achieve anything significant on their behalf he needs the co-operation of powerful allies and connections.

In conclusion then, we can see that the Deputy's membership of the French elite remains ambiguous. On the one hand we have the contrast between the national and local levels: at local level his leading role in local elite structures is a stable, long-term and seemingly assured phenomenon; while his membership of the national elite is unstable and fluctuating, including periods in which he may virtually drop out of the elite altogether. Again, while at local level he is a member primarily of a status elite, a position he enjoys by both ascriptive and accepted right, at national level he is a member (when a member at all) of the power elite. In this latter instance there is an added element of instability: not only does the Deputy move into and out of the power elite over time, but the attitudinal origins of his membership have also changed; membership by ascription but with low internal elite acceptance has given way to membership by internal acceptance but with low mass ascription. If the Deputy's role and status today is modest by contrast with half a century ago, it is certainly greater than it was twenty years ago: it may indeed stand favourable comparison with his counterpart in the Bundestag or even — dare one suggest? — the House of Commons.

Notes

1 Philip M. Williams, *The French Parliament, 1958-1967* (London, 1968). In addition there is of course a small number of specialised case studies, perhaps the best known of which are: Pierre Delvolvé and Henry Lesguillons, *Le Contrôle parlementaire sur la politique économique et budgétaire* (Paris, 1964); and Eliane Guichard-Ayoub, Charles Roig and Jean Grangé, *Études sur le parlement de la Cinquième République* (Paris, 1965).

2 From Ezra N. Suleiman, *Power, Politics and Bureaucracy in France: The Administrative Elite* (Princeton, N.J., 1974) — the best and most complete statement of this perspective on the French political system. A diluted British variant of this view can be found in Jack Hayward, *The One and Indivisible French Republic* (London, 1973).

3 Oliver H. Woshinsky, *The French Deputy* (Lexington, Mass., 1973).

4 Roland Cayrol, Jean-Luc Parodi and Colette Ysmal, *Le Député français* (Paris, 1973; Fondation Nationale des Sciences Politiques, Série 'Travaux et Recherches de Science Politique', no. 23).

5 For an excellent introductory survey of the major types of elite theory, see Geraint Parry, *Political Elites* (London, 1969). It might be worth mentioning here that one of the central problems facing all attempts to construct theories of elites is to formulate a definition of an elite which avoids, on the one hand, the pitfall of circularity (in which elites are defined in terms of the groups who hold elite positions), and on the other hand avoids the danger of committment to a rather paranoid form of conspiracy theory — 'tightly-knit groups of politically motivated men'.

6 It would be impossible to cite specific sources for the generalisations contained in this paragraph, which are a distillation of years of accumulated snippets and impressions from a diversity of sources. Perhaps the work that most closely conveys the flavour of what this paragraph is attempting to describe is Theodore Zeldin, *France 1848-1945*, Vol. I, *Love, Ambition, Politics* (Oxford, 1973).

7 See, for example, J. P. T. Bury, *France 1814-1940* (London, 1949), passim; Herbert Luethy, *France Against Herself* (New York, 1955), pp. 5-27.

8 Michel Debré, *Ces Princes qui nous gouvernent* (Paris, 1957).

9 La Documentation Française, *Textes et documents sur la pratique de la Ve République* (Paris, 1978), p. 232.

10 Ibid., pp. 266-7.

11 The procedure whereby the government can force controversial legislation through Parliament by insisting on a single vote being taken on an entire bill or any part of it.

12 La Documentation Française, op. cit., p. 219.

13 The interviews were conducted with other purposes in mind, and questionnaires where used did not contain questions specifically designed to tap Deputies' attitudes about their role as an elite group. The conclusions reported below are taken mainly from open-ended and unstructured conversations conducted after the main purpose of the interview had been accomplished. As a result the reported generalisations are inevitably couched in impressionistic and unquantified terms.

14 Cayrol et al. found that 67 per cent of their sample of Deputies had held elective local office prior to their first election to the Assembly, while a further 7 per cent had attempted unsuccessfully to do so. Although they do not state how many subsequently dropped their local responsibilities, the number is unlikely to be great judging from the importance Deputies typically attach to maintaining a local power base; in any case these are likely to be offset by those who gained local office subsequent to their first election as Deputy. See Roland Cayrol et al., op. cit., pp. 116, 122.

15 The best accounts of the local importance of the Deputy are found in Mark Kesselman, *The Ambiguous Consensus: A Study of Local Government in France* (New York, 1967); and Sidney Tarrow, *Between Centre and Periphery: Grassroots Politicians in Italy and France* (New Haven, 1977).

12 The 'closed' worlds of Socialist and Gaullist elites

WILLIAM R. SCHONFELD
University of California, Irvine

This chapter describes and analyses the routine behaviour of French party elites towards their partisan adversaries. Most data, but not all, are drawn from interviewing and observation of the Gaullist (RPR) and Socialist (PS) national leaderships. What shape do interparty relations take? How conflictual are they? Are there ties which bind opponents together? How closed are the personal and structural networks of party leaders?

The everyday dissociations and linkages between competitive partisan elites are a neglected topic of inquiry. The degree of integration among national elites has been extensively discussed.[1] A few empirical studies have examined communication and friendship ties among the economic, political, and social leaders of a country.[2] The broad scope of this research, however, tends to preclude gathering (or at least presenting) data on interparty connections.[3]

The absence of grounded insights into the frequency, style and form of cross-partisan contacts is particularly regrettable because there is an extensive and growing body of literature on the critical role of relations between party elites in fostering stable, effective democratic rule. Patterns of 'amical agreement', 'accommodation', and 'consociational' decision-making among competitive political leaders can bind together a society cleaved into distinct subcultural groups.[4] The Dutch and Swiss cases demonstrate that partisan elites drawn from and rooted in distinct segments of society can govern together effectively.[5]

In consociational democracies, in systems where amical agreement prevails, competitors collaborate to manage the nation. Are they bound together through dense communication links and strong personal friendships? The researchers have not provided a response. This may not be a major lacuna, since the elites do, in fact, co-operate.[6]

However, in regimes where the relationship between partisan elites is formally antagonistic, information on the structural and personal networks of the opposing elites may be critical to an understanding of the stability and intensity of the adversarial style. Conflict may well be reduced

through contact, exacerbated through distance. The host
competitors engaged in what appears to be, or is presented ¿
between polarised, incompatible goals, might be moderated
partisan connections which cement together an otherwise frag.ɛ system.
Alternatively, mutual isolation and ignorance could become a breeding
ground for accentuated conflict.

Succinctly put, party leaders live in more or less closed, homogeneous
political worlds. The extent to which their bias and preferences are reinforced or challenged in their working and personal relations should
be a critical factor for understanding and explaining the strength, bases
and solidity of partisan conflict.

Perhaps the most noted feature of French democracy is the high degree
of political competition and conflict. The struggle for the people's vote
is a sharp confrontation between parties and coalitions claiming to represent mutually exclusive economic, social and political options. The 1981
electorate was offered, in the words of party candidates seeking their
support, *'un choix de société'*. In this context, politics is war not compromise, elections are battles not contests, parties are enemies not
opponents, and their leaders are commanding officers not rivals.

Since French parties are very antagonistic, diatribing rather than
debating with each other, we would expect their elites to have structural
and personal networks which tend to be hermetically sealed from their
opponents. After all, to maintain severe conflict, you must dehumanise
your adversaries, turning them into stereotypes. The type of contact
associated with ordinary day-to-day casual interaction would undermine
antagonism.

Although party politics in France is first and foremost antagonistic,
the imagery of irreconcilable rivalry may be overdrawn.[7] There are
indications that perhaps extreme hostility is somewhat contrived, a general
consensus on the rules of the adversarial game might exist, and the highly
competitive elites may even combine to preserve their common interests.

First, no significant group is calling for fundamental institutional
changes. Rather the formerly controversial framework of the Fifth
Republic is now considered legitimate. Such agreement is inhabitual in
France.

Second, in spite of the vehemence of electoral campaigns and the
narrowness of victory, those who are defeated do not protest or demonstrate. The accept their loss with the calmness and reserve of a profoundly
democratic and moderate people.

Third, the accentuated nature of party conflict does not seem to be a
reflection of profound, reinforcing social, economic, and political cleavages

in the society. The traditional divisions which fueled partisan discord — clerical and anti-clerical sentiments, republican and anti-republican feelings — have lost their potency. New bases for fundamental conflict have not arisen to take their place.

Fourth, the President of the Republic from 1974–81, Valéry Giscard d'Estaing, in a radical departure from the precedent set by de Gaulle and Pompidou, advocated a reduction of political tension and a 'reasonable cohabitation' between the majority and the opposition. Most French have sympathised with this call; this suggests that the population is not wedded to the politics of confrontation but rather seeks a more moderate style of partisan conflict. The leaderships of the Communist, Socialist and Gaullist parties have, in unison, strongly challenged the President's argument as a ploy designed to improve his electoral chances and reduce theirs; this reinforces the sense that acute partisan conflict is not entirely responsive to the electorate's attitude.

Fifth, the partisan elites refuse to capitalise on certain events which could undermine their 'implacable' adversary and strengthen themselves. For example, long before Pompidou's death, it was generally known in political elite circles that the President was suffering with terminal cancer. Yet the Socialist and Communist press and leaders avoided making Pompidou's capacity to carry out his functions a subject of public debate. Similarly, when in 1980 *L'Express* made an issue out of Georges Marchais's 'voluntary' work in Nazi Germany, all segments of the political elite came to the defence of the Communist General Secretary, and refused to seek political profit from his supposed unpatriotic activities during World War Two. Both incidents suggest a certain collaboration and cooperation among party elites which fails to fit the model of irreconcilable foes.

Thus, the extreme adversarial style of French partisan elites seems somewhat unwarranted and at times contradictory: unwarranted because of the electorate's democratic decorum; contradictory because the mortal enemies occasionally seem to come to each other's defence.

This paper will examine similar inconsistencies and tensions in the everyday relations between Socialist and Gaullist national leaders. We will begin with an examination of the structural features of the PS and the RPR which tend to isolate the two elites from each other and generate animosity. Then the personal styles and behaviours, a factor which tends to mitigate antagonism, will be analysed. A tension exists between organisational pressures purely for reinforcing partisan contacts and personal non-sectarianism; the final section explores the capacity of this contradiction to persist.

Structural isolation and animosity: the maintenance of hostility

The democratic struggle for the people's support is competitive. The gains of one coalition or party can only occur at the expense of its rivals. Success requires undermining foes. As a result, each side in the political battle may be expected energetically to seek information about its opponents and their activities.

Surprisingly, the Gaullist and Socialist national elites violate this logic; they show little if any interest in each other.[8] Mutual ignorance is supported by an absence of any effort to obtain insights into the projects and difficulties of the other side. In fact, leaders seem to avoid the acquisition of information even when it is easily within their grasp.

This is unexpected not only because it runs counter to the basic demands of a politically conflictual context but also because French party leaders discuss politics in ways which emphasise the significance of their competitors. Speeches systematically analyse and criticise the policies and proposals of adversaries. When members of the elite describe politics in private discussions, they often turn to metaphors which highlight the need to understand one's rivals. For example, parties are most commonly compared to armies in battle, an image which implies frequent reconnaissance missions. Occasionally, leaders draw parallels between contemporary French politics and a doubles tennis match, thereby suggesting the importance of observing and understanding adversaries and partners alike.

Nonetheless, Gaullist and Socialist elites tend not only to lack knowledge about each other but also to go out of their way to maintain mutual ignorance. After considering the evidence from which this description is drawn, we will examine everyday patterns of interaction which nourish partisan hostility.

The most readily accessible source for information about political opponents is the press. The party elites are avid consumers of newspapers and magazines. At the very least, everyone having a position of national responsibility gets *Le Monde*. All the top leaders receive the major weeklies and at least three of the national dailies, judging simply from the distribution made by party headquarters to them at their personal request. The reading material obtained by the Gaullists and Socialists strongly overlaps. From this it might be assumed that the party leaderships share a common information base.[9] In fact, they do not.

The Gaullist scan the press for articles about their own movement and the right-wing coalition. The Socialists search for and scrutinise information about the PS and the Left in general. Both elites ignore reports about the activities of their adversaries.

I began to suspect this pattern of selection from the comments about the news which I overheard party leaders make to each other. Descriptions and analyses of their own organisations were the only ones discussed, and these, interestingly, were not treated critically but rather as sources of new information.[10]

Later when I began observing the closed meetings of the PS's and RPR's decision-making structures, I glanced at the articles leaders were reading as they waited for a session to begin or during a break. Invariably, they exclusively looked at the news about their own party. The members of the elite with whom I travelled, in their constituency or around the country, had similar reading habits.

During the year preceding the 1978 legislative elections, certain journalists published books about the national leaderships of political parties. Thierry Pfister, at the time *Le Monde*'s correspondent on the PS, wrote *Les Socialistes* (Paris, 1977). Pierre Crisol, of the radio-television station RTL, collaborated with Jean-Yves Lhomeau on *La Machine RPR* (Paris, 1977). Each of these works purported to provide insights into the 'secret' workings of the party and offered biographical sketches of many members of the elite. Pfister's study was widely read by Socialists and for more than a month was frequently discussed. The Gaullists responded in an identical fashion to the publication of the Crisol-Lhomeau volume. Neither group seemed even remotely aware of the book published about their adversaries.

After completing my basic research (structured interviewing and systematic observation), I maintained contact with a certain number of the leaders, some but not all of whom had positions of major national responsibility. While discussing preliminary findings, I offered my impressions about how each elite ignored the other. Often I jokingly suggested the two parties could save a great deal of money if they shared subscriptions, since the leaders read different parts of the same papers. No one challenged the validity of this observation.

To conclude, consider the following illustrative anecdote.

On Sunday, June 12 1977, the RPR held its first *Congrès extraordinaire* — a gathering of delegates to vote on an issue of special importance. Summoned to the Sheraton Hotel in Paris, the Gaullists elected 100 members of the Central Committee and examined the report on 'participation' prepared under the auspices of Philippe Dechartre, former junior minister to General de Gaulle, historic leader of the Gaullists of the left, and member of the RPR's executive committee.

After Dechartre spoke, people with direct experience in participatory environments addressed the Congress. These speeches furnished concrete examples of the functioning and benefits of participation. One report described the Hotel Plaza-Athénée's experiment. According to the preliminary schedule, the general manager, Paul Bougenaux, was not to appear personally. However, after the major portion of his speech was delivered by someone else, he mounted the platform to address the delegates. This segment of the Extraordinary Congress was not held behind closed doors.

The press gave extensive coverage to the Gaullist meeting. In particular, the presentation of the Plaza-Athénée's experience as a model of participation and Monsieur Bougenaux's personal appearance were reported.

About three weeks later, on Tuesday July 5 1977, I had an extensive discussion with an important Socialist administrator. Our conversation was wide-ranging, and at one point, turned to party doctrine, including the notion of 'autogestion'. When I asked was not this idea really the same as the RPR's concept of participation, my interlocutor protested strongly saying that 'autogestion' had no parallel whatsoever with the ideas of the 'right'. Then I asked: to what precisely does the idea of 'autogestion' refer? After offering a general and abstract view, he suggested − after further coaxing on my part for a specific case − that perhaps I should look at the Hotel Plaza-Athénée, an enterprise that ran according to this Socialist principle. He also indicated that the manager of the hotel, a certain Paul Bougenaux, was 'obviously' a PS sympathiser, maybe even a party member.

The PS leader could never have selected this concrete example of 'autogestion' − a very poorly chosen case from his perspective since it raised questions about the 'fundamental difference' between the two parties − if he had read the press reports on Gaullist activities.

Reading habits are not the only indicator of the special efforts taken by party elites to ignore each other. In seeking authorisation to conduct my research, a sizeable number of contacts were made. When describing the project, I always informed Gaullists that Socialists were also to be studied and vice versa. Similarly, in discussions with respondents after the structured interview was completed I often mentioned the comparative nature of my inquiry. Finally, the many members of the elites who I saw frequently knew their adversaries were also being investigated.

During the earliest phase of fieldwork, I anticipated probing questions from the members of one elite about the activities of their foes. Much to my surprise, and relief, this problem was never posed. Quite to the contrary, even those leaders with whom I developed friendly relations after many hours of casual discussion, were only concerned with eliciting my impressions of their party. No Socialist or Gaullist exhibited the slightest penchant for exploiting my 'expertise' about their opponent. Surely this is a powerful, even if personal, indicator of the 'pains' taken by leaders not to gather information about their adversaries.

A final indicator of the leaderships' inattention to competitors' activities stems from the personal contacts a few members of each elite have with their peers on the other side of the political fence. Typically due to shared experiences during the Resistance and/or in Mendesist circles of the 1950s, real friendships link certain Gaullists and Socialists. These people, in many cases, continue to interact. At times they exchange information about their parties' affairs. This knowledge is not ordinarily transmitted to members of one's own elite. Moreover, when this is done, the confidences drawn from such personal ties are ignored.

For example, an important Gaullist met François Mitterrand by chance on September 15 1977; they were booked on the same flight. The two men knew each other well. At the instigation of the RPR leader, they decided to sit together and spoke for about an hour. The day before, Robert Fabre, head of the Radicaux de Gauche, walked out from the left's negotiating session on their common programme. This critical event and its implications for cooperation between the Communists and the Socialists in the forthcoming legislative elections, was the basic subject of conversation between Mitterrand and the Gaullist.

The RPR leader felt that he had acquired information of great significance to the movement. He quickly flew back to Paris and called Marie-France Garaud – one of Jacques Chirac's two closest advisers – to make an appointment to see her and pass on his special knowledge. A meeting was set. The Gaullist arrived on time. After a frustrating two-hour long wait, he told the secretary he was leaving, and if Mme Garaud wanted to find out what François Mitterrand was thinking, she should telephone him. No one ever called.

As a result of the special efforts to avoid gathering information about adversaries – even when it is readily accessible – the PS and the RPR have little knowledge or understanding of each other's activities. Such ignorance, within a highly competitive environment, facilitates the generation of extreme hostility. Under conditions of belligerence and mutual isolation, exaggerated and stereotypical images can flourish unchallenged.

Isolation and animosity are also supported by patterns of everyday interaction. Gaullists and Socialists alike work with people who share, or at least do not openly contest, their partisan biases and beliefs.

Holding a position of national responsibility in the PS or the RPR is very time-consuming. The majority of the interview sample were neither salaried employees of the party nor deputies, senators, or mayors of cities: they earned their livelihoods from non-political activies. Yet 63 per cent of the Gaullist respondents and 70 per cent of the Socialists claimed to spend more than 40 hours every week in partisan activities.

Political roles are demanding in all societies. For two reasons this general tendency may be accentuated for French party elites. The practice of accumulating party posts and elected positions[11] means that respondents either occupy or seek a series of distinct responsibilities, each requiring a certain expenditure of effort. In addition, there is an enormous amount of turnover in the ranks of the party leaders.[12] The tendency for tenure in office to be short nourishes feelings of insecurity and drives people toward a total commitment to retain their positions.

The elites generally spend their work time with other party members: coordinating action with fellow leaders, mobilising and directing activists, and handling organisational matters with party or parliamentary group staffs.

The partisan role, of course, also entails contact with outsiders. First and foremost, the leader is a campaigner seeking the support of ordinary citizens for himself and/or his party. He may be asked to intercede with the governmental authorities on behalf of a constituent, who, as a petitioner, will surely avoid calling into question his partisan beliefs. The leaders' only other source of contact with the general public occurs through door-to-door canvassing and open meetings. Here their views are challenged, often forcefully, but their task is to undermine and discredit such criticism. Hence, this context is not propitious to developing a more open political perspective.

Party leaders interact with other influential members of their society. In particular, they may deal with government officials, representatives of interest groups, and journalists. The Socialists and Gaullists have such contacts, but ones which typically reinforce rather than challenge their basic partisan beliefs.

Respondents were presented with a list of fifteen groups 'with which deputies and party leaders have more or less frequent professional contact'. Each was asked to rank-order on a ten rung self-anchoring ladder,[13] the frequency with which he personally encountered representatives of each group. The Socialists claimed to interact most with: locally elected officials (8.5), trade union leaders (7.9), journalists (7.8), representatives of teachers' unions (6.7), and intellectuals (6.6). The Gaullists claimed to have most contact with members of ministers' staffs (7.6), locally elected officials (7.4), journalists (7.4), other high level civil servants (excluding directors of the central administration and members of ministerial staffs) (7.0), and ministers (6.5).

A certain difference between the two lists is immediately obvious. Trade unions and teachers' unions oppose the Government's policies; the Socialists, but not the Gaullists, often associate with representatives of these groups. Ministers, their personal staffs, and other high-level civil servants work to promote the Government's policies; the RPR leaders, but not those of the PS, frequently interact with these people. 'Intellectuals' is a vague category, but one which in France is more generally linked with the left than with the majority; in fact, the intellectuals seen by the Socialists are at least party sympathisers.

Both sets of respondents mix with reporters and local politicians. However, they do not see the same types of people. The local officials with whom they interact are often of the same party; otherwise, the local politician is contacting the party leader (who in this case is typically a deputy, senator, or candidate for such an office) so he can intercede with the national authorities and help solve a local problem. Finally, most journalists, although not necessarily partisan, do work on one side or the other of the political divide. Reporters tend to be 'incorporated' within an elite in the sense that their contacts, knowledge, and interests are focused on a party. Moreover, the journalists's role is to describe and perhaps uncover, not to cross-fertilise; as a result, he does not challenge the biases of his contacts.

The party leader, thus, tends to interact with like-minded individuals. This propensity, is in part, due to the demands of holding a position of national responsibility, which places him in a structured, reinforcing organisational network. But the pattern of interaction is also a response to pressures, especially within the PS, against association with 'the enemy'. These constraints are important for counteracting the pull of ties which might draw certain Socialists and Gaullists closer together. In particular, many leaders have connections with opponents based on camaraderie during the Resistance and/or common support of Pierre Mendès-France. The discouragement of cross-partisan contact has not destroyed these links but it does mute their salience. Moreover, certain deputies and senators, either to enrich their personal parliamentary experience or to further specific legislative goals, would like to interact more frequently and more casually with their colleagues on the other side; Socialist party pressure all but prohibits establishing such contacts.

Mingling with political adversaries is suspect within the PS; a member of Parliament or of the hierarchy who mixes with foes cannot be fully trusted; he is regarded as a potential pollutant. Consider three distinct examples of this attitude.

(a) In conversations with Socialists who had played important roles during the Resistance, I would ask if they continued to see their comrades of the war years who had become Gaullist leaders. Many shrugged off the question; the others 'pleaded guilty' to having such contacts but noted that they took place in the privacy of their homes and that politics was not discussed.

(b) A well-known, young PS leader and deputy was taking a drink at the National Assembly's bar. He noticed an old army buddy and went over to say hello. The two men knew each other well and quickly became engaged in an animated conversation. It so happened that the military friend had just taken a position as legislative assistant to a major figure in the RPR. When the Socialist found this out, he quickly broke off the discussion. Afterwards, when the two men's paths crossed, the PS leader acted as if he did not know the other fellow.

(c) An ordinary Socialist deputy informed me how he would like to have contact with colleagues from the majority, simply as a way of enriching his parliamentary experience. However, were he to meet openly with political adversaries, his Socialist colleagues would banish him. Finally, he had figured out a way of having discussions with RPR and UDF deputies away from the prying eyes of his PS colleagues: for transportation to the airport when returning to his electoral district, he would systematically use the National Assembly's limousine service and wait for a car with political adversaries.

Personal non-sectarianism: the limits of partisan enmity

The organisational environments of the PS and RPR support a pattern of structural isolation. The two national elites ignore each others' activities; in fact, they make special efforts to avoid gathering easily accessible information about competitors. Job demands push the leaders into contact with people who share or at least do not openly challenge their partisan biases and beliefs. The inclination to live in a closed world is further reinforced by pressures within the PS against associating with adversaries.

The pattern of interaction adopted by individual leaders *tend* to satisfy collective expectations. In spite of group pressures, however, personal relations between some Gaullists and Socialists do persist; similarly, at least certain PS leaders conceal contacts with RPR colleagues and others invent ploys for encountering political adversaries. What is the significance of these deviant acts?

The answer depends upon the relationship between the organisations' demands and the personal styles and behaviours of the individual leaders. If the members of the elite are sectarian, then structural isolation at the group level is a logical consequence. In this context, the nonconformist behaviour of a small subset of Gaullist and Socialists would probably simply reflect their atypical personal openness. Alternatively, a good proportion, perhaps even a majority, of the leaders might not be sectarian. If so, structural isolation would be a pattern of interaction enforced by the collectivity upon its members who most often comply, but only reluctantly. The deviant members of the elite would differ from their peers in terms of how they balance personal tastes and style against group constraints.

To select between these alternatives, we need to know if sectarianism is widespread among members of the elite. Do leaders talk and behave as if they belonged to segregated subcultures? In discourse, are adversaries dehumanised? Is contact with people of opposing political persuasions spoken about as though it were contaminating? Are the leaders' personal networks of friends totally reinforcing?

Considering the statements made by Socialists and Gaullists during structured interviews, in casual conversations, or while observing them, there is little evidence of sectarianism. In fact there were only four incidents.

(a) An interview item asked: 'Do you have Socialist/Gaullist friends?' One PS leader, a member of the *comité directeur*, responded that friendship with an RPR sympathizer or member was 'morally impossible'. This sectarian response was totally atypical. The other 86 Socialists and all the Gaullists answered the question in a straightforward fashion with no suggestion or hint that PS-RPR friendships were unthinkable on principled grounds.

(b) In discussions with members of thé elites as well as during a section of the interview dealing with channels of communication, the issue of reading the press was often broached. Only a single respondent offered the sectarian view that to avoid gathering misinformation, you have to exert self-censorship and not consult the 'wrong' newspapers and magazines. Specifically, a member of the RPR's central committee explained that he was not well educated. As a result, he might have difficulty critically dissecting 'false' views. To maintain a 'correct' perspective and to avoid 'contamination', he only read *La Lettre de la Nation* — the movement's daily four-page newsletter.

(c) As already noted, many members of the elites as well as employees of the parties knew I was studying both the PS and the RPR. They seemed uninterested in the work being done on their adversaries. Some could not understand the logic behind such a comparative inquiry. Only one person, a PS employee who became a *secrétaire nationale* after the 1979 congress at Metz, responded to the description of my research in a way suggesting that since I was in contact with adversaries, I must be an enemy. An important party administrator introduced me to this person, succinctly explained my project, and asked if this individual would please help me get some specific information I needed. The sectarian Socialist immediately replied: 'I'm too busy to help you; . . . the PS has over 160,000 members for whom I work.' The tirade continued for about ten minutes during which time I repeatedly, but to no avail, tried to explain how much I admired the PS and simply sought a better understanding of the party. My remarks never penetrated; obviously my interlocutor was convinced that since I had contact with the RPR, I could never objectively appreciate the PS.

(d) All party leaders spoke of the legislative elections as involving an important choice. Most publicly and privately strongly attacked their adversaries' policies and proposals, as being wrong for France. Only one member of the elite, a very important Gaullist, ever expressed a sectarian view of the meaning of the electoral outcome. This individual, whom I eventually came to know very well, told me during our first casual conversation, that if the left won, the majority's leaders would be thrown into prison. In spite of my lack of receptivity to this perspective, he persisted in expressing the view that if his side lost, a dictatorial system would be established.

These four incidents are significant, not because of their presence but because of their rarity. The structural isolation and antagonism between the PS and the RPR could, perhaps even should, generate frequent expressions of partisan sectarianism. Yet, this hardly ever occurred. Rather, adversaries were viewed as opponents with different interests, ideas and practices, not as contaminating, evil, dehumanised enemies.

Similarly, the individual members of the elites do not tend to live their personal lives in politically self-reinforcing, segregated subcultures. Quite to the contrary, large proportions of Gaullists and Socialists have friends who hold opposing partisan beliefs. The data on the leaders' personal networks is interesting: it reveals not only the absence of sectarianism but also differences in acknowledging cross-partisan friendships.

Two types of indicators were used. First, respondents were told: 'Just like all human beings, politicians and party leaders have family lives, social lives, leisure lives and professional lives. To better appreciate your environment, I would like to get some insights into both the types of people who are your friends and those who you see most often. However, to avoid in any way probing into your personal life, I will ask you to label these people by simply using their first name or the initial of their first name; that way we will have a set of people who you, but not I, can specifically identify. What are the first names or initials of your friends?' [Respondents could provide as many as eight names, but usually gave three, four, or five.] 'Now, what are the first names or initials of the people you see most frequently? These people may or may not be friends.' [Again 8 names were coded.] Once these lists were generated, I asked the respondent for the profession and then the political preference of each person identified. From these data, we could determine the proportion of Socialists and Gaullists who included political antagonists in their lists and use this as a measure of heterogeneity in personal associations.

Second, later in the interview, respondents were posed two close-ended questions: 'Do you have Communist friends?', and then 'Do you have Socialist friends?' [for the RPR respondents] 'Gaullist friends?' [for the PS respondents].

In conjunction, the two indicators provide insights into respondent bias concerning the desirability of presenting oneself to others as having friends with diverse political preferences. The item asking for a list of friends, forced respondents to identify a small number of people, without knowing what further questions would be asked about these individuals. The result might have been a sample of friends from distinct contexts or a purely random selection; more likely, however, these are the most intimate friends. One thing is absolutely certain: the composition of the list could not have been shaped by the respondent's beliefs about whether it was better to be seen as having a friendship group with diverse or with reinforcing partisan preferences.

The close-ended item not only tapped such beliefs but also permitted a much looser notion of friendship. For example, consider a Socialist who highly values left unity. None of his intimates are Communist, but he is friendly with certain party members. When asked 'Do you have Communist friends?' he will probably respond positively, even though he would not have included anyone belonging to the PCF in his list. Moreover, the do-you-have questions may even elicit positive responses from respondents who, for whatever reason, wish to present themselves as 'open', even though they do not really have friendly relations with such people. (Remember the anti-Semite's statement that some of his best friends are Jews.) Finally, respondents with diverse partisan friendships may respond negatively to the close-ended questions, because their environment discourages any but reinforcing contacts.

With this background, we can analyse the data. 33 per cent of the Gaullists and 43 per cent of the Socialists claimed to have PCF friends when explicitly asked. Yet, only 5 per cent and 6 per cent, respectively, included Communists in their lists of friends. The difference in responses is dramatic: the close-ended item suggests that the RPR leaders and, to an even higher degree, those of the PS have extensive personal ties with Communists; the list item suggests the absence of such contacts. This incongruity may simply reflect the much larger network tapped by the close-ended question. Alternatively, it may indicate a very strong Socialist value and a strong Gaullist value attributed to having Communist friends; a value hardly realised in practice.

The two indicators, when applied to Socialist-Gaullist friendships, provided different results. 70 per cent of the RPR leaders, when explicitly asked, claimed to have PS friends; 35 per cent had included Socialists or left partisans in their list of friends (31 per cent in their list of people most frequently seen). In contrast, 28 per cent of the PS leaders claimed RPR friends on the close-ended question, but 43 per cent had included Gaullists and right partisans in their list of friends (24 per cent in their list of people most frequently seen).

These findings indicate a strong inclination among Gaullist and Socialist national leaders to include friends with opposing political preferences within their personal networks. This characteristic is not universal. Yet, since respondents are party elites within a society where political conflict is very strong and appears to pit proponents of irreconcilable views against each other, it is quite noteworthy that 70 per cent of the RPR sample claimed to have Socialist friends and 43 per cent of the PS sample included right partisans in their short lists of friends.[14] These data are not compatible with the image of a society cleaved into party subcultures. The pattern of personal sectarianism consonant with and supportive of structural isolation is not present.

An obvious question remains: What is the meaning of the disjunction between findings drawn from the listing and the close-ended items? The two types of questions could be seen as simply tapping more or less extensive networks: the list item was very restrictive allowing respondents to identify only a few of their friends; in contrast, the close-ended items drew on the individual's entire circle of friends. This interpretation does not fit the Socialist responses concerning right-wing friends. This exception is difficult to explain. Obviously the PS leaders included in their lists people identified not only as Gaullists but also as the majority, the right, and occasionally, Giscardian. In other words, the question coded as right partisan a category of people with opposing political views that is much larger than RPR member or sympathisers. But, the same is true for the Gaullist lists which included not only Socialists but also Communists and friends of the left.

Thus, the most obvious interpretation is inadequate. One way in which we can make sense out of the differences between responses to the listing and close-ended items is in the more general context of the tension between organisational constraints which generate isolation and animosity, and personal styles and networks which tend to be non-sectarian.

The tension between structural isolation and personal non-sectarianism

The findings on structural isolation indicated that much stronger pressures were placed on Socialists to avoid contact with Gaullists, than vice versa. In any dyad, if one partner avoids contact with the other, then the other partner will necessarily have few ties with the first. Thus, the absence of formal links between PS and RPR leaders may in large part be due to organisational constraints exerted by the Socialist Party. These pressures are applied to a set of non-sectarian individuals, many of whom have open personal networks. A tension results between private patterns of thought and interaction and the expectations of a group to which the individual not only belongs but also attributes enormous salience. One indication of this tension is that certain PS leaders have contacts with their RPR counterparts but conceal these, while others devise ploys for encountering political adversaries.

The discrepancy between the Socialist listing of right-wing friends and their responses to the close-ended question on RPR friends may be a second indication of this tension. When asked 'who are your friends?' almost half of the PS leaders revealed that their personal networks are heterogeneous. However, when posed the specific 'do you have RPR friends?' the respondents had to deal openly with their party's discouragement of such contacts. As a result there was no exaggeration of such friendships, which otherwise might have stemmed from a reasonably universal value among non-sectarians that one should be friends with all kinds of people. This value, perhaps supplemented by the PS's organisational commitment to left-wing cooperation, does explain the discrepant images of Socialist friendship with Communists: 43 per cent, when explicitly asked, claimed PCF friends even though only 6 per cent included Communists in their lists.

The same interpretation accounts for the disjunction in RPR responses. In regard to both Socialists and Communists, many more Gaullists claimed such friends in the close-ended question than those who included partisan adversaries in their lists. The RPR responses reflect the non-sectarian's bias for openness in contacts, uncurbed by organisational pressures against interaction with political adversaries.[15]

The tension between structural isolation and non-sectarianism should be reduced if the Socialist Party stopped discouraging cross-partisan links. If the organisation simply ignored such ties among leaders — as the RPR seems to — there is every indication that much larger proportions of the two national elites would have contact with their counterparts. The dissonance generated by open personal styles and patterns of interaction would be reduced. Moreover, the level of partisan hostility would be moderated. Hence the lynchpin of the existing adversarial pattern is the organisational pressure within the PS against interaction with adversaries. Why does it exist?

One answer, drawn from a common view of the PS often offered by party members as well as certain observers, focuses on the special character of a left-wing organisation, in particular the ties which bind it into a close community and its working-class heritage, which drive members to be wary of outside attempts at infiltration. No argument based on these characteristics could explain Socialist isolation because there is significant evidence drawn from the RPR fieldwork that Gaullist leaders have frequent contact with their Communist counterparts. And the PCF is certainly as much of the left, working-class, and a community as is the PS. Consider the following examples of casual Gaullist-Communist interaction.

(a) Every Monday or Tuesday, many RPR deputies and leaders return from a long weekend in their provincial electoral district. In private discussions, occasionally in executive committee sessions and in other small party meetings, they refer to conversations they have had with local Communist leaders, often members of the Central Committee. Such contact seems rather widespread; interaction with Socialists having national or local responsibilities appears to be rare.

(b) An important RPR leader went to lunch with his collaborators in the constituency where he was campaigning. As they sat down, the Gaullist noted a major national Communist personality, whom he knew, dining with a group of PCF colleagues in the same restaurant. Both tables had a leisurely meal. Eventually they were the only customers left in the restaurant. At that point the Communist leader got up and went to the Gaullist, using his first name and the familiar 'tu' form, to say: you don't even say hello any more? A friendly conversation ensured. (Although the RPR leader also knew many Socialists, he claimed always to initiate contacts with those in the PS, who were more reserved than his PCF friends.)

(c) One day at the Gaullist offices in the National Assembly, I overheard a conversation in which a former minister was describing a recent experience. He received a call the other evening from Roland Leroy, editor of the Communist daily, who wondered if he would like to come over to *L'Humanité* that night to see how a paper was produced. (Apparently, at some earlier encounter the Gaullist had expressed such an interest.) The former minister explained that he didn't want any publicity or photos, to which Leroy responded: 'Of course, this is just a get-together between friends.' And, that's exactly what the meeting was. (Obviously such events are rare, but when I asked a sample of Socialists, who for one reason or another had a relationship with Leroy, if they or anyone they knew had ever received such an invitation, they not only never had such an experience but could not imagine it ever happening.)

These anecdotes suggest that leadership dissociation between the PS and the RPR is even greater than that between the RPR and the PCF. The degree of structural isolation between Socialists and Gaullists is so extreme that one wonders whether it is not somewhat contrived. The PS's discouragement of connections with RPR leaders, buttressed by mutual ignorance and the lack of formal contacts, may be an organisational mechanism which counterbalances the pull of non-sectarianism, old personal ties and friendships that might permit these 'moral enemies' to live calmly with each other, even to cooperate.

The similarities between the RPR and the PS are great enough that formal interaction among leaders might facilitate collaboration. This in turn would undermine the current structure of political opposition in France. If the Socialists were to cooperate with their adversaries of the right, they would lose the possibility of dominating an omnipotent coalition of the left, in order to be a minority partner in government. Moreover, for more than a decade the PS has presented itself as a proponent of economic, political and social policies distinct from those of the Gaullists and Giscardians. This platform has brought the party a great deal of success, even if victory at the national legislative and presidential elections eluded it until 1981. To change their positions would have run the risk of undermining the Socialists' credibility, especially since the transformation would obviously have compromised their claim to be the only alternative to continued right-wing dominance.

There is no possibility that the Communists and Gaullists could ever govern together. Their fundamentally different world views and electoral bases prevent such cooperation. Consequently, contact between RPR and PCF leaders does not run the risk of establishing meaningful organisational links, and need not be avoided. Such connections, in fact, may serve the interests of both organisations. Gaullists and Communists alike have seen their coalition partners as weak links, tempted by a potential change in alliances. Cooperation between Socialists and Giscardians would have driven both the RPR and the PCF into sterile opposition, with no chance of even sharing in national power. Casual contact may have been seen as useful to prevent such cooperation. After all, in the words of one Gaullist leader: 'As long as we and the Communists have the majority, France is safe.'

Succinctly put, might it be that structural isolation between the PS and RPR is a major safeguard against cooperation, cooperation which could develop on the basis of personal non-sectarianism? Such cooperation, it has been thought, could only reward centrist-dominated coalition-building, and thus undermine the bipolar structure of inter-coalition competition which has been a salient feature of the Fifth Republic party system. Yet party elites are not embedded in antagonistic, mutually exclusive subcultures. As such, the virulence of partisan hostility is unexpected. This contradictory pattern however, does resemble an inversion of consociational democracy, where political elites drawn from antagonistic subcultures cooperate in government.[16] The extreme adversarial style in France helps to maintain a system and a set of rules of the game from which Socialists and Gaullists expect to derive important benefits — benefits which the Gaullists realised in the 1960s, and which have worked very much to the Socialists' advantage in 1981. In addition, a change in pattern would bring with it the risk of electoral sanctions. Finally, commitment to the existing arrangement combined with non-sectarian styles and personal interactions, permit the entire political elite to combine when necessary for their general defence. As long as the parties, especially the PS, remain wedded to this system, as long as there is a broad elite consensus in favour of adversarial politics, 'dissociational' democracy is likely to persist.

Notes

The fieldwork upon which this chapter is based took place over an eighteen-month period which began in January 1977. A random sample of almost 50 per cent of the national elites of the Socialist and Gaullists parties were formally interviewed: 87 PS and 91 RPR leaders. In addition, there were extensive conversations with almost all of the most influential leaders, as well as many other members of the elites, party workers and employees of central headquarters. Finally, for a period of approximately six months, I observed the closed sessions of the two parties' decision-making structures.

I am particularly indebted to Michel Charzat, Jean-Pierre Cot, the late Georges Dayan, Claude Estier, Claude Labbé, Yves Guéna, Jérôme Monod, and Charles Pasqua for making my basic research on the PS and the RPR possible. (A full list of acknowledgements will be included in future publications reporting my findings.)

The Ford Foundation, the Centre National de la Recherche Scientifique, the

Centre de Sociologie des Organisations, and the Group d'Étude des Méthodes de l'Analyse Sociologique, provided critical support.

I benefitted from discussing certain of the ideas presented in this paper with Harry Eckstein and Linton Freeman.

1 The classical theorists, Michels, Mosca and Pareto, stimulated analysis of elite integration. For reviews of the extensive literature, see: Robert D. Putnam, *The Comparative Study of Political Elites* (Englewood Cliffs, N.J., 1976), pp. 107–32; and Gwen Moore, 'The structure of a national elite network', *American Sociological Review*, 44 (October, 1979), pp. 673–5.

2 Frank Bonilla, *The Failure of Elites* (Cambridge, Mass. and London, 1970), pp. 149–246; Charles Kadushin and Peter Abrams, 'Social structure of Yugoslav opinion-makers: Part I, Informal leadership', and 'Social structure of Yugoslav opinion-makers: Part II, Formal and informal influences and their consequences for opinion', in Allen H. Barton, Bogdan Denitch and Charles Kadushin (eds), *Opinion-Making Elites in Yugoslavia* (New York, Washington, and London, 1973), pp. 155–219; and Gwen Moore, op. cit., pp. 673–92.

3 An exception to this general rule is Bonilla, op. cit., who suggests that party affiliation is an important variable in explaining patterns of elite association in Venezuela.

4 See, in particular: Arend Lijphart, *Democracy in Plural Societies: A Comparative Exploration* (New Haven and London, 1977); Arend Lijphart, *The Politics of Accommodation: Pluralism and Democracy in the Netherlands*, second edition (Berkeley, Los Angeles and London, 1975); Jeffrey Obler, Jürg Steiner, and Guido Dierickx, *Decision-Making in Smaller Democracies: The Consociational 'Burden'* (Beverly Hills and London, Sage Professional Papers in Comparative Politics, Series Number 01-064, 1977); and Jürg Steiner, *Amicable Agreement versus Majority Rule: Conflict Resolution in Switzerland* (Chapel Hill, N.C., 1974).

5 This finding modifies, in important way, Gabriel Almond's earlier formulation of the determinate role of political culture. See, in particular, his: 'Comparative political systems', *The Journal of Politics*, 18 (August, 1956), pp. 391–409; and 'A functional approach to comparative politics', in Gabriel A. Almond and James S. Coleman (eds), *The Politics of the Developing Areas* (Princeton, N.J., 1960).

6 Nonetheless, such data should be quite useful for understanding the development and persistence of consociational decision-making. Can such elite collaboration develop or endure without personal networks which bind together the leaders from distinct subcultures? Minimally, such ties seem necessary for the pattern to persist.

7 P. G. Cerny, 'Cleavage, aggregation and change in French politics', *British Journal of Political Science*, 2 (October, 1972), pp. 443–55; John Frears, 'Conflict in France: The decline and fall of a stereotype', *Political Studies*, 20 (March, 1972); and J. R. Frears and Jean-Luc Parodi, *War Will Not Take Place: The French Parliamentary Elections, March 1978* (London, 1979), pp. 1–4 and 105–25.

8 In contrast, consider the Austrian case. G. Bingham Powell (*Social Fragmentation and Political Hostility: An Austrian Case Study* [Stanford, Cal., 1970], p. 80) suggests that the leaders of the two major parties made 'elaborate efforts to find people with friendly contacts in the opposite party so that they could get some inkling of its plans'.

9 For example, on the basis of a synthesis of existing literature, Robert Putnam concludes: 'Elite integration is increased where intra-elite communication is monopolised by a single newspaper, such as *The Times, Le Monde*, and (to a lesser extent) the *New York Times*.' (op. cit., p. 114.)

10 In fact, certain French journalists play the unexpected role of conduit for information *within* a partisan elite. By reading their published articles, a very large proportion of the leadership, including at times major party personalities, learns about decisions taken by their party as well as positions taken by their peers. This role of the media will be analysed in a forthcoming book on the PS and RPR elites, tentatively entitled: *Les éléphants et l'aveugle.*

11 I am referring to a *cumul des mandats* including local, regional and national party posts as well as elected positions such as deputy or senator, mayor, and departmental councillor.

12 William R. Schonfeld, 'La stabilité des dirigeants des partis politiques: le personnel des directions nationales du Parti socialiste et du mouvement gaulliste', *Revue Française de Science Politique*, 30 (June, 1980), pp. 477–505.

13 The technique was developed and used by Hadley Cantril in *The Patterns of Human Concern* (New Brunswick, N.J., 1965).

14 Unfortunately, I have been unable to locate comparable data on other national partisan elites. There are, however, findings on French local elites. Denis Lacorne, in a study of Socialist and Communist elites in Picardie and Languedoc (*The Red Notables: French Communism and Socialism at the Grassroots* [Ph.D. dissertation, Yale, 1976], pp. 278–80) found a higher degree of Socialist sectarianism toward Gaullists than we found. Almost 10 per cent of his sample volunteered the opinion that 'the very idea of having a right-wing friend was unthinkable'. 31 per cent of his PS respondents, when explicitly asked, claimed to have right-wing friends; this proportion is comparable to the responses on our close-ended question, but much less than revealed by the listing item.

The comparison is interesting for two reasons. First, 'elite integration should be markedly greater in local communities than at the national level' (Putnam, op. cit., p. 114), and integration should be, but apparently is not in the French case, facilitated by a reduction in sectarian attitudes and interactions. Second, an important study of local partisan elites discovered: 'It was only among the Socialists in France that we found the kind of open and accessible partisanship that appears more promising for political contact and political exchange.' (Sidney Tarrow, *Partisanship and Political Exchange in French and Italian Local Politics: A Contribution to the Typology of Party Systems* [Beverly Hills and London, Sage Professional Paper in Contemporary Political Sociology, no. 06–004, 1974], p. 41.) The PS's national elites appear more open than their local elites, yet they seem to totally reject political contact and exchange with their partisan adversaries.

15 The effect of organisational constraint is perhaps also visible in the Socialists' responses to the question: who are the people you most frequently see? The two lists developed by RPR leaders offer similar images of openness to cross-partisan contact: 35 per cent identified left-wing friends and 31 per cent included left partisans among the individuals they most frequently saw. The responses of the PS leaders are quite different: 43 per cent identify right-wing friends, but only 24 per cent included right-wing sympathisers in their list of people with whom they more often interact. Socialist party pressures against contact with adversaries could account for this difference.

16 Arend Lijphart's typology of democratic regimes includes the category of 'centripetal democracy', which in principle is the mirror-image of consociational democracy. However, he argues that in centripetal democracies 'the government versus-opposition pattern . . . has not meant an extreme adversarial style'; furthermore, 'in practice, politics is not consistently played in the adversarial style'. (*Democracy in Plural Societies*, p. 111.) This concrete description does not fit the French case of elite behaviour.

13   Problems in the study of France's regional political elites: the case of post-war Brittany

JILL LOVECY
University of Manchester
Institute of Science and Technology

In the West European liberal democratic states a major characteristic of the processes through which the exercise of state power has been democratically legitimated in the modern period has been the elective representation of a variety of territorial units. In the case of France for the greater part of the last hundred years this principle has been embodied in an electoral system for the National Assembly based on single-member constituencies, with a double ballot. Of course the operation of this principle of territorial representation, at the level of both national and local governments, was from its origins profoundly affected by the influence of political ideologies which were constructed around non-geographical forms of identity, and which gave rise to the development of party systems in these states which were for the most part organised around the defence of socio-economic interests and religious affiliation. (Moreover in the recent period this form of representation has increasingly been supplemented by procedures which institutionalise representation of a corporatist nature.)[1]

Nevertheless, the incorporation in the institutions of the state of this principle of territorial representation, it could be argued, has engendered a certain tendency among those members of the political elite who are able to influence the making of legally binding decisions by virtue of holding elective political office to seek to legitimise their role to their own electorates, at least to some degree, in terms of the existence of a specifically local configuration of interests which they claim to represent. That is to say, quite apart from those parties and political elites claiming to represent ethnic, cultural or religious groupings which do correspond to fairly clearly defined geographical locations, other political elites at the national and local level have also become involved in sustaining to varying (and often quite minor) degrees a geographical mode of conceptualisation of the national social formation. This tendency has been especially marked in France among politicians of the centre and right and it is this mode of representation which the term local political *'notable'* is widely employed as signifying.[2]

At the outset of the post-war period no official regional units existed in France for purposes of elective representation. Increasingly over this period, however, a regional dimension has been incorporated into France's political institutions and official decision-making procedures, and the region, in 1972, finally won recognition from the state as a legitimate unit for at least limited procedures of (indirect) democratic representation. Thus by the end of this period the term regional political elite must be taken to refer not just to a few exceptional politicians in France who have, for example, succeeded in winning a position of leadership over many of the politicians in the region surrounding their own immediate political base, who are able to influence public opinion throughout a wide area by their control of a regional press, or whose views have considerable weight at the national level for all decisions affecting the wider region around their own constituency; nor even to the limited phenomenon of politicians whose *only* political identity is a regionalist one – the claim to defend the interests of a specific region. More specifically the term designates that stratum of politicians who occupy positions in official decision-making or consultative bodies at the regional level and whose representative status therefore incorporates to a greater or lesser extent a geographical dimension of this kind. It is in this sense that the French state itself has been forced to accept and could be said now to legitimate – and to have disseminated in areas where they had not previously success-fully established themselves – at least limited forms of regionalist ideology.

In investigating the role of France's regional political elites in the post-war period two questions would therefore seem to be of especial interest. Firstly, in what particular circumstances in the post-war period was the argument taken up in specific areas of France, that a shared regional identity existed – a regional interest which required official, institutionalised forms of representation? Secondly, what were the circumstances in which the specifically regional political actors who advanced this argument succeeded in winning not only support from organised interests and from a wider public opinion, but also recognition from the state? It is perhaps necessary to stress the importance of exploring the historically specific context in which an officially recognised political elite has established itself at the regional level in France because, *pace* those writers who focus essentially on such long-term historical factors as ethnicity or the experience of political incorporation and economic exploitation imposed by internal colonialism, what needs to be explained is precisely why in this period the sense of a regional identity and a shared regional interest became politically salient to the extent that some re-organisation of the state's institutions did finally take place.[3] This is not to deny the relevance of distinctive cultures with their own patterns of historical development within the French nation-state, or of earlier region-alist movements, but these cannot be regarded as constituting of them-selves sufficient conditions for the successful establishment of officially recognised political elites at the regional level in the period since 1945.[4]

At this stage it would perhaps be useful to reformulate our two initial questions in order to distinguish between the different spheres of political activity whose interplay we shall need to examine. In the first place, what was it about the experiences of different socio-economic groups in particular areas in France that facilitated their perception of their own problems and opportunities in this period in terms of a shared regional identity, and provided a suitable basis for aspirant political elites at the regional level? Secondly, what political actors took up the argument that specifically regional interests existed requiring appropriate procedures of representation, and in what forms did they present this argument? Thirdly, why, and in what form, was the state (or those in charge of it at particular times) prepared to make concessions to these kinds of regionalist claims?

It is perhaps surprising that despite renewed academic, as well as political, interest in the regional dimension of politics in France, and despite the appearance in the last decade or more of numerous studies of the post-war period dealing not only with the role of regional and local elites, but also with intra- and inter-regional relations and with the specific phenomenon of regionalism, those questions have not been directly addressed in the literature.[5] It is the argument of this chapter that the reason for this lies in the prevalence in this literature of what is essentially a geographical mode of conceptualisation. In part this may reflect the fact that a territorial principle of representation is, as has been previously noted, institutionalised in France and her neighbouring states: the claims for regional representation may thus be seen merely as an extension of this principle, and the existence of separate regional interests accepted as a fact which does not require direct investigation. Much more specific-ally, legitimate concern with the high degree of centralisation of the French state has in recent years, it is argued here, become entangled with a particular conceptual approach focusing on 'centre-periphery' relations. This conceptual approach appears to have established a pervasive presence in the literature on regional and local elites, even in works which seek primarily to pursue other, quite different, theoretical concerns.

This chapter will therefore seek to explore the implications of this mode of conceptualisation by investigating its influences in a number of contrasting studies of regional elites, including the work of J.-P. Worms and P. Grémion, notably the latter's *Le Pouvoir périphérique: Bureaucrates et notables dans le système politique français* (Paris, 1976); R. Lafont's *La Révolution régionaliste* (Paris, 1967), and R. Dulong's *La Question Bretonne* (Paris, 1975).[6] The chapter will then examine, by way of a case study, the emergence and activities of one such regional elite grouping in post-war Brittany.

Centre-periphery relations and France's regional elites

The approach adopted here is not intended to minimise the important contrasts of interpretation that are offered in these works. On the one hand, what may be termed 'revisionist' writing on *'le phénomène notabiliaire'* has been concerned with identifying the degree of mutuality of interest, and the degree of mutual constraint, which has developed historically between local elites and local agents of the central state (J.-P. Worms, 1966; P. Grémion, 1966); works of this kind have served to underline the *'pieds d'argile'* of the centralised state machine, its dependence on elites at the periphery for the successful implementation of its policy initiatives and their capacity for resistance (Grémion and Worms, 1967; Grémion, 1976).

In contrast, studies like Lafont's, elaborated within the framework of the internal colonialism model, have effectively taken up and reformulated the contention that France's centralised state does indeed enjoy the capacity to impose its own chosen (and inimical) pattern of development on the diversity of regional interests present in France, not least through its predominant role in disseminating an exclusively nationalist (i.e. French) political culture which actors — elite and otherwise — within these regions internalise, a process which Lafont, in particular, identifies as the crucial component of internal colonialism (Lafont, 1967). Dulong, working within an Althusserian framework, has mapped out a third and quite distinctive position in his study of Brittany (Dulong, 1975). Like Grémion and Worms, Dulong also has characterised the role of the elite of the periphery in terms of resistance, but for him Brittany's political notables until the mid-1960s should primarily be understood as leading a sustained, but ultimately unsuccessful, defensive action against the restructuring of the regional economy by externally located forces of monopoly capitalism.

Despite these contrasts of interpretation, each of these studies is nevertheless informed by a mode of conceptualisation whose two major analytic categories are characterised essentially in terms of their geographical separation. For the purposes of this chapter the generic terms 'centre' and 'periphery' will be used to refer to these two categories, although, as will be discussed more fully below, each study adopts its own particular conceptual vocabulary, and there are notable differences between these. However, the argument being pursued here is that a similar conceptualisation, one that is in a fundamental sense based on a geographical approach, is present in each of these studies. The more important implications of this mode of conceptualism would seem to be three-fold.

In the first place, local and regional political notables are in each case firmly located in and of local and regional societies; that is, the particular patterns of socio-economic groupings present in a given locality are assumed to constitute a specific entity — local or regional society — whose interests the political elite represent more, or less, effectively. Secondly the centre is located 'elsewhere'; that is, there is a corresponding, inherent tendency in this approach to define the centre negatively, in terms of its exteriority to the historically concrete local societies which constitute the periphery. As a consequence it is not possible to develop from these concepts a rigorous and systematic treatment of the relationship of the French state to French society. Finally, what this conceptual approach identifies as crucial to understanding the role of regional elites is the relationship between these two referants — 'centre' and 'periphery'.

This chapter, however, contends that these basic conceptual categories are unsatisfactory; that the role of the regional elites can be more effectively treated in terms of a different problematic, one focusing on the relationship between state and national social formation; and that in consequence, a number of the more significant insights contained in these works are not adequately explored and developed because they sit uneasily with the conceptual framework employed.

In the case of Grémion and Worms their research strategy specifically privileges reference to this geographical dimension at the expense of any wider framework of identity and behaviour that may be relevant to the social actors they study, for they set out to investigate responses to the territorial re-organisation of certain state agencies, rather than, for example, responses to a particular economic or political strategy which it may be possible to identify as informing that territorial re-organisation. It is not possible to judge whether such inter- and intra-regional differences as are revealed are sufficient to invalidate analysis in terms of national socio-economic groupings or whether what are dealt with as specifically local phenomena could fruitfully be subsumed within an alternative — non-geographical — framework of analysis.

Grémion and Worms's work has the considerable merit of explicitly acknowledging the priorities implicit in their research strategy. As Grémion (1976) notes:

> la théorie du pouvoir local que nous présentons est une théorie organisationnelle du pouvoir . . . elle privilégie les stratégies d'acteur au détriment des structures sociales.[7]

The centre in their work is therefore conceived in essentially organisational terms, as the centralised institutions of the state (located in Paris). In their case, adoption of this conceptual vocabulary seems to correspond to a deep-seated belief that the state is indeed located outside of society. In a further elaboration of their conception of the state's externality to the social order Grémion has argued that within the French state one component, the Ministry of Finance, exercises an overall regulative function, embodying *'une logique bureaucratique pure'* which ensures the state administration's coherence and unity in face of the diversity of competing interests in society seeking to influence it.[8] Thus while in their studies both the state's externality to French society and also its internal coherence are never presented in simplistic fashion — Grémion in particular developing a discussion of the mutual interiorisation of values between state agencies and their client groupings in French society (in Crozier, 1974; see also Grémion and Worms, 1967; Grémion, 1976) — the sophistication and subtlety of much of their work seems nevertheless to be circumscribed by their adoption of a research strategy which relegates questions concerning the character of France's contemporary social order and its relationship to the state from the centre of their enquiry.

As regards the emergence of a regional elite, one consciously seeking to create a regional consensus, they do however demonstrate that this is associated, in the first place, with particular interests and elites who are favoured, because of their geographical location in the regional prefect's department, with better access to the centre as a result of the regional reforms; and secondly with the existence of a sense of their own past failure among interests and elites, not locationally favoured in this way, who thereby attach greater credibility to the promise of economic modernisation offered by a regional strategy.

Much of Grémion and Worms's work, it is true, is concerned with the argument that to a considerable degree the role of local and regional elites in general, and of political notables in particular, is determined by their relationship to the state, but their study (1967), develops this argument primarily in terms of elucidating the strategies which these actors pursue in response to the organisationally structured context which the state provides. Their subsequent analysis (1974) of the process of mutual interiorisation of *'rationalités d'attribution'* between state agencies and their client groupings in society is incorporated by Grémion (1976) in the form of a discussion centering on the extent to which these elites who enjoy officially representative status do so in forms and through processes controlled by the state, this latter therefore in part determining the modes of representation and legitimation which they adopt. The role of such elites, Grémion argues, is therefore not so much to articulate or aggregate specific interests in society, as to synthesise such interest articulation into political forms that are consistent with the state's *'rationalité'*.

However, this account of relations operating until the '60s is largely deduced back from the problems encountered by the 1964 reforms; no empirical investigation is offered of the specific content of the state's *'rationalité'* in different historical periods; rather the picture presented is one of overall historical continuity for almost a century prior to these reforms.

The forms in which regional elites were already operating in the 1950s, before the state recognised these units for consultative purposes, is not an issue of any particular importance for them; neither indeed is the question of whether these elites' activities contributed to the decision to introduce the 1964 reforms: rather these reforms, whose subsequent implementation is portrayed as an historical watershed leading from a balance of power between centre and periphery embodied in the role of the local political notable to a new pattern of corporatist politics, are presented unambiguously as an initiative of the 'centre', and one that failed.

Lafont's rather different methodology involves the constant reassertion of the existence in France of *'cet être collectif spontané, la région'* — regions that are distinct entities with their own specific regional interests.[9] These are treated as though constituting separate social and economic (but not, as yet, political) formations from the centre, but nowhere does he adduce substantive social and economic data to validate this claim. These regions are counterposed to *'L'État centralisé autoritaire'*, and a major theme of his work concerns precisely the necessity of dealing with the state in terms of its overall role in the specific historical context of the rise and consolidation of industrial capitalism in France. However the geographical mode of conceptualisation, so fundamental to his internal colonialism model, appears to militate against a clear and consistent analysis of the state's role. For Lafont the 'centre' is composed of an alliance between state institutions and dominant socio-economic forces, but it is an *a priori* assumption of his work that these latter can be characterised in terms of their geographical location: the French state therefore serves *'le capitalisme parisien'*. In places he seems diffident about the validity of isolating specifically 'Parisian' capital in this way, introducing a less exclusive, but still geographically-based, formula: *'le capitalisme parisien et ses relais du Nord, de l'Est et lyonnais'*, but this bears with it the danger of dissolving France's regions into a single national social formation; elsewhere the social structure of capitalism is itself dissolved instead into the natural landscape of France, and the state is deemed to serve the interests of *'le bassin parisien'*.[10] His account thus turns on social geography rather than social class.

For Lafont, however, France's regional economic and political leaders have traditionally acted unwittingly on the basis of values that are hostile to their own interests precisely because they have interiorised the values inculcated by the powerful and highly centralised machinery of the French state and its *'politique de centralisation culturelle'*. As a result *'les régionaux eux-mêmes . . . formés à la mentalité centraliste . . . ne peuvent concevoir la défense de leur région'*.[11] The actions of these regional elites, and most especially of the regional bourgeoisies, are thus in his account fundamentally irrational. That they too could in any sense be the beneficiaries of the state's role in sustaining a particular social order is *a priori* excluded; their role can therefore only be accounted for by resort to the special terminology of *'servilité'*, *'duperie'*, *'trahison'* and *'folie'*.

For Dulong the geographical mode of conceptualisation of 'centre' and 'periphery' takes the form of counterposing Brittany's precapitalist social formation to the external, and dominant, economic forces of monopoly capitalism. In effect, this mode of conceptualisation is pursued to its logical conclusion in his work, with the characterisation of Brittany as constituting a separate social and economic formation from that of France, for he contends that Brittany in 1945 formed *'un îlot précapitaliste dans le stade du capitalisme libéral . . . une structure à dominante précapitaliste . . . confrontée à l'ensemble (de la France)'*.[12] Dulong thus attempts to offer an explicit basis for marrying the concept of 'periphery' with the Marxist categories of social class and mode of production. Although his general theoretical stance certainly prioritises the investigation of socio-economic forces, it does so in a quite particular form which does not require direct analysis of the state itself. Developments in the political arena and the role of the state are both curiously marginalised by what is presented as an inevitable progression of stages of capitalism, a progression which eventuates in the transformation of productive processes and is characterised above all by the sequential predominance and elimination of successive hegemonic fractions of capital. In this scheme the state as a crucial conceptual category is all but redundant.

In spite of numerous insights into the three dimensions which he distinguishes within the regionalist movement in Brittany, into the themes these have promoted and into the conflicting interests which have assumed a regional guise, Dulong's analysis is constricted by his understanding of the region as a distinctive social formation. The regional political elite's role is fundamentally characterised in relation to this latter. The leads him to treat Brittany's regional elite and its economic regionalist ideology in isolation from similar developments elsewhere in France for which the precapitalist characterisation would be even less appropriate. Moreover, while the political notables are presented as distanced from those they claim to represent, nevertheless in seeking to preserve their own status and role they are inevitably involved in furthering regional resistance to integration with France's modern capitalist economy; and, at least until the late 1960s, in taking up and articulating this resistance their role is characterised by their relationship to specific classes rather than to the state:

> à la fois délégués de la paysannerie pour défendre ses intérêts politiques dans les instances de l'État et instrument de domination de cette paysannerie pour la bourgeoisie industrielle.[13]

In Dulong's account the crucial relationship is the confrontation between two sets of economic forces, those of a precapitalist social formation and those of monopoly capitalism, a confrontation in which the state's role is not of central importance:

> le mouvement breton pose son problème au dehors du lieu où s'exerce la contradiction principale (i.e., between capital and labour) que tente de régler l'existence de l'État.[14]

It is only from the late 1960s, when this struggle has been lost and the regional political elite has been decisively re-aligned with the dominant forces of French capitalism (with the emergence at the forefront of the regional stage of political actors who can be characterised by Dulong as belonging, personally, to the 'techno-Bourgeoisie') that the regional elite's relationship to the state becomes a salient feature of their role:

le CELIB était tenu de taire le contenu novateur de sa demande et finalement de la remplacer par le contenu idéologique de la bourgeoisie détenant les appareils de l'État . . . le CELIB devenait instrument de domination'.[15]

The case of 'Le Comité d'Étude et de Liason des Intérêts Bretons' (CELIB) in post-war Brittany

Where the approach of these writers presents the role of regional elites as Janus-headed, relating on the one side to specific regional interests and on the other to the centre, the alternative approach adopted here situates regional, along with other, elites at the interface between the state and conflicting interests (primarily of a socio-economic kind) in French society — as occupying a privileged role in renewing and sustaining the negotiated social order. From this perspective the two faces requiring consideration — and whose range of historical variation would be the subject of empirical investigation — would be, on the one side, the extent to which the elite is representative of and responsive to those it claims to represent, and on the other side, the ways in which the state is able to influence the forms of representation which these elites undertake, including the forms in which they seek to legitimate their role of representation. In the case of regional political elites, their role would specifically involve responding to problems, grievances and opportunities in given localities and would to a degree involve translating these into claims on the nation-state that are mediated by a form of regionalist ideology (i.e., drawing on an argument concerning the significance of some kind of regional identity of interests). In their case, we would face a double task: of attempting to identify what particular interests they respond to and seek to represent in a given period, and how they feed these, as regional claims, into the process of producing a re-negotiated social order; and of exploring their relationship to the state and to the collective goals and values which it promotes, a task that would involve sensitivity to what Steven Lukes has termed the third dimension of power.[16]

An investigation of the emergence and successful establishment of a regional elite grouping in Brittany in the post-war period, would therefore involve examining three interlinked processes: firstly the range of problems, grievances and opportunities that have arisen within the specific configuration of social classes present in this region; secondly, the way in which regional political actors have articulated these in the form of specifically *regional* claims on the state; and thirdly, the general features characterising the state's role in this period and the ways in which these may have influenced the activities of this regional elite. To employ a spatial metaphor, their role would be assessed in terms of their relative responsiveness to pressures from 'below' and from 'above'.

The concern of this chapter has been most particularly with the limited treatment accorded to this latter dimension of their role. It is therefore with the relationship of Brittany's post-war regional political elite to the French state that the following case study will be primarily concerned, that is with the second and third of the interlinked processes noted above. Moreover, a preliminary survey of the origins of the regional interest group, Le Comité d'Étude et de Liaison des Intérêts Bretons, which provided the organisational focus for this regional elite, suggests, moreover, that a further distinction should be incorporated in the second of these processes, distinguishing among the new regional political actors of this period: between, on the one hand, those arguing a 'regionalist' case who did not already enjoy elite status of some kind in the four departments which were later to be recognised as the region of Brittany; and, on the other, established political notables who at some point sought to restructure the basis of their representative role and establish a correspondingly new form of legitimacy around the idea of the region's unity, of a shared regional interest.

In the early post-war years the particular form of regionalism that came to be identified with CELIB was most consistently argued from the first category of activists. But the key to a *successful* regional political elite establishing itself and winning a considerable echo in public opinion and some recognition from the state, as representing such a *regional* interest, was the subsequent massive adherence of established political notables. In the last years of the 1940s, two individuals in particular contributed to winning recognition among limited circles of opinion for arguments that were to become the main platform of the region's political elite, arguments which primarily identified the region's shared interest in economic terms. One of these, Joseph Martray, had belonged to Vichy Brittany's regional political elite, as a member of the *Conseil Consultatif de la Bretagne*, the only regional body of its kind under the Vichy régime.[17] The composition of this committee had itself testified to the strength of Breton sentiment in the war period, a sentiment focused largely on cultural questions. This tradition of cultural defence, and also that other strand of political separation represented by the *Parti Nationaliste Breton* since 1932, was ruptured in the Liberation period, with widespread purging of nationalists and the repression of some leaders of the cultural movement: developments which may in turn have enhanced the attractions of new arguments focusing on the region's demographic decline and peripheral geographic situation, and presented in the 'apolitical' vocabulary of regional economic solidarity.

Martray himself still enjoyed a certain influence as a journalist, and extensive contacts, at the national and also international levels, as a fervent regionalist. His belief in the reality of Brittany as a culturally distinct entity led him in this period to involvement not only in the European Federalist movement, but also with the issue of winning more extensive democratic rights for local government in France. This latter movement, too, had antecedent influences, in the *Fédération Régionaliste Française*'s campaigns for administrative reform under the previous Republic.[18] However under the impact of the Liberation period, and also, surely, of the process of economic reconstruction underway under the aegis of a national plan, he increasingly translated the whole issue of regional aspirations into an argument about the urgency and desirability of economic modernisation, but his initial attempt to establish a regional committee on these lines met with only a fragmented response from among the region's established political and economic notables.

At the same time a wider range of business opinion in the region began to be exposed to similar arguments developed by an academic at the University of Rennes, Michel Phlipponneau, in a series of articles arguing for large scale, selective and planned investment in the region, published in *La Bretagne Industrielle et Commerciale*, the organ of the regional Chamber of Industry and Commerce. An economic geographer, not of Breton origin himself, M. Phlipponneau at this time was essentially a believer in the rational utilisation of economic resources, much influenced by certain examples of planned economic development in Britain and Denmark, and concerned by the backwardness and poverty of the region in which he now worked.

What seems clear at this point is the extent to which the specific form in which Brittany's regional identity was now being portrayed was influenced by the new practice and claims of national economic planning. This nascent economic regionalism, a decisive development for the later emergence of a specifically regional political elite in Brittany, cannot be properly understood if analysis is confined to the region itself: concentration on the economic backwardness of the four departments, posed now as a specifically *regional* problem, indeed as providing the basis for their unity as a region, was in large measure a response to fundamental changes in the national economic context, to the expectations generated at the national level by the break with the French state's previous politics of economic Malthusianism which suggested that the way forward for

Brittany, as for the French national economy, was systematically to pursue a strategy of economic modernisation. Moreover, in this respect developments in Brittany in the late '40s and early '50s were by no means unique but formed part of a wider movement of economic regionalism underway in various localities and regions and which gave rise in 1952 to the founding of *La Conférence Nationale des Economies Régionales.*[19]

In Brittany, however, the tentative and limited character of this movement was to be dramatically transformed in 1950 by the entry onto the regional scene of a whole number of established politicians based in the four departments. These were to take over the themes already being separately developed by Martray and Phlipponneau. Before examining their activities, some attention must be paid to the circumstances in which such political figures at this point become exponents of the region's unity, and sought to redefine their own role in terms of representing the region's shared economic interests. It is worth noting, in the first place, that those four departments under the Third Republic had been the terrain *par excellence* of the politics of the French centre and right, revolving around the figure of the locally based political notable (although in traditionally radical voting areas in the Breton-speaking western parts of Côtes-du-Nord, Morbihan and the coast of South Finistère both the SFIO and more recently the PCF had established a different pattern of organised party politics). With the establishment of the Fourth Republic this pattern of political activity had been disrupted not only because a good part of the traditional political notables were in discredit following from their association with Vichy, but also because the introduction of an electoral system based on party lists at the departmental level required locally based politicians at the least to acquire a somewhat different identity within a departmental political alliance.

However by 1950 the shift that had taken place in the regime's political centre of gravity since 1947 — when the search began for Third Force alliances at the national level to replace *Tripartisme* — posed special problems for the legislative elections due in the following year. The electoral system was amended, but at the local level the longstanding political division between *'laïcs'* and *'cléricaux'* made it difficult for the political groupings now forced to work together in government to organise joint lists in an attempt to limit the number of seats won by parties wholly opposed to the regime. It was in this context that the themes of economic regionalism, hitherto taken up by a few more or less isolated propagandists, were suddenly metamorphosed into the platform of a vocal and powerful elite grouping. A series of meetings, initially concerned with

La Fédération's national campaign for strengthening local government, and culminating in a banquet held in Paris in May 1950, brought together an impressive array of political and economic notables from the four departments and also Loire-Atlantique, to debate the region's economic, administrative and cultural problems.

Martray's most notable political recruits at this stage were the leading SFIO and MRP deputies from the region, Tanguy-Prigent and Paul Ihuel. CELIB was now successfully relaunched with the task of assembling and co-ordinating information and expertise to mobilise elite opinion – and through them a wider public – and it was the specifically economic dimension of the region's problems that soon came to predominate in the new organisation's activities. Although there was only one Third Force alliance list presented in the four departments, that headed by R. Pleven in Côtes-du-Nord, bringing together UDSR, SFIO and MRP, a programme of regional action submitted by CELIB to all candidates standing in the four departments was signed by every candidate except those of the PCF, and CELIB's theme of regional unity thus served to defuse party divisions in the electoral period in an area where the religious division made joint action between politicians from left to right-of-centre particularly difficult. It was in this context that economic regionalism with its 'apolitical' and conciliatory aspirations came to the fore in Brittany.

At this point René Pleven, Prime Minister from July 1950 to March 1951, former Minister of Finance in de Gaulle's Provisional Government, and President of the UDSR – one of the pivotal components of any governmental majority in this period – became involved in CELIB. When in July 1951 Martray had his first meeting with Pleven in his office at the Ministry of Defence, Pleven was clearly attracted by the possibility of reorganising the established politicians of the area as a specifically regional political elite: 'L'idée de réaliser en Bretagne et autour de nos problèmes une entente entre tous les élus, cette idée le séduisait'.[20] Within a month Pleven was again Prime Minister and had been elected CELIB's first president at its General Assembly, a post he was to retain for the next twenty years.

The conversion of such a leading national figure as Pleven was of major importance in establishing the credibility of political action at the regional level, but here too analysis would be distorted by a narrowly regional focus, for it was the national political context which was decisive in the adoption of this theme of a regional unity of economic interests by established politicians both here in Brittany and elsewhere. This restructuring of their political role, however, outlived the particular circumstances of this electoral period.

France now witnessed the consolidation of the most vocal and highly publicised regional political lobby of the post-1945 period, a grouping for which CELIB's 'Commission des Élus' provided the main organisational forum. From November 1951 to June 1970 they held a total of 172 meetings, but their heyday was under the second legislature of the Fourth Republic. Governments dependent on shifting and insecure majorities were particularly vulnerable to determined lobbying, and Brittany's political representatives belonged for the most part to the undisciplined groupings of the centre and right — although some SFIO parliamentarians played a prominent role. In this period it regularly assembled virtually all the deputies and senators of the five departments once a month in a committee room of the Palais Bourbon. Its chairmanship circulated periodically, for Brittany's new regional political elite recognised that 'il était indispensable de confier à un élu de la majorité, quelle qu'elle soit, la tâche de parler au nom de l'ensemble de ses collègues.'[21]

Martray's highly idealised account of their meetings, published in 1970, is worth recording, underlining as it does the essentially economic character of their perception of the region's shared identity of interest:

Chaque séance se déroulait autour d'un ordre du jour précis, technique, avec un rapporteur qui était généralement le secrétaire général du CELIB, lui-même en étroite liaison avec les collectivités et organismes économiques de la région. La commission procédait ensuite à l'audition de hauts-fonctionnaires ou de chefs de grands services nationaux qui ne savaient très bien devant quelle instance parlementaire il se trouvaient convoqués mais qui gardaient ensuite l'impression d'avoir comparu devant un pouvoir régional singulièrement efficace. Chaque réunion se terminait de manière identique: le jour même, ou au plus tard 24 heures après, une délégation se rendait chez le ministre dont dépendait l'affaire évoquée. Il faut avoir connu l'étonnement de ces ministres lorsqu'ils voyaient entrer dans leur cabinet quinze ou vingt parle-mentaires appartenant à tous les groupes de l'Assemblée Nationale et du Sénat et réclamant d'une même voix pour la Bretagne, à partir d'une documentation solide, la même mesure avec décision immédiate! Le lendemain matin *L'Ouest-France* pouvait presque toujours annoncer aux Bretons que leurs parlementaires avaient enfin obtenu autre chose que l'habituelle 'lettre d'attente', mais tels crédits, tels investissements, telles décisions essentielles pour l'économie régionale.[22]

Several regional and national factors served to make their continuing action more viable in this period than it might otherwise have been. In the first place, as has been noted, the Fourth Republic's assembly-based regime and, in this period, the search for governmental majorities con-structed around France's divided political centre, made a substantial parliamentary lobby of this kind particularly effective. Their successes helped establish, among organised interests and a wider public, the credentials of their claim to be defenders of 'the region', at the same time the concessions granted to this political lobby amounted to *de facto* recognition by successive French governments of the existence of specific interests at the regional level in Brittany, and of the legitimacy of their claims to represent these interests. Moreover there can be no doubt that the backwardness characteristic of so much industrial pro-duction located in the four departments and the problems they faced in holding their markets as the restructuring of France's national economy proceeded, together with the particular difficulties experienced by so many of Brittany's small polycultural family farms in this period, made for a continually renewed supply of claims for special treatment, claims well suited to the piecemeal lobbying which the regional elite could undertake.

However to reduce the role of this regional elite to what Martray portrays as the traditional lobbying of the Third Republic local political notable — now transferred for greater effectiveness to the regional level and marked, of course, by *'une documentation solide'* — is to view it primarily as a reflection of the region's socio-economic structure, the logic of this approach being to stress its backward-looking and defensive character, or even, as Dulong does, to interpret their activities primarily in terms of resistance to change.

For beyond the winning of piecemeal and temporary concessions, and quite crucial for a general assessment of these groupings as a specifically regional elite, was the nature of the dominant themes which they con-stantly reiterated in this period. These provided a quite different content to their relationship to organised interests in Brittany, and a different basis for ultimately winning official recognition (from the Mendès-France government in December 1954) of the need for properly constituted consultative bodies at the regional level in France. These themes focused above all on the necessity and desirability of initiating a process of economic modernisation for the region as a whole; indeed this was increas-ingly identified as *the* common interest uniting the region and which, despite protests and indignation about existing patterns of state expendi-ture and population movement, suggested that the region's interest lay in its *more* thorough integration with the national economy.

The analysis of economic regionalism presented earlier pointed to a causal linkage operating downwards from the state, spreading the new ethos of modernisation. What gave coherence to this and other regional elites in this period was the expectation raised by the new mode of state intervention in the economy that available resources should and could now be rationally developed. In their turn, Brittany's regional elite acted to influence both the way in which the organisations affiliated to CELIB interpreted their experience in this period, and through this their behaviour. This is not to discount CELIB's role in the upward articulation of interests and demands. Nor is it to deny that many specific measures that they supported were purely protective in character. But in assessing the regional elite's role as an intermediary between the state and the organised interests located in Brittany, the argument here is that their primary historical function was as agents of modernisation within the region.

Their tone throughout was primarily an optimistic one. What they preached was the possibility of the region winning 'modernisation on its own terms', that is, a process adapted to the region's particular configuration of resources and skills, and benefitting its inhabitants. More specifically, they rapidly became involved in encouraging the affiliated organisations of CELIB to reorient their activities in line with the national modernisation effort, and to reformulate their demands on the state within such a perspective. This role was to find its clearest expression in the work of preparing a regional plan, but from its earliest days CELIB's persistent emphasis on expertise, the importance it assigned to compiling detailed technical dossiers, were symptomatic of its efforts in this direction. And the earliest study groups of CELIB, established to work out policy priorities for individual sectors, introduced a particularly crucial mechanism, for in these representatives of relevant professional organisations worked together with local officials of the appropriate state administration — mirroring the procedures which at the national level had already been established — embodying the ideal of *'une économie concertée'*.

The regional elite thus remained firmly located within the wider movement of economic regionalism in France and within one year of the 1951 elections they found themselves embarking with CELIB on a most ambitious and quite unparalleled project, the elaboration of a regional plan for Brittany. This initiative itself reflects the degree to which the modernising ethos of the French state in this period had permeated French society; Brittany's regional elite thus found themselves absorbed into, and in turn contributing to, the *économie concertée*'s climate of economic rationality. The real sense of grievance that served to stimulate a new awareness of local identity within the movement of economic regionalism seems thus to have been subsumed within the promise of modernisation within this movement. The unsettling process of post-war economic restructuring served as a catalyst, for the most part, for a sense of identity operating at a quite localised level. In the case of Brittany, and equally of Alsace-Lorraine, larger regional identities were involved, drawing on distinctive patterns of history and culture; but here too what emerged were two of the earliest and strongest examples of economic regionalist organisation and not, at this stage, neo-nationalist politics. The affirmation that all local and sectional interests could be reconciled at a regional level was, it seems, easily projected on to the national level and translated into a voluntarist faith in the possibility of an harmonious inter-regional development, breaking with the existing patterns of inequality.

The idea of an economic plan for Brittany had first been advocated by M. Phlipponneau at the end of 1951 in an article in *La Bretagne Industrielle et Commerciale* which was subsequently reprinted in February 1952 in *La Vie Bretonne*, the monthly journal owned by Joseph Martray which was closely associated with the activities of CELIB and its supporters. At this period several industries in the region, notably food-canners and the Forges d'Hennebont, were developing proposals for governmental aid for modernisation programmes. But it was the project of another industry in the region, that processing iodine from seaweed, which led the Commission des Élus to establish its first contact with the Commissariat Général au Plan and arrange for a delegation of the latter's staff to visit the region. And it was following their visit that CELIB took up the idea of elaborating a regional plan for Brittany. Phlipponneau now became involved in CELIB and was to be responsible for the final drafting of the *Rapport d'ensemble sur un plan d'aménagement, de modernisation et d'équipement de la Bretagne, 1954–1958* (the *Rapport Vert*).

One hundred and fifty representatives of affiliated professional organisations, local councils and the four departmental councils, as well as thirty members of the National Assembly and Senate, attended the General Assembly of CELIB at Vannes in June 1952 where the decision was taken to draw up a 'Plan Breton'. Strenuous efforts were made to gain official status for the enterprise and were partially successful. The working parties established from October 1952 were able to utilise documentation from a wide range of governmental departments and public sector enterprises, and prominent members of the regional staff of both these types of body acted as rapporteurs for many of the thirty-four separate sector reports that were prepared. But while the Commissariat Général du Plan was prepared to intervene in order to exert its influence over the plan's content, it ensured that the whole project remained an unofficial undertaking. Pleven explained to CELIB's 'États-Généraux de St Brieuc' in

March 1953, where the results of all this activity were presented to four hundred delegates from affiliated organisations, that 'le CELIB a reçu la mission non pas d'élaborer lui-même un plan, mais d'en provoquer l'élaboration';[23] but in the absence of an official sponsor the regional plan remained CELIB's own responsibility. The rapporteurs for the separate sector reports were invited to present progress reports to leading members of the CGP and the Délégation Général à l'Aménagement du Territoire at a series of meetings held at the CGP's headquarters in early 1953. Robert Hirsch, the Planning Commissioner, attended the St Brieuc meeting in person and (together with the head of DGAT) was a *'membre de droit'* of the Commission Ihuel which met after St Brieuc to synthesise the sector reports.

For the CGP at this point in the development of national planning in France, the incorporation of a regional dimension presented certain advantages, but obvious dangers too. For this constituted a logical development for the national plan, one that had been recognised by the CGP as early as 1946 in its 'Rapport Général'. Moreover, in the aftermath of the breakdown of the political consensus which had initially underpinned the national plan, these regional pressure groups with their themes of national resource development and their strategic position of influence around the centre of France's party political spectrum, did also offer a certain potential for legitimising and promoting the systematic pursuit of economic modernisation. However the operation of the *'économie concertée'* had increasingly become subordinated in practice to the need to restructure French capital on an internationally competitive basis, and the exclusion of electorally important but economically marginal sectors, like those in Brittany, from the planning process, and the relative autonomy from parliamentary politics which this had hitherto enjoyed, had been crucial to the pursuit of that objective.

In seeking the representation of declining and backward regions within the planning process CELIB and its sister organisations now challenged the French planners to control the new pattern of regional inequalities which had developed within the *'économie concertée'*. The planners themselves were sensitive to the high 'hidden' economic costs entailed by concentration of growth in limited areas, most particularly around Paris, but they could not easily act to contain either the economic or political problems which the process of capital restructuring was generating, even though these posed a challenge to their claim to be able to discipline the operation of capitalism in France to a longer-term general interest.[24] Rather the changed conditions of the early '50s combined to cast uncertainty over the status of the national plan and to introduce a new note of caution into proceedings at the Planning Commissariat.

Brittany's regional elite had to reconcile themselves to their failure to win any official commitment to implement the 'Plan Breton' at this stage but the elaboration of this plan had clarified their role in the region and consolidated their linkages with the state's strategy of capital restructuring in France. As intermediaries between the state and organised interests in Brittany, the regional elite acted not only as carriers of the state's dominant ideological themes concerning the necessity and desirability of 'modernisation' but had more specifically taken on the task of propagandising in the region for the specific forms of economic restructuring which the national planners were pursuing.

In the most general terms this involved the regional elite in promoting a decisive shift in the climate of opinion in Brittany. They themselves had become convinced of this necessity, and that without it no amount of government funds could effect a solution to the problems of the region: 'c'est l'opinion bretonne qu'il s'agit de convaincre et d'entraîner.'[25] In similar fashion to the national plan, the Breton plan's elaboration rapidly developed in a large-scale educational exercise for the region. At its apex were the working parties which brought together representatives of professional organisations with appropriate technical and state experts, the results of their collaboration then being subjected to the scrutiny of officials of the CGP. Like the Modernisation Commissions of the national plan, these favoured consensus-building and the acceptance of externally imposed constraints, filtering out demands judged 'unrealistic' on the prevailing wisdom. Beyond these working groups, the two large meetings held at Vannes and St. Brieuc in 1952-3 associated a broad cross-section of Brittany's political and economic notability with the new perspectives being elaborated for the region and their underlying ideological themes. These perspectives and themes moreover were now able to reach a far wider audience than hitherto, through the campaign which the region's leading daily paper *L'Ouest-France*, conducted in its columns in favour of 'le Plan Breton'.

Crucially, in Brittany, it was opinion in the agricultural sector that needed to be influenced, and it was in relation to this sector that the ambiguity of the regional elite's intermediary position between the state and the region was to be most clearly revealed, as was the elusive nature of its quest for a specifically Breton path to modernisation. For the plan was not, fundamentally, an extrapolation from the demands currently being raised within the region, but was undertaken specifically within the framework provided by the Second National Plan. The attitudes entrenched among Brittany's farming organisations embodied a philosophy radically opposed to that informing the national plan — epitomised by

Jean Meynaud as 'the habit of regarding the state as a universal insurance fund which operates without collecting premiums'. Confrontation between these two views, already present at earlier meetings, dominated the first plenary session of the agricultural commission at Quimper in October 1952, when it became clear that not only the representatives of the farmers own organisations but also departmental officials of the Ministry of Agriculture were committed to a strategy of maximising state support for the agricultural community, through social investments in the countryside, whereas representatives of the CGP, and other experts influenced by its brand of economic rationality, notably M. Phlipponneau, argued for priority to be accorded to measures that would directly stimulate production.

The confrontation posed an embarrassing challenge to CELIB's leadership. *La Vie Bretonne* responded with an editorial entitled 'Limites d'un programme' asserting that modernisation in Brittany would not mean an end to the system of polyculture *'chère au cultivateur de Bretagne'*. More prudently, other leading figures sought to defuse the situation, first by proposing that decisions on costing and prioritising the proposals for agriculture be postponed until the St Brieuc meeting, and then, at St Brieuc, by arguing successfully that they be remitted to the 'Commission Ihuel'. Ultimately it was the wisdom of the CGP which prevailed. The leaders of Brittany's farmers were forced to face up to the implications of the economic strategy adopted nationally and to concede the need to adapt their own perspectives to it. And Martray's 'Avant-Propos' to the published plan acknowledged that 'il fallait rappeler aux Bretons leurs propres responsabilités dans le retard économique de leur province'.[26]

Thus the attempt, with the elaboration of the Breton Plan, to align the region onto the national economic perspectives embodied in the Second Plan, led to significant shifts in the terms in which the regional elite formulated Brittany's problems to its regional audience. And two aspects of this process were to prove of continuing importance to their role in the region. In the first place, the recognition that the Bretons themselves bore a part of the responsibility for their region's failure to modernise ensured that in this period when 'le CELIB incarna pour beaucoup la conscience régionale' the Bretons were not portrayed simply as victims of external forces — the implication being that the region's own efforts could contribute significantly to altering its fate. And indeed this conclusion was given considerable emphasis. At the same time Brittany's declining population was now isolated as the decisive feature of its predicament and one which could be expected to be further exacerbated since any attempt by the agricultural sector to secure its future and contribute to the national export effort would require a major effort to raise the level of labour productivity and thus would entail large-scale job losses. From this analysis the 'Plan Breton' developed a major new perspective for the region, arguing that the key to the region's future lay in the urgent provision of new employment opportunities, primarily in light industry, and primarily by the influx of new capital into the region.

One proposal included in the 'Plan Breton' had been taken up by the Mayer government and provided the basis for a new phase of vigorous campaigning by the regional elite within Brittany, bringing to the fore their argument that new employment, whatever the source, held the key to Brittany's future and that the region must be prepared to make some sacrifices in this cause. This proposal (which had originated with the Regional Chamber of Commerce and Industry), was that any new industrial enterprise establishing itself in the region should be liable to exemption from up to 50 per cent of the local tax, the *patente*, for a period of five years; this was incorporated in the Finance Bill of 7 February 1953. Within eighteen months CELIB's campaign had resulted in all four departmental councils and twenty-seven municipal authorities implementing the tax exemption.

By this time, as the implementation of the Second National Plan got under way, the establishment of the Mendès-France government in June 1954, committed to co-ordinate a broad range of policies in support of the planners' strategy of national economic expansion, finally provided the context for the regional elites of Brittany and other areas to win official recognition for themselves and for the contribution that a regional development perspective could make to this national effort. The Mendès-France government was the first to attempt to tackle the wider social and political implications of economic modernisation in France, proposing an ambitious 'programme d'équilibre financier, d'expansion économique et de progrès social' while at the same time seeking to insulate itself from the parliamentary lobbying strength of sectors which would be disadvantaged by the impact of modernisation by requesting decree powers from the National Assembly in order to put this programme into effect. But its programme did accept that the task of securing the participation of new layers of France's economy in the national modernisation effort could be promoted by functionally representative bodies at the local level with a consultative role within the planning process. It therefore proposed, as one of six measures designed to promote economic expansion, to institute 'une organisation régionale, départementale ou locale chargée de mettre au point le développement économique dans le cadre du Plan.' The corresponding decree 'relatif à l'institution de comités d'expansion économique et de commissions régionales de co-ordination' was published on 11 December 1954. Under its provisions recognition was to be extended to the existing organisations within the economic regionalist movement, with CELIB the first to be accorded consultative status in October 1955.[27]

This chapter has been primarily concerned with examining the ways in which regional elites in France since the Second World War have been influenced by certain national economic and political developments, and most particularly by specific aspects of the state's role. In contrast, it has been suggested, many recent studies of regional elites have, in spite of other contrasting theoretical concerns, been informed by an essentially geographical mode of conceptualisation which has constricted their investigation of this crucial dimension of their role.

In the case study of Brittany that has been presented here it has not been possible to deal in any detail with the other dimension of their role which requires investigation from within a problematic placing regional elites at the interface of state and interests in French society — the nature of the problems arising in Brittany. This case study has concentrated on discussing the circumstances in which established politicians in this region took up regionalist themes, the form that these themes took — that of economic regionalism — and the ways in which these linked Brittany's regional political elite into the state in this period. Through their role which they assumed as agents of a modernisation strategy initiated by the state, disseminating within a traditionalist and primarily rural area the modernising ideological climate of the *économie concertée*, Brittany's regional elite thus contributed to the two distinctive processes by which economic activities in this region have been restructured in the post-war period — the industrialisation of agriculture and the penetration of national, and indeed international, industrial capital.

Notes

1 In France the post-war establishment of national economic planning and the corresponding ideal of '*une economie concertée*' are of particular importance in this respect.

2 An explanation of the strength of this anti-party political tradition as an essentially rural political phenomenon influenced by a number of specific historical developments is offered in S. Tarrow, 'The urban-rural cleavage', *American Political Science Review* (1971).

3 Cf. K. Webb, *The Growth of Nationalism in Scotland*, revised edn (Harmondsworth, Middx, 1978).

4 See below, p. 226. On the pre-war regionalist movement, see in particular *Le Mouvement régionaliste français. Sources et documents* (Paris, 1966).

5 With the exception of Dulong's study, which does explicitly pursue the first two of these questions. His work is discussed below, pp. 223–225.

6 In addition to Grémion's study (Paris, 1976) reference will also be made below to their joint work, *Les Institutions régionales et la société locale: Rapport d'enquête* (Paris, 1968); to J. P. Worms, 'Le Prefet et ses notables', *Sociologie du Travail* (1966); P. Grémion, 'Résistance au changement de l'administration territoriale: le cas des institutions régionales', *Sociologie du Travail* (1966); and to P. Grémion, 'La Concertation', in M. Crozier (ed.), *Où va l'administration française?* (Paris, 1974).

7 *Le Pouvoir péripherique . . .*, p. 12.

8 'La Concertation', in M. Crozier, op. cit., p. 174.

9 *La Révolution régionaliste*, p. 41.

10 Ibid., p. 192.

11 Ibid., pp. 17 and 134.

12 *La Question Bretonne*, pp. 37–40, 70.

13 Ibid., p. 45.

14 Ibid., p. 203

15 Ibid., p. 205.

16 S. Lukes, *Power: A Radical View* (London, 1974), especially chs 3 and 4.

17 See Y. Gicquel, *Le Comité consultatif de Bretagne* (Rennes, 1961).

18 See n. 4 above; also P. Barral, 'Idéal et pratique du régionalisme dans le régime de Vichy', *Revue Française de Science Politique* (1974).

19 See J. Tessier, 'Les comités régionaux d'expansion économique et leur conférence nationale', *Revue Administrative* (1955).

20 J. Martray, *La Région: Pour un état moderne* (Paris, 1970), p. 57.

21 Ibid., p. 59.

22 Ibid., pp. 59–60.

23 *La Vie Bretonne,* no. 16 (June, 1953), p. 3.

24 See the special issue of *Revue Française de Science Politique*, vol. VI, no. 2 (April-June, 1956).

25 Cited in P. M. Williams, *Crisis and Compromise* (London, 1964), p. 375.

26 *Le Rapport Vert*, p. 8.

27 Assemblée Nationale, *Recueil des lois* (1954), p. 444 (loi numéro 54–809).

Analytical afterword
Towards a prosopography of elites in modern and contemporary France*

JEAN-MARIE MAYEUR
University of Paris IV

Although a specialist neither in the history of elites nor in the problems of prosopography, I became involved in the prosopography of elites when this subject was chosen by the CNRS as one of the major projects of the Institute for Modern and Contemporary History (IHMC), a special unit of the CNRS, for which I am responsible.

It is hardly surprising that such a task should be confided to an emerging research unit which aspires to serve the historical community as a centre for information and reflection on history and its methods and which aims to provide the working tools which are so sadly lacking at present. Indeed the constitution of a vast biographical body of knowledge is without doubt just the type of undertaking which is always talked about and never achieved, precisely because it is beyond the capacity and the means of a single individual or even a team. It is a lengthy task which can only be carried out collectively and whose materials will gradually be stocked cumulatively in a historical data bank.

In order to understand the nature of our project, it is essential to consider briefly what is meant by a prosopography of elites, to sketch the outlines of recent research into French elites and to underscore the problems which a prosopographical analysis can help resolve. In the following pages, I shall make use of a number of points made during the Round Table discussions at the IHMC on 23 October 1979.[1]

Definitions

Without becoming entangled in the problem of definitions, it is nevertheless essential to make one or two points about the notion of elites. There is little point in stressing the fact that the use of elites in the plural is regarded by the *Robert* dictionary as a neologism dating from 1954.

* Translated by Jolyon Howorth

In fact, the term, which derives from political sociology, from Mosca and Pareto to Max Weber and Raymond Aron, was used by essayists in the 1930s[2] and is now an integral part of the terminology of sociologists, political scientists and historians. It is one of the tools the historian uses, conscious of the limitations of vocabulary, to describe and understand the realities he encounters. It is true that seventeenth and eighteenth century historians, steeped in a society defined by the notion of order and rank, did not have recourse to the term. When, after the Revolution, a society emerged which was based on the theoretical principle of civil equality, terms like 'notables', 'social authorities', 'upper classes' and 'ruling classes' began to acquire currency. It is, of course, the groups – the social minorities – encompassed by these terms which must in the first place be classed as elites: 'people of the first rank in every field', according to the *Robert*.

What criteria for selection can we adopt? The question is basic to a project such as ours. Two main solutions are available. The first is to start with functions and institutions: lists of office-holders under the *ancien régime*, members of the civil or military state *corps*. And yet it is often the most obvious cases which are unreliable. The same function or the same title can, over the decades, lose its prestige: an *agrégé* at one of the Parisian *lycées* before 1914 must have ranked among the elite of the university; but it is difficult to say the same today. At a more generalised level, a diploma like the *baccalauréat*, 'a barrier and levelling device' in France at the turn of the century (10,000 *bacheliers* a year), no longer plays this role in 1981 with 160,000 *bacheliers* a year. Another point which suggests the limits of selection based on function and title is that such selection takes account of power in only one domain, one determined field, and does not take into consideration the 'social surface' which is precisely the characteristic of elites. The majority of the former students of ENA, wielders of power in the administrative hierarchy of their ministerial departments, are by no means destined to be part of the ruling class and to participate in economic and political power.

Finally, and this hardly needs stating, selection through function does not help to identify social and economic elites. In order to classify these categories, we must see them through the eyes of their contemporaries, through their historical image, identifying not only those whom the state honoured with the responsibility of office, but also those on whom it conferred honours and decorations – in other words those who were recognised by their peers and fellow-citizens as belonging to an elite. The definition which one historical period can give to elites does not always respond fully to social reality. We know that in the Empire and Restoration periods, elites were defined by property while intellectual ability or productive capacity was ignored. Saint-Simon, in the 'Parabola' (1819) draws an opposition between on the one hand the '3,000 principal scholars, artists and artisans in France' and, on the other, the '10,000 landowners living as noblemen, and the 80,000 individuals regarded as the most important in the state'. The historian is not called upon to choose between different elites but strives, through the application of various criteria, to embrace the totality of the elites – those of the past and those of the future, both coexisting, of course, at the same point in time. The last question is the most difficult: where does one draw the line? The cut-off point must of course differ according to the group or the period. But the upper echelons of the bourgeoisie and of the nobility must undoubtedly be included.

In the history of elites, prosopography offers a particularly useful approach. The term and the method were first used in Roman history: through the juxtaposition of individual biographical sketches it was possible to pinpoint the various families of the Roman *nobilitas*, and to trace their matrimonial alliances and political following.[3] Space does not allow us to consider what the prosopographical method has contributed to our knowledge of medieval and modern history. It is enough to note that prosopography is restricted neither to a purely genealogical type of research, nor to contributions to a biographical dictionary (which is usually no more than a collection of individual biographies selected more or less at random). The aim of prosopography is to create a working instrument, a reference tool at the service of different researchers, but also to describe elites in the light of political sociology. The aim, above all, is to retrace individual destinies in the context of family networks, interest groups, educational, religious and ideological solidarity. This approach allows emphasis on duration and diachrony, while avoiding the pitfalls of purely statistical studies of social groups. Prosopography allows us to integrate the individual and the event into social history.

Retrospective survey

It would be impossible to offer up a complete account of recent work on French elites, still less to draw up a bibliography.[4] I shall limit myself to sketching out the principal approaches, with more particular reference to prosopographical studies than to simple exercises in social history. Published work relating to the modern period has above all indexed the *corps* of crown officials, particularly in the eighteenth century. These *corps* had clear-cut boundaries and their members were relatively few in number. François Bluche, in his study of some 600 law officers in the Paris Parlement, has established their ascendancy and descendancy from 1715 to 1771; Michel Antoine, examining the members of the King's Privy Council, has, thanks to the meticulously kept ledgers of the Paris *notaires*, been able to examine marriage contracts, details of estates and inheritance. Civilian office-holders are better known than leading military personnel on whom documentation is scarcer, whose numbers are larger (more than one thousand). Anne Blanchard has provided detailed information on 1,500 military engineers. Apart from office holders, the upper clergy and the upper nobility have been the object of various studies. Much less is known about businessmen, contractors or traders. Little is known about municipal or cultural elites.

Since the IHMC's project concerned with both the modern and contemporary periods, and cuts across the revolutionary divide, I have allowed myself this brief glimpse into the early period. I am, however, more familiar with the contemporary period and will therefore spend more time looking at the examples it has to offer. At the outset, one has to stress yet again the value of the magnificent book by André Tudesq: *Les Grands notables en France, 1840–1849*. At the crossroads of the *ancien régime* and the new France born of the Revolution, a recent study by Louis Bergeron and Guy Chaussinand-Nogaret on the *notables* of the First Empire, is nearing completion.[5] They have chosen a particularly important period in which the regime was keen to inventory its elites which were a blending of the nobility and bourgeoisie of the *ancien régime* with the new bourgeoisie born of the Revolution. The authors' criteria of selection was based on three series of lists: the thirty leading tax-payers in each department, the 'sixty most distinguished landowners in terms of their private wealth and public and private qualities', and above all, the 'most noteworthy individuals' of the late Empire period. They have thus selected the 'most notable of the notables', about 6,000 or 7,000 individuals in a vast 'social biography' to whose approach and method the IHMC project is greatly indebted.[6]

The prefectoral documents used by L. Bergeron lead to an underrepresentation of commercial and industrial elites: wealth alone, in the eyes of the administration, was an inadequate criteria for belonging to the ranks of the 'most noteworthy individuals'. This attitude was not peculiar to the prefects; moreover it lasted throughout the century. The *Biographie Normande* by the *rouennais* Théodore Lebreton, in 1857, includes 'the most renowned names in the sciences, letters and the arts . . . the names of scholarly ecclesiastics, eminent magistrates and jurists, soldiers, sailors and navigators, and finally the names of promoters of progress in commerce and industry'.

The work of historians of the post-revolutionary period — as with the modern period (and for the same reason: the easy availability of sources) — is dominated by studies of state functionaries. The history of administrators is undergoing a revival;[7] witness the series of colloquia organised by the fourth section of the EPHE and the birth of the Association for the History of French Administration, which has given rise to histories of a number of the *grands corps*. The first volume was concerned with the *Conseil d'État*; another is to follow on the *Ingénieurs des Ponts et Chausées*. Mention must be made here of the seminal contribution of Guy Thuillier — *conseiller référendaire à la cour des Comptes*, and an infatigable historian. We must also draw attention to the fine work done by Vincent Wright on the *Conseil d'État* and the prefectoral system. Research is starting on the directors of the Finance Ministry and the Inspectorate of Finances. These studies of administrative history, without being systematically prosopographical in approach nevertheless contribute a great deal to the understanding of the administrative elites. The same could be said of studies of the university elite by Paul Gerbod, a pioneer in the field, or, more recently, by Victor Karady, whose knowledge of the upper spheres of the University since the end of the nineteenth century is exceptional. William Serman has recently shed light on the officials of the Second Empire. Political elites have, on the whole, been less scrutinised, despite the recent thesis by Jean Estèbe on the ministers of the Third Republic. Jolly's *Dictionnaire des Parlementaires* is poor in indications of social origins and private wealth. Above all the major approaches of economic history — prices and growth — seem for a long time to have distracted attention away from the personality of bankers, industrialists and big businessmen.

Moving from the national to the regional dimension, which is a favourite concern of French historiography, one is struck by the limited number of studies of local elites.[8] It is as though the dominant perspective of total social and political history of the departments and regions, as well as the concern to integrate popular classes into the historical picture, had led to the neglect of the elites, with the exception of the *conseillers généraux*. The first study to take up the trail blazed by Adeline Daumard in 1963 with her thesis on the Parisian bourgeoisie from 1815 to 1848, is the major still-unpublished thesis by Jean-Pierre Chaline (1979) on the bourgeoisie of Rouen in the nineteenth century.[9] Through the use of a wide variety of sources — registry and notarial archives — and by adopting differing criteria — wealth, expenditure on rent, number of servants, mentality as revealed by the possession of certain goods, collections, libraries, place in the cemetery — he has identified the reality of the local elite. He shows how the bourgeoisie was formed from 1800 to 1914 through a complex process of social ascent. On the whole, the bourgeois milieu constitutes from 10 to 15 per cent of the urban population and possesses 85 per cent of inherited wealth. Within the bourgeoisie, about one tenth of the upper middle classes make up the families whose names dominate the nineteenth century in the Rouen area. One would like to have space to stress the richness of this study, a remarkably sensitive combination of quantitative and qualitative analyses, teeming with new sources. Many historians will follow up the approach to the bourgeois cemetery in Rouen, to this town of the dead within the town. It is impossible not to be reminded of Daniel Halévy, speaking in *Pays parisiens* of the tomb of the Halévys in the Jewish section of Montmartre cemetery: 'It is at the high point of the cemetery. Their rich tombs dominate all the others and that of the Halévys is more visible than most. A bust of the author of *La Juive* sits resplendent at the very top.'

J.-P. Chaline explores the part played within this bourgeoisie by foreign immigrants who wielded great power in the industrial world. These families were either British in origin, like the Waddingtons, or from the Rhineland. He describes the various strata of this bourgeoisie: descendants of the old trading classes which had, under the *ancien régime*, finally arrived at the threshold of nobility, then the 'cotton bourgeoisie' and finally the members of the 'port bourgeoisie'. But he also brings out, as others have done, the durability of a traditional elite, based on private income and linked to the liberal professions, especially lawyers and *notaires*.

While an interest in the elites of the nineteenth century has recently been revived, the ruling elites of France in the twentieth century have never ceased to be the subject of intense curiosity. Years ago, Mattei Dogan drew attention to the political elites. A vast literature exists on technocrats in general and now, since the 1967 pamphlet on the 'Enarchy', the growing role played in administrative and political decision-making by the former students of the ENA. This subject gave rise to much controversy before the joint study of Jean-Louis Bodiguel and Marie-Christine Kessler produced an interpretation which was as profound as it was incontrovertible. One might well ask whether the interest provoked by the ENA, the myth and the reality, has not masked the more general problem raised both by the *grandes écoles* and by the situation of the upper civil service and the *grands corps d'État*.[10] Last but by no means least, there is the research of P. Birnbaum, who in 1977 published a short book entitled, *Les Sommets de l'État: Essai sur l'élite du pouvoir en France*, and of Pierre Bourdieu and his team. It is worth noting that Bourdieu makes widespread use of the prosopographical method, through the exploitation of entries in year-books, biographical dictionaries and other forms of *Who's Who*. There remains, as P. Favre noted *à propos* of Birnbaum's work, the problem of the limits of these sources.[11] But neither the history nor the contemporary prosopography of elites can rely entirely on archival sources. Above all, it is much easier — even more so than in the past — to get to know the administrative and political elites than it is to analyse the business elite, despite recent attempts in this direction by M. Lévy-Leboyer.

Methods and perspectives

This sadly inadequate overview, which is neither a full account nor a 'distribution of prizes', is simply intended to sketch out the main lines of recent research into elites. This research is most often informed by a quantitative approach to historical sociology and is not, in the first instance, prosopographical in intent. The IHMC project, on the other hand, will be consciously and deliberately prosopographical. For the coming years, four main lines of research can be identified:

(1) *An inventory of the existing working instruments*: printed matter, tables of contents of certain works, card indexes of archival collections, libraries, research centres and individual researchers. One only needs to think of the card indexes accumulated during the writing of a thesis. Other researchers could glean so much from them, yet in fact they are rarely used and often disappear altogether.

To this should be added an inventory of existing printed or manuscript sources, family record books, private archives . . . In a word, our aim is to constitute a fund of documentation and a working library. Our project has already led to an attempt to put together a collection of *L'Almanach National.*

(2) *The publication, in a specific area, of working instruments* such as M. Perrichet's general, alphabetical and methodical table of the minute books of Parisian lawyers; or Jean Nagle's *Dictionary of Administrative Offices.* There is also the need to publish entries for sub-groups such as the University elites.

(3) *The collection of data.* Here, there are three main areas:

— to undertake, with the aid of technical collaborators, the systematic combing of vital first-hand sources;

— to gather together card indexes (or copies of them) which have been drawn up by isolated researchers and which would then be accessible to everybody;

– to assemble all existing printed data from whatever sources: entries in dictionaries or reviews, obituaries, biographical or genealogical studies, often of a confidential nature, which have remained in family hands, such as the family books which are commonly prized among the bourgeoisie of the department of the Nord.

(4) *To compare these data.* The main value of the project lies precisely in being able, eventually, to compare and contrast these index cards, to bring together information stemming from various sources on a single individual. Since the power of the elites is many-sided, it is particularly important to assemble data from different areas of reality – economic, political, cultural, religious. The diversity of the elites will no doubt prevent the construction of a uniform pattern of data collection. But, as Louis Bergeron has suggested, one can at least bring together information relating to training, professional career, politics, family connections, wealth, social activities, study circles, learned societies, academies.

In the long run, computerisation of these data is desirable. Ideally this would allow the constitution of an easily accessible, cross-referenced databank. But that is still far in the future. However, we are already studying the methdological problems involved in a computerised biographical index.

In conclusion, it seems useful to mention some of the problems of the history of elites which a project such as ours can help elucidate. Whatever the purely documentary interest of the project or its usefulness as a working instrument, it can only fully justify itself if it provides answers to the major questions being posed by historians and sociologists.

Prosopography, by taking account of *la longue durée*, by looking at several generations, can provide a reply to essential questions about social mobility – upward, but also (and this is sometimes forgotten) downward – and about the reproduction of elites. When one establishes that the majority of the members of the upper civil service come from the upper classes (a concept, incidentally, which remains vague and which, in J.-L. Bodiguel's work, includes secondary school teachers), the occupation of the grandparents, which would perhaps produce quite another impression, is left out of account.[12] Among the industrial bourgeoisie of Rouen, J.-P. Chaline has discovered a degree of real social mobility during the first half of the nineteenth century, although this later subsided.

Prosopography restores the place of the family in historical reality. History is all too often made up of statistical groups or individuals. In fact 'the history of what is commonly called social elites is above all, in modern France, a history of families' (M. Perrichet). This is equally true of contemporary France. A sociologist recently spoke, in her study of families, of 'these networks of belonging and solidarity which cut across statistical categories'.[13] These family relationships and strategies are so evident in the world of the employer in Lille, Lyon, Mulhouse and Rouen. We are today well aware of the role of the family in preserving and reproducing inequalities which the education system merely condones. Our project will hopefully contribute towards the recognition of an aspect of reality which is often neglected.

Thus we shall rediscover the continuity of these 'bourgeois dynasties' whose 'responsibility', from Bonaparte to Pétain, was established in 1943 by Emmanuel Beau de Loménie in a polemical, often exaggerated, but well-informed book. Do we need to recall what he wrote of the family of M. de Montalivet, Louis-Philippe's Minister of the Interior, the son of one of Napoleon's ministers, who rallied to the Republic with his left-of-centre friends and became a senator in 1877? One of his sons-in-law, Georges Picot, a magistrate, in charge of criminal affairs and pardons under Dufaure and a member of the *Académie des Sciences Morales* founded a line of diplomats, *inspecteurs des finances*, and high ranking officers. His daughter married Jacques Bardoux, the son of Agénor Bardoux, one of the leading personalities of the centre-left. He in turn became senator for the Puy-de-Dôme, member of the *Académie des Sciences Morales* and member of the *Conseil National.* His daughter married an inspector of finances, Edmond Giscard. The rest of course is common knowledge.[14]

Another area in which prosopography has a contribution to make is in considering the role of the diploma in the power of the elite. It is often forgotten that the nineteenth century witnessed elites without diplomas: this was the case with the first generation of the Rouen *patronat*. Their sons, however, were to go on to the *lycée* and attempt the *baccalauréat*. Francis Demier, in his recent thesis, has shown that as eminent an economist as Adolphe Blanqui did not possess the *baccalauréat.* This is a far cry from the situation today in which elite positions are secured by means of multiple high-level diplomas: the rue d'Ulm and ENA for a socialist like Laurent Fabius or the former Assistant General Secretary to the Presidency, Yves Cannac; or the École Polytechnique and ENA for many another leading personality. These developments were foreseen by the founder of the École Libre des Sciences Politiques, Emile Boutmy, when he wrote in 1871 to E. Vinet, a co-founder of the school:

Privilege no longer exists; democracy will not recede. Those classes which consider themselves to be the upper crust are now obliged to submit to the law of numbers; they can only preserve their hegemony by playing on the rights of competence. Behind the crumbling break-water of their traditional prerogatives, the democratic wave will have to cope with this second barrier composed of striking and useful qualities, of a type of superiority whose prestige is incontrovertible, of skills which cannot reasonably be ignored.

There is also a vast subject which can only be touched on: the relationship between national and local elites. There are several questions here. First, how to explain the amazing contrasts from region to region. Louis Bergeron has wondered 'why certain departments hardly ever produce a figure whose influence goes beyond the *canton* or the *arrondissement* whereas others seem to specialise in providing leaders of national stature?' Secondly, what are the criteria for defining local elites? They probably vary from region to region; in certain areas, one has to look lower down the social ladder, whereas in others office, esteem and wealth are the cardinal features. Another question: how does one move from the local elite to the national, or vice versa in the case of the 'parachuting' into the provinces of political leaders?

Other themes can be tackled via a prosopography, for instance that of the relation between elites and religious minorities (one thinks immediately of the role of protestants among the intellectual, economic and political elites).

Finally one must ask a far-reaching question about the unity or the diversity of elites. The point of departure must be groups of elites – social, economic, intellectual or political. These groups are both independent and interdependent. The value of prosopographical analysis is to bring out these links and relationships, to note their 'multipositionality' in various 'fields' (to use the terminology of the Bourdieu school). This phenomenon was noted long before our modern sociologists by astute observers like Alain who, in the *Dépêche de Rouen* in 1910, denounced the partisans of 'appeasement' who rallied to the now moderate Briand:

These are people with private incomes or huge salaries; they wield immense power in the State – material power – for they direct events, make appointments, and occupy, through their family and friends, some particular sphere of influence or some highly profitable situation which allows them a cultured and well-endowed lifestyle. They also enjoy almost unlimited moral power. . . . Within this elite there are lawyers, professors, and high-ranking officers in the forces; all are cousins of industrialists and bankers. It is true that antisemitism divides them into two camps, but they are brought together by the fact that they speak the same language – the hatred of demagogy.

This final sentence needs quoting because it underscores the divisions within the French elite before the Dreyfus Affair and ought even afterwards to serve as a warning against the simplistic notion of a ruling class with a united and coherent strategy. Beau de Loménie, eager as he was to denounce the 'bourgeois dynasties', nevertheless saw the conflict between centre-left and centre-right as simple shadow-boxing; indeed in his view the failure of the 'conjunction of the centre' can be seen as the key to the early history of the Republic. Much contemporary work also provides the impression of a type of conspiracy of the elites which serves as the supreme explanation for the various twists and turns of our national history. Yet, to take but one of the Republics, the elites were never unanimous — not on the 16 May, not at the time of Dreyfus, nor of the *Front Populaire*, nor during Vichy. Perhaps the most valuable contribution of the prosopographical approach will be to remind historians of the singularity of individual destiny and choice.

Notes

1 *Pour une prosopographie des élites françaises*, XVIe-XXe siècles.
2 Cf. C. Heyraud, *La Grande faute: Le problème des élites* (Paris, 1929); or M. Muret, *Grandeur des élites* (Paris, 1939).
3 Cf. C. Nicolet, 'Prosopographie et histoire sociale: Rome et l'Italie à l'époque républicaine', *Annales* (September–October, 1970), pp. 1209–28; and A. Chastagnol, 'La prosopographie: Méthode de recherche sur l'histoire du Bas-Empire', ibid., pp. 1229–35.
4 Most of the work referred to below is listed in the bibliography of *Prosopographie des élites françaises (XVIe-XXe siècles): Guide de recherche*, and will therefore not be referenced here.
5 Centre National de Recherche Scientifique, *Grands notables du Premier Empire: Notices de biographie sociale*, vol. I (Paris, 1978). The same authors study the electoral registers of the Empire in *Les 'masses de granit': Cent mille notables du Premier Empire* (Paris, 1979).
6 D. Woronoff and M. Richard have been participants of long standing in the seminar led by L. Bergeron.
7 See the excellent survey by Christophe Charle, *Les Hauts fonctionnaires en France au XIXème siècle* (Paris, 1980).
8 One study stands out: Pierre Barral, *Les Périer dans l'Isère au XIXe siècle, d'après leur correspondance familiale* (Paris, 1964).
9 The substance of his thesis can be found in 'La bourgeoisie rouennaise au XIXe siècle', *Annales de Normandie* (March, 1980), pp. 55–63.
10 See Ezra Suleiman, *Politics, Power and Bureaucracy in France* (Princeton, N.J., 1974).
11 In the *Revue Française de Science Politique* (December, 1978).
12 In criticising Pierre Birnbaum, P. Favre observes that the higher civil service, if studied over several generations, can be seen equally well as an arena of upward social mobility, ibid., p. 1106. A student who enters ENA can be classed as having a military background when his father is a *gendarme* and the son of a peasant!
13 S. Chalvon-Demersay, *La Sagesse et le désordre: France 1980* (Paris, 1980).
14 Compare another '*dynastie bourgeoise*', the Périer family: Barral, op. cit.

INDEX